LEGAL ETHICS

LEGAL ETHICS

A GUIDE FOR FUTURE PRACTITIONERS

FIRST EDITION

Anitha Cadambi And Mona R. Shah

University of Southern California

cognella®
SAN DIEGO

Bassim Hamadeh, CEO and Publisher
Danielle Gradisher, Project Editor
Arielle Lewis, Editorial Assistant
Casey Hands, Production Editor
Jess Estrella, Senior Graphic Designer
Greg Isales, Licensing Coordinator
Natalie Piccotti, Director of Marketing
Kassie Graves, Senior Vice President, Editorial
Jamie Giganti, Director of Academic Publishing

Copyright © 2023 by Cognella, Inc. All rights reserved. No part of this publication may be reprinted, reproduced, transmitted, or utilized in any form or by any electronic, mechanical, or other means, now known or hereafter invented, including photocopying, microfilming, and recording, or in any information retrieval system without the written permission of Cognella, Inc. For inquiries regarding permissions, translations, foreign rights, audio rights, and any other forms of reproduction, please contact the Cognella Licensing Department at rights@cognella.com.

Trademark Notice: Product or corporate names may be trademarks or registered trademarks and are used only for identification and explanation without intent to infringe.

Printed in the United States of America.

CONTENTS

INTRODUCTION   vii

CHAPTER 1   ETHICS, MORALITY, AND REGULATION OF THE LEGAL PROFESSION   1

CHAPTER 2   ESTABLISHING AND TERMINATING THE ATTORNEY-CLIENT RELATIONSHIP   27

CHAPTER 3   COMPETENCY AND DILIGENCE   47

CHAPTER 4   ATTORNEY FEES   61

CHAPTER 5   COMMUNICATION, CONFIDENTIALITY, AND PRIVILEGE   83

CHAPTER 6   CONFLICT OF INTEREST [PART 1]   107

CHAPTER 6   CONFLICT OF INTEREST [PART 2]   139

CHAPTER 7   THE LAWYER AS ADVOCATE   157

CHAPTER 8   DECISION-MAKING IN A LAWYER-CLIENT RELATIONSHIP   171

CHAPTER 9   ADVERTISING AND SOLICITATION   183

GLOSSARY   195

ACTIVE LEARNING

This book has interactive activities available to complement your reading.

Your instructor may have customized the selection of activities available for your unique course. Please check with your professor to verify whether your class will access this content through the Cognella Active Learning portal (http://active.cognella.com) or through your home learning management system.

INTRODUCTION

"Once you are a lawyer, you are always a lawyer."

This is a phrase that you will often see in this book. We include it to make you think about what you are embarking on. Going into the legal profession is not just about starting a new career, but about a new way of thinking, a new way of identifying really. We include this phrase in this book often to remind you of this new way of thinking, this new identity for yourself.

As you go through this textbook, you will soon see this is not your traditional textbook. Definitely not your traditional legal textbook! We do not emphasize grammar, punctuation, citations (you will have legal writing for that!). This is not even a traditional legal ethics textbook. Frankly, there are plenty of excellent, more conventional legal ethics textbooks on the market. We did not want to create that, and there is no need for another one of those.

What we wanted to create was something new, something different. We hope many of you can refer to for years to come after you graduate law school and practice law. We wanted to produce something that will make you think! We chose to write something to make you discuss, debate, argue about the different scenarios that can make up ethical dilemmas in the legal world. That was our goal here. We drew upon our own personal experiences, colleagues' experiences, and real-life legal, ethical issues in this book to understand how the ethical rules are applied, how they should be used. So, why do we do this? Because showing you the application of the rules to real-life facts will make you remember the rules. And, if you remember the rules, you will hopefully not break the ethical rules when you are a practicing lawyer. See what we did there?

Here is the thing. Legal ethics is something you will need to remember far beyond your legal ethics class. It will be something you will need to remember far beyond an exam. The ethical rules are applied every single day of your legal career. There is no avoiding it. You cannot be a lawyer without being an ethical lawyer. Our legal profession requires it. For this system to work, lawyers need to have integrity. There is no way around it. Learn it here and understand it.

So, who are we? We are two legal ethics professors who taught from outstanding traditional legal ethics textbooks for many years. We love legal ethics (but never fully appreciated it when we were in law school)! We often text each other legal ethics articles for fun! After many years of teaching from very traditional textbooks, however, we knew we needed something different. We needed to develop a book that addressed the practical application of legal ethics—applying the ethical rules to real-life practice.

We adopted a direct and straightforward approach. Many books will tell you what you cannot do. We tell you what you can. We attempt to *give it to you straight* with the caveat that we are "recovering" lawyers. We still like to say, "it depends," as many ethical issues can go either way.

Our book pulls from our lives. We are two practicing lawyers – one a litigation attorney and one a transaction attorney – who bring their real-life experience into this book. How do you keep client confidentiality? What does it mean to avoid a conflict of interest? How do you know if you are a competent attorney? We drew upon our own day-to-day practice and the stories of our lawyer friends, colleagues, families (including husbands) to answer these questions for you here. At the end of each chapter, we ask questions that do not have clear answers but instead make you think about whether the rules serve the purpose they are intended to address.

At no point in this book do we want to come off as preaching a higher moral ground. You will shape your own professional identity. That said, we would like to change your perspective on the legal profession. A student once remarked that most successful and renowned lawyers routinely "bend" the rules to win or record more billable hours. It is normal and accepted behavior in their circles." As future lawyers, you can influence what is otherwise normal and accepted behavior. We attempt to share a few nuggets of wisdom in this book to help you think about positive change in the profession.

We want to thank everyone who helped us along the way with this incredibly special work. This was an endeavor of countless hours that became more and more of a passion project. Thank you to Jerusha D'Souza, Ipeleng Motuba, William Enger for your revisions, rewrites, and plain 'You don't make any sense." comments. Thank you to our incredible team at Cognella for your support along each step. Thank you to our husbands and families for your constant love and encouragement.

Thank you finally to our past students. It is because of all of you and your feedback we started this project.

This book gave us an incredible appreciation for the sacred place that ethics has in our legal profession. We hope that it does the same for you.

CHAPTER 1

Ethics, Morality, and Regulation of the Legal Profession

Visit your interactive ebook to download the Chapter 1 Outline.

Learning Objectives

In this lesson, students will:

- Define legal ethics.
- Assess the interplay between ethics and morality.
- Learn relevant ethics terminology.
- Outline the lawyer disciplinary process.

Key Terms

- **ABA**: The American Bar Association is a national organization of lawyers who participate in law reform, law-school accreditation, and continuing legal education for lawyers to help improve the legal system.
- **Model Rules of Professional Responsibility:** A set of ethical guidelines for lawyers, some of which are mandatory while others are not. Each rule has comments that help explain the rule.
- **State Bar (or Bar Association):** An organization of members of the legal profession that license and discipline lawyers.
- **Discipline:** A penalty ranging from a permanent loss of a law license to a private warning, imposed for violating the ethical rules.
- **Sanctions:** Serious fines or other penalties for violating the ethical rules. These usually come from a judge.

- **Suspend:** To temporarily remove an attorney's right to practice law.
- **Disbarment:** The revocation of an attorney's right to practice law.
- **Complaint:** An expression of dissatisfaction with legal services that is filed with the state bar.
- **Ethics:** A system of moral tenets or principles; the collective doctrines relating to the ideals of human conduct and character.
- **Morality:** The doctrine of right and wrong in human conduct.
- **Managing partner:** A managing partner for a law firm manages the operations of a law firm and delegates responsibilities to employees within the law firm, including attorneys, secretaries, firm executives, and paralegals.
- **Reasonable** or reasonably: When used in relation to conduct by a lawyer denotes the conduct of a reasonably prudent and competent lawyer (ABA Model Rules, Rule 1.0(a) Terminology, 2020 Edition).
- **Reasonable belief** or reasonably believes: When used in reference to a lawyer, it denotes that the lawyer believes the matter in question and that the circumstances are such that the belief is reasonable (ABA Model Rules, Rule 1.0(h) Terminology, 2020 Edition).
- **Reasonably should know:** When used in reference to a lawyer, it denotes that a lawyer of reasonable prudence and competence would ascertain the matter in question (ABA Model Rules, Rule 1.0(j) Terminology, 2020 Edition).

Introduction

"Once you are a lawyer, you are always a lawyer."

This is a phrase that you will often see in this book. You are embarking on the transformational journey of becoming a lawyer. We sound a bit dramatic, but this is a very true statement. Even as law students, you will soon recognize that the rest of society will see you no longer as who you were before, but often first as an expert in the legal realm. You will be the holders of key legal advice, solvers of problems, those who take legal burdens off the shoulders of people. Your words will carry a heavier weight as lawyers, and this is where legal ethics comes in.

The preamble to the ABA Model Rules states:

> Compliance with the rules, as well with all laws in an open society, depends primarily upon understanding and voluntary compliance, secondarily upon reinforcement by peer and public opinion and finally, when necessary, upon enforcement through disciplinary proceedings. The rules do not, however, exhaust the moral and ethical considerations that inform a lawyer, for no worthwhile human activity can be completely defined by legal rules. The rules simply provide a framework for the ethical practice of law.

FIGURE 1.1   Law vs. Ethics.

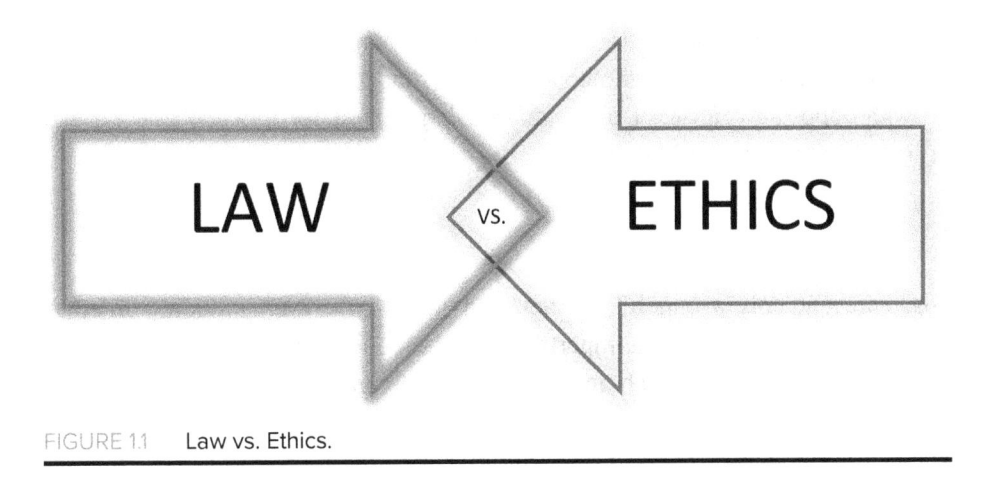

The preamble is insightful as it reminds us that the ABA Model Rules are a suggested framework for practicing law. Legal ethics are the minimum requirements that lawyers need to follow. Peer and public opinion and a lawyer's own morals and instincts often play just as important a role.

What Are Legal Ethics? Why Do We Discuss Legal Ethics? Why Do You Need to Know about Legal Ethics?

PICTURE ANY OF THE FOLLOWING ETHICAL SCENARIOS AND ASK YOURSELF, HOW WOULD YOU PROCEED?

- Would you defend a baker in a lawsuit from a gay or lesbian couple who sued the baker because the baker refused to bake a wedding cake for the couple because of their sexual orientation?
- You are a partner in a law firm with over 50 lawyers in your office and over 30 offices worldwide. What would you do if you learned that another partner is discriminating against female junior associates in your office?
- You recently discovered that your firm brings in a new client who is a high-profile movie producer being sued for sexual harassment. How would you proceed if your firm decides to represent such a person, but you strongly disagree?
- You are worried that an attorney in another law firm is an alcoholic. You have recently heard rumors that the lawyer has started neglecting clients and files. What do you do? Should you report the lawyer to the state bar?
- What if you missed a filing deadline and you know you may be sued for malpractice by your client? Do you change the postmark date on the mailing machine in your office to commit fraud to avoid malpractice?

> - Would you expect a judicial officer to recuse him- or herself voluntarily? If so, in what situations? What if someone tells you that the judge is in a basketball league with opposing counsel? Do you make a big deal about this and ask the judge to recuse him- or herself?

These scenarios represent only a handful of thousands, or maybe even millions, of ethical and moral situations you may face as a lawyer. More importantly, these are real-life situations. You can imagine these happening. How you emotionally approach any one of these circumstances will be vastly different from the way some of your classmates will approach them. Your morality—your internal "what is right and wrong" meter—is what guides you. What you do in response may be in part due to morality, but also in part due to ethics (how the law expects you to respond). The rules governing lawyers in the United States require that lawyers be ethical; however, they also recognize it is hard to remove one's morality from the equation. Lawyers are, after all, just human. We tend to forget that sometimes, but we are. Humans are emotional creatures. We cannot take emotions out of the law. However, our legal training will teach us to separate emotions from the law. Whether you end up doing this will largely shape the type of lawyer you become.

> **WHAT WOULD YOU DO?**
> Read the following article from the *New Republic* about well-respected and former solicitor general Neal Katyal. https://newrepublic.com/article/160481/neal-katyal-depravity-big-law
>
> After reading the article, ask yourself: do you agree with the author that it is hypocritical to criticize an attorney for representing a corporation that is currently being sued by formally enslaved children?

Structure of Legal Ethics in the United States

Attorneys in the United States are provided ethical guidance by two sources: the American Bar Association's (ABA) Model Rules of Professional Responsibility and their state's ethical rules. In California, those are the California Rules of Professional Responsibility. Statutes and case law sometimes also provide guidance, but for purposes of this book, we focus on the ABA Model Rules and California Rules.

You will note that we use the term *guidance*. Guidance is what the rules provide, not absolute strictness. As we begin to examine the rules, you will see the authors themselves provide much room for interpretation. This extra latitude allows us to apply, when appropriate, specific facts to the rules to determine if we can call the actions of lawyers ethical. Ethics must be determined on a case-by-case basis.

AMERICAN BAR ASSOCIATION MODEL RULES OF PROFESSIONAL RESPONSIBILITY

The American Bar Association (ABA) *Model Rules of Professional Responsibility* were adopted by the ABA House of Delegates in 1983. They serve as models for the ethics rules of most jurisdictions. Before the adoption of the ABA Model Rules, the ABA model was the 1969 Model Code of Professional Responsibility. Preceding the Model Code were the 1908 Canons of Professional Ethics (last amended in 1963). Today, almost every jurisdiction has adopted all or a majority of the ABA Model Rules with some modifications. The bar exam and the Model Professional Responsibility Exam (MPRE) test on the ABA Model Rules.

CALIFORNIA RULES OF PROFESSIONAL CONDUCT (CRPC)

The California Rules of Professional Conduct are intended to regulate the professional conduct of attorneys licensed by the California State Bar through discipline. They have been adopted by the Board of Trustees (the State Bar's governing body which develops guiding policies and principles) and approved by the California Supreme Court pursuant to statute to protect the public and to promote respect and confidence in the legal profession. The rules and any related standards adopted by the board are binding on all attorneys licensed by the state bar. In 2018, California updated the CRPC to be in more line with the ABA Model Rules. Before 2018, California was the only state to have rules that did not follow the ABA Model Rules, especially as it pertained to the organization and structure of the rules.

Other Rules

The Restatement of the Law, Third, The Law Governing Lawyers is an important source for legal ethics. It covers topics not specifically addressed in the ABA Model Rules; namely, contracts and liability for malpractice. Thus, lawyers and courts will refer to it to better understand how contract law might govern the attorney-client relationship and what happens when a client sues for malpractice. Candidly, many practicing lawyers will never open the Restatement when researching legal ethics questions. However, judges often cite them in ethics opinions which is why we include them in our discussion.

Many state bars also publish opinions (called formal opinions) that respond to an ethical question posed by a lawyer. Lawyers use state bar formal opinions to guide them in researching certain ethical gray areas.

It should not be forgotten that because a lawyer practices before different federal and state courts and administrative agencies (like the Securities and Exchange Commission), these tribunals have their own set of rules. Lawyers must follow these rules.

Lastly, other federal and state statutes might require lawyers to follow certain guidelines. For example, in California, the Business and Professions Code provides certain definitions and requirements for lawyers to follow.

Thus, the ABA Model Rules and state rules are only the beginning. Lawyer conduct is always under scrutiny.

Ethics and Morality

What are ethics and morality? Ethics are the moral principles that govern one's behavior or one's conduct of an activity. It is the collective drive (obeying company rules, stopping at a stop sign even when there are no cars or persons in the vicinity, waiting your turn in line at the cashier) that makes an individual person do something or not do something. The collective doing of things makes living among one another better and easier. Morality, on the other hand, is behavior distinguishing right from wrong. What is the difference? Ethics and morals both relate to right and wrong conduct. While they can be sometimes used interchangeably, they are different:

- *Ethics* refers to rules provided by an external source (code of conduct in a workplace).
- Morality refers to an individual's own principles regarding what's right and wrong (our personal and individual upbringings).

Both morality and ethics are ever changing and are always fluid. Our notions of what is right and wrong is constantly at risk of being upended. This is true in both society and within our own personal concepts of what we consider to be moral.

So, what do we expect of lawyers? We expect them to be reasonable. The term *reasonable*, when used in relation to conduct by a lawyer, denotes the conduct of a reasonably prudent and competent lawyer (ABA Model Rule 1.0 Terminology).

We expect lawyers to look at every client, case, situation, and consider, how can I best handle this? What that actually means is what we will discuss in this book.

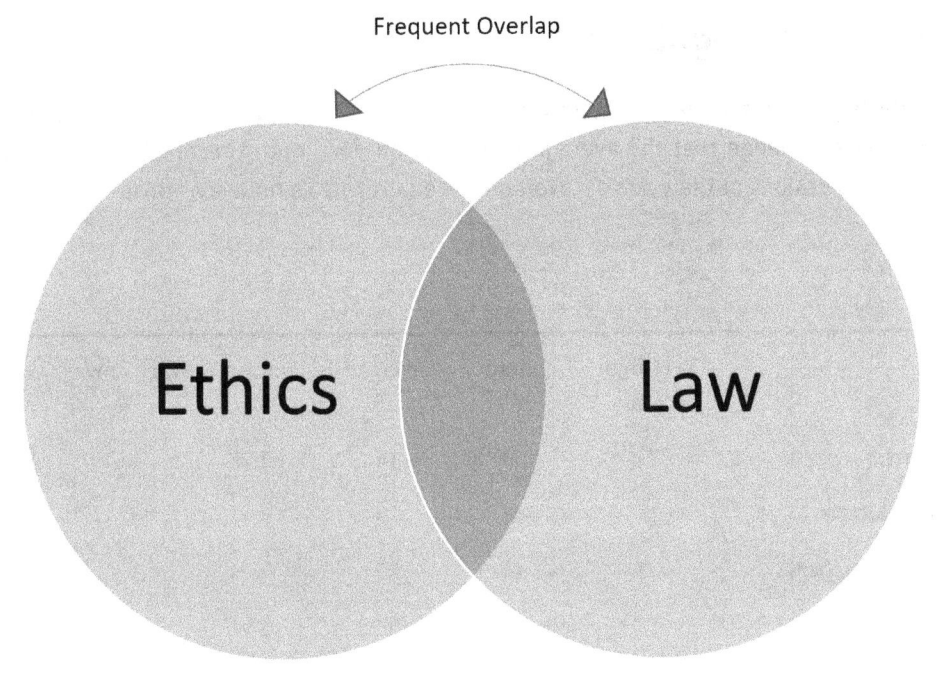

FIGURE 1.2   Law often represents an ethical minimum. Ethics often represents a standard that exceeds the legal minimum.

Let's go back to our original questions: Why do we discuss legal ethics? And why do you need to know about legal ethics? There are many different reasons.

- At their core, the ABA Model Rules focus on regulating three categories of relationships.
    - The relationship between a lawyer and their client.
    - The relationship between a lawyer and the public.
    - The relationship a lawyer has with other lawyers, whether in litigation or as part of a transaction.

Each of these relationships are scrutinized by the public and the profession. Therefore, lawyers should care about legal ethics. However, even in the absence of scrutiny, ethics give real and practical guidance to lawyers. It gives the legal profession purpose.

- Are attorneys disciplined for ethical violations? Should they be? Many lawyers believe that the risk of violating an ethical rule is simply: the price of misconduct discounted by the probability of enforcement. Lawyers must be "caught" and "turned in" before they can be disciplined. How is that done? Should it be done more often? Who should do it?

Why Are Lawyers Regulated?

Courts and state legislatures believe that lawyer regulation is needed to "protect the public."[1] Lawyers possess specialized knowledge that the average client/person does not. A recent Gallup Poll that assesses honesty/ethics in professions put lawyers at "average" when it came to honesty/ethics.

Table 1.1 Response to Gallup poll question: Please tell me how you would rate the honesty and ethical standards of people in these different fields — very high, high, average, low or very low?

	Very high %	High %	Average %	Low %	Very Low %	No opinion %
Nurses	27	54	16	2	1	—
Medical doctors	17	50	25	5	3	*
Grade school teachers	18	46	25	7	4	1
Pharmacists	17	46	30	4	2	1
Military officers	16	45	31	6	2	1
Police officers	13	40	32	9	6	*
Day care providers	10	40	42	4	2	2
Judges	8	30	43	13	5	*
Clergy	8	28	48	10	4	1
Auto mechanics	5	30	51	11	3	*
Nursing home operators	6	21	46	18	9	1
Bankers	3	24	52	14	6	*
Local officeholders	2	20	54	17	7	1
Lawyers	3	16	50	21	9	1
Newspaper reporters	4	13	39	26	17	*
Business executives	2	13	50	25	9	1
TV reporters	2	12	38	27	21	*
State officeholders	1	11	48	29	10	*

---

1. Fred C. Zacharias, "The Purpose of Lawyer Discipline," *William & Mary Law Review* 45, no. 2 (December 2003): 675–745, https://scholarship.law.wm.edu/wmlr/vol45/iss2/6.

Advertising practitioners	1	10	44	31	12	2
Members of Congress	3	6	29	37	25	1
Car salespeople	1	7	49	31	11	1
Lobbyists	1	4	28	35	28	4

Law often represents an ethical minimum. Ethics often represents a standard that exceeds the legal minimum.

Source: https://news.gallup.com/poll/1654/honesty-ethics-professions.aspx

For this reason, state bar associations provide a forum for clients to register complaints against lawyers. These complaints usually pertain to situations where the attorney has acted unethically. However, often complaints are initiated because clients are unhappy with the outcome in a case or have a problem with their billing or attorney fees. Interestingly, many states do not have a statute of limitation on complaints. However, once a complaint is filed, a state bar has a set time frame within which it must start disciplinary proceedings against an attorney.

In many states, besides filing a complaint, the public can search the state bar's website to check whether an attorney has a public record of prior discipline. Additionally, in instances where there is a fee dispute, a client may resolve such dispute "through an informal, confidential, and low-cost alternative called Mandatory Fee Arbitration."[2] See the Additional Resources section at the end of the chapter for a sample complaint form and a "Look Up a Lawyer" example.

---

2. "Resolving Fee Disputes with Your Attorney," The State Bar of California, n.d., http://www.calbar.ca.gov/Public/Free-Legal-Information/Resolving-Problems/Lawyer-Fee-Dispute.

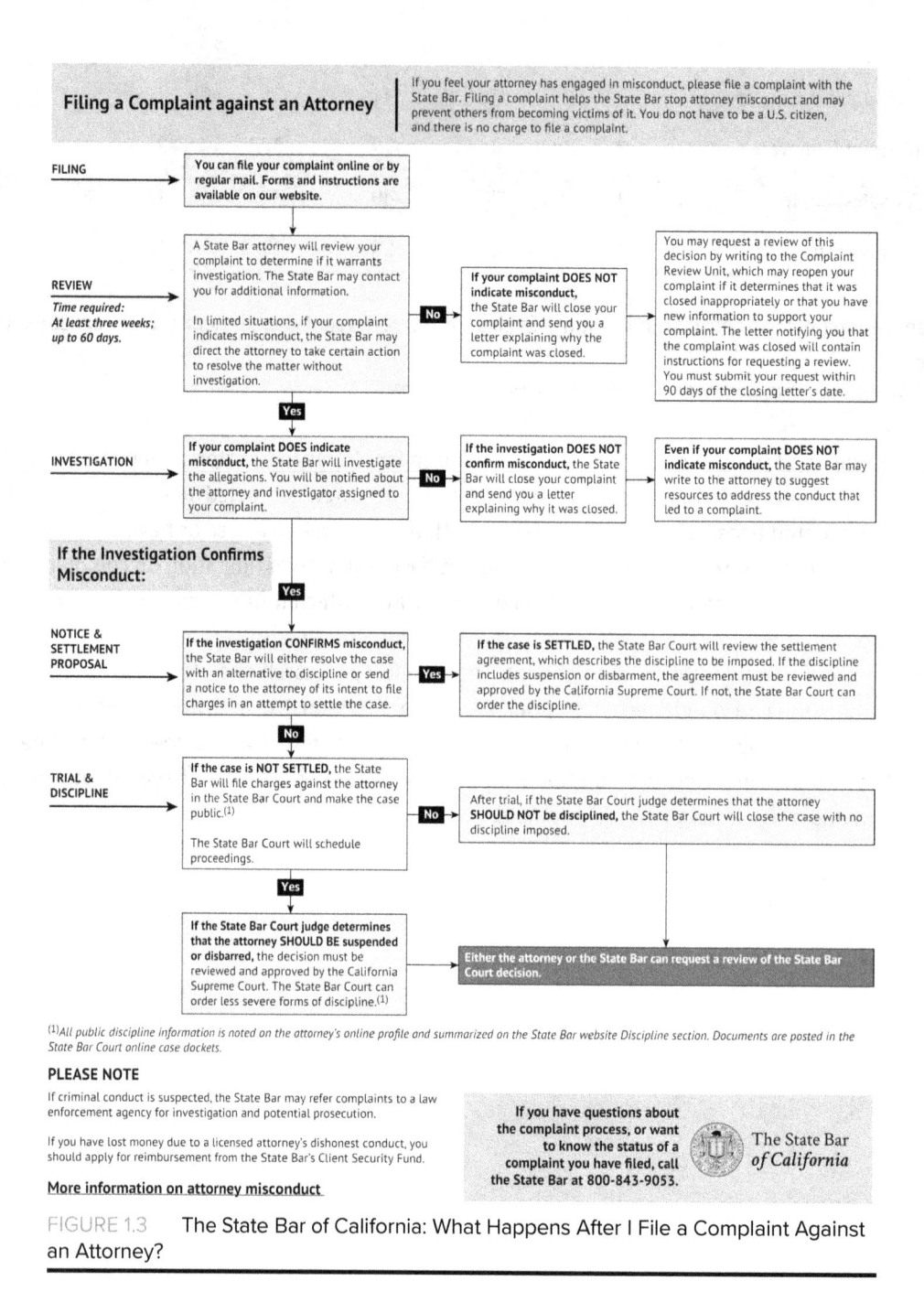

FIGURE 1.3   The State Bar of California: What Happens After I File a Complaint Against an Attorney?

Discipline

If the state bar imposes discipline, it can range from private reprimand to disbarment. The state bar can:

- issue a private reprimand (usually a letter sent to the lawyer)

- issue a public reprimand (usually published on the state bar's website and attorney newsletter)
- **suspend** the lawyer (the lawyer cannot practice law for a specific time)
- disbar the lawyer (the lawyer loses his or her license to practice law)

Note that a private reprimand is the lowest form of discipline under the rules, while disbarment is the most serious.

Reciprocal Discipline

Reciprocal discipline means that a lawyer who is subject to discipline in one state may also be disciplined for the same misconduct in any other state where the lawyer is licensed to practice law. Why? *To protect the public in other jurisdictions.* Permitting a lawyer who is suspended or disciplined in another state exposes the public to harm, undermines the integrity of the legal profession, and erodes public confidence in the legal profession.

Reporting Obligation

The "Snitch" Rule

ABA Model Rule 8.3 requires lawyers to report other lawyers' misconduct when they **know** that the lawyer has committed an ethical violation that raises questions about that lawyer's honesty, trustworthiness, or fitness to practice law. ABA Model Rule 8.3 does not require lawyers to breach confidentiality to comply with the rule. In other words, if a client insists that the information required to make the report remain confidential, the lawyer cannot report it. A lawyer can encourage their client to allow them to report so long as disclosure would not substantially prejudice the client.

Know is defined as "actual knowledge." A person's knowledge can be inferred from the circumstances. Ask any lawyer whether they are certain on whether a violation occurred, and they will likely pause to ask you, "does one ever really know?"

Comment 3 of the rule is helpful in such situations. "If a lawyer were obliged to report every violation of the Rules, the failure to report any violation would itself be a professional misconduct. Such a requirement existed in many jurisdictions but proved to be unenforceable. This Rule limits the reporting obligation to those offenses that a self-regulating profession must vigorously endeavor to prevent. A measure of **judgment** is, therefore, required in complying with the provisions of this rule." Calling out a colleague for misconduct can be tricky. Trusting your instincts in these situations is important. Some helpful factors in determining whether to report include the possibility of future harm and the extent to which the misconduct will otherwise go unnoticed.

Ultimately, the "Snitch Rule" is almost rarely enforced. However, the rule's importance should not go unnoticed, given the self-regulating nature of the profession. The state of California decided not to adopt ABA Model Rule 8.3. Was this the right decision?

Are lawyers required to self-report? In some states, yes. For example, California outlines a series of triggering events (like an entry of judgment for fraud or misrepresentation or a misdemeanor conviction) in which lawyers must report their conduct to the state bar. Failure to report is misconduct.

A Lawyer's Obligation to Supervise Their Subordinates

Partners in law firms and other lawyers with "managerial authority" over other employees at a law firm have a duty to make "reasonable efforts" to ensure all lawyers (their subordinates) conform with the rules of professional responsibility. Failure to do so can lead to discipline. ABA Model Rules 5.1(a) and (b) cover a managing attorney's responsibilities.

The ABA does not define *reasonable efforts* but recommends that lawyers have internal policies that ensure that all lawyers in the firm conform to the rules. This includes

- designing policies to detect and resolve conflicts of interest
- identifying dates by which actions must be taken in pending matters
- accounting for client funds and property
- ensuring inexperienced lawyers and staff are properly supervised
- billing measures to prevent overbilling
- participation in continuing legal education (CLE)

Thus, a good employee onboarding system is a must. Here, new lawyers can learn more about the law firm culture, the importance of following the ethical rules, and whom to contact if there is an ethical issue. Establishing a culture in which a law firm takes ethical issues seriously is a must. That way, new and junior lawyers understand the importance of following ethical standards.

A lawyer is always responsible for their own misconduct. There are three situations in which a lawyer may be responsible for another lawyer's misconduct [ABA Model Rule 5.1(c)]:

- When a managing attorney orders the misconduct
- When a managing attorney with knowledge of the specific misconduct ratifies it
- When a managing attorney learns of conduct at a time when its consequences could have been avoided or mitigated and does nothing.

HYPOTHETICAL 1.1: WHEN IS A SUPERVISING ATTORNEY RESPONSIBLE FOR SUBORDINATE ATTORNEY MISCONDUCT?

In each of the situations below, identify if the supervisory rules under ABA Model Rule 5.1 have been violated.

- A managing attorney orders her associate to follow ambulances around town and to hand out the firm's business cards whenever an ambulance drops a patient off at the hospital.
- A managing attorney learns that the last three clients the firm signed were because an

associate at the firm solicited clients from a hospital. In desperate need to bring in clients, the associate went into the local hospital and approached the Information Desk to leave business cards. The volunteer on staff then asked the attorney if he would like to talk to patients in the ICU – where the most critically injured patients were cared for. The associate said yes. After visiting the ICU and speaking with patients, the associate was able to sign on three new clients. The managing attorney continues to represent them.

- A managing attorney learns that a few associates plan to visit a nursing home nearby to solicit clients and does nothing.

Complete the following activity to confirm whether the rules have been violated.

> Please refer to the interactive ebook in Cognella Active Learning for interactive/media content.

Recap

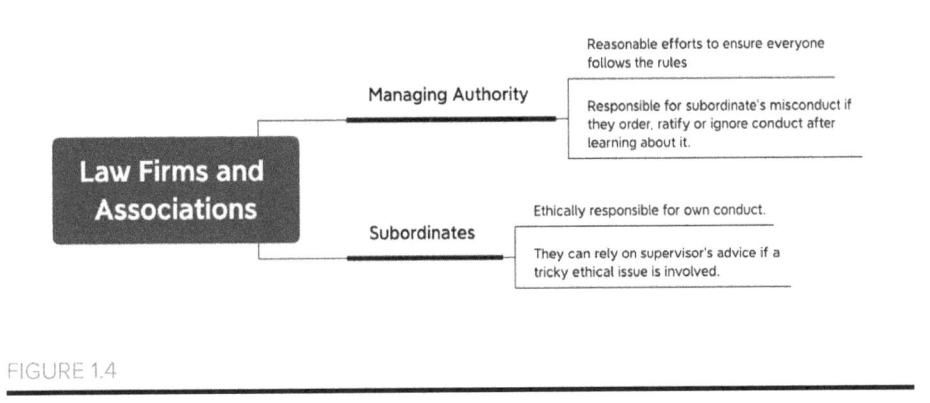

Law Firms and Associations

- **Managing Authority**
  - Reasonable efforts to ensure everyone follows the rules
  - Responsible for subordinate's misconduct if they order, ratify or ignore conduct after learning about it.
- **Subordinates**
  - Ethically responsible for own conduct.
  - They can rely on supervisor's advice if a tricky ethical issue is involved.

FIGURE 1.4

Who Is Regulated and What Is the "Practice of Law?"

The state bar regulates licensed attorneys and non-attorneys engaging in the unauthorized practice of law. Remember Mike Ross from the hit TV show *Suits*?

What Is the Practice of Law?

ABA Model Rule 5.5, Comment 2 indicates that states determine what the practice of law means. Included in Comment 2 is an acknowledgment that the practice of law is limited to members of the bar only. This protects the public from unqualified persons.

Many states follow California's definition of the practice of law. In California, the practice of law includes

- performing services in a court case/litigation;
- preparing legal documents like contracts and wills that secure legal rights; and

- giving legal advice.[3]

To practice law, one must be licensed in that state. Each state is free to determine how and what type of licensing they want to administer. Every state in the United States administers a bar exam and a multistate professional responsibility exam (MPRE).[4] To pass, applicants must receive a predetermined score, which varies with each state.

Additionally, the state bar assesses each candidate's moral character based on a compilation of many details of the applicant's life. The state bar reviews each applicant's history. If there are pending questions about the applicant's good moral character, the applicant will be invited to attend an informal conference with the state bar to convince state bar officials of their moral character and qualification to practice law in such state.

> Practice of law → must be licensed/active member of the state bar
>
> Unauthorized practice of law → not licensed/inactive or suspended member of the state bar

FIGURE 1.5   Practice of Law and Unauthorized Practice of Law.

> Read or listen to the following article: "Infamous Reporter Stephen Glass Vies for Bar Admission." The California bar ultimately decided against admitting Stephen Glass for admission to the bar. Do you agree or disagree with this decision?

---

3. *In re Garcia* (9th Cir. BAP 2005) 335 B.R. 717, 728.
4. It should be noted that Wisconsin is the only state with diploma privilege, where applicants must meet a set of course and grade requirements. They may practice law without taking a bar exam if they fulfill these requirements.

Temporary Practice of Law in Another Jurisdiction

In some cases, lawyers may practice law temporarily in another jurisdiction. Usually, this requires special permission from the tribunal where the lawyer wants to appear (called *pro-hac vice admission*) or by associating with local counsel in that jurisdiction.[5] In some cases, like in mediation or arbitration, the lawyer may participate without special permission due to the non-trial nature of these proceedings. Such participation must arise out of or be reasonably related to a pending arbitration or mediation— for example, a cruise ship passage contract that provides that disputes are to be resolved in California, even though an incident or injury may arise in another jurisdiction where the cruise ship traveled to.

ABA Model Rule 5.5(c)(4) accounts for situations not covered above but arising from or reasonably related to the attorney's practice in a jurisdiction where that attorney is admitted to practice law. For example, in today's global marketplace, we may have an American corporation that employs individuals all over the country or even throughout the world. Each employee is governed by the employment laws of the individual state that the employee resides in. An employment lawyer from that company would need to understand, and maybe even practice, if necessary, the laws of any state where an employment claim would be filed. We provide this example as more of a hypothetical as most corporations would hire local counsel in the state who could already practice law in that state to handle any lawsuits. However, it is not unheard of for a company's own lawyers to handle litigation in another state for various reasons, including costs, knowledge of the matter, or a business-related interest.

When Have Lawyers Violated This Rule?

Lawyers should be careful to ensure that a temporary practice remains temporary. In Gould v. Florida Bar, the 11th Circuit confirmed the district court's finding that a New York attorney, who was not admitted to the Florida bar, does not have the authority to practice New York law in Florida state courts. In this case, the attorney attempted to regularly practice New York law in Florida, which was prohibited.

We acknowledge that the recent pandemic (COVID-19) has changed the practice of law. Today, many state bars have waived strict enforcement of UPL laws (see below) when lawyers practice law in another state. With virtual practices growing in popularity, we suspect many lawyers will live in one state while practicing the law of another state, similar to the attorney in *Gould*. Thus, the decision in Gould could have little applicability today as states adapt to this new normal.

Other Exceptions

ABA Model Rule 5.5(d)-(e) creates a safe harbor for in-house counsel admitted in a US jurisdiction but may not be practicing in the jurisdiction where they are licensed. For example, Attorney A is admitted in New York but works in-house for ABC Corporation, headquartered in California. Although Attorney A is only licensed in New York and not in California, he has not engaged in the unauthorized practice of law by working in

---

5. ABA Model Rule 5.5(c)(1)(2).

California so long as he registers with the California state bar. Like many other states, California still requires in-house counsel to register with their state bar as "registered in-house counsel."

What Is the Unauthorized Practice of Law?

Simply put, practicing law without a license is the unauthorized practice of law (UPL). In many jurisdictions, UPL is a crime. As legal services become more digital, robots and artificial intelligence take over, concerns about UPL have increased. Furthermore, with some state bars expanding access to justice by permitting non-lawyers or paraprofessionals to provide limited legal services, UPL is back in the spotlight.

Common UPL Issues

- Paralegals or legal support staff drafting legal documents (for example, legal pleadings like the complaint, an answer, response to discovery, etc.) for a client.
- A suspended or disbarred attorney continuing to offer legal services to existing clients.
- A recent law school graduate (still awaiting bar results) helping a friend with their legal issue.
- Advising clients about the laws of another state or foreign country where an attorney is not licensed (absent any ABA Model Rule 5.5(c) exceptions).

CASE ALERT: IN RE CHARGES OF UNPROFESSIONAL CONDUCT IN PANEL FILE NO. 39302.

In a per curiam opinion (an opinion in the name of the court), the Supreme Court of Minnesota agreed with the Office of Lawyers Professional Responsibility director, who had issued a private admonition to a Colorado lawyer for engaging in UPL in Minnesota.[6] The lawyer represented his in-laws (a Minnesota couple) by defending a judgment against them for $2,368.13. The couple asked the lawyer to assist them in negotiating payment of the outstanding judgment. The lawyer attempted to negotiate via email regarding the satisfaction of the judgment with another Minnesota lawyer. The lawyer admitted through these emails that he was not licensed to practice law in Minnesota and that he would associate with a local attorney to assist with the matter. The lawyer's practice in Colorado involved a few cases and he had experience in debt collection, but his legal practice was primarily focused on other areas of law.

The disciplinary panel held that engaging in email communications with people in Minnesota may constitute the unauthorized practice of law in Minnesota, in violation of Minn. R. Prof. Conduct 5.5(a), even if the lawyer is not physically present in Minnesota. The court concluded that the lawyer's conduct was non-serious and agreed that an admonition was sufficient given the facts.

---

6. *In re Charges of Unprofessional Conduct in Panel File No. 39302* 884 N.W.2d 661 (Minn. 2016)

In re Charges of Unprofessional Conduct in Panel File No. 39302.

The Director of the Office of Lawyers Professional Responsibility (the Director) issued a private admonition to appellant for engaging in the unauthorized practice of law in Minnesota. [...]

I.

Appellant is an attorney licensed to practice law in the state of Colorado, where he maintains an office and has been practicing environmental law since 1986. He has also practiced personal injury law for approximately 7 years. Part of his litigation practice includes debt collection. Appellant is admitted to practice law in New York, Florida, and Alaska, but is currently on inactive status in those states. Appellant is also admitted to practice in federal court in the District of Colorado, the District of Alaska, the Southern and Western Districts of New York, and the United States Court of Appeals for the Ninth and Tenth Circuits. Appellant is not licensed to practice law in Minnesota.

Appellant's mother- and father-in-law live in Minnesota. They contacted appellant in May 2014 to obtain assistance regarding a judgment entered against them in conciliation court in Minnesota for $2,368.13 in favor of their condominium association, Voyager Condominium Homeowners' Association, Inc. (VCHA). The couple told appellant that VCHA's attorney, D.R., a Minnesota-based lawyer and the complainant in this case, was harassing them with telephone calls attempting to collect on the judgment. The couple asked appellant for his assistance in negotiating with D.R. regarding payment of the outstanding judgment.

Appellant sent an e-mail to D.R. in late May 2014, informing D.R. that he was representing his in-laws and instructing D.R. to direct all future communications to him instead. Appellant and D.R. exchanged approximately two dozen e-mails between May 2014 and September 2014. In his first responsive e-mail to appellant, D.R. asked whether appellant was licensed to practice law in Minnesota. Appellant replied that he was not licensed in Minnesota and that if he needed to file suit in Minnesota he would hire local counsel. The subsequent e-mails consisted of discussions regarding the in-laws' assets and ability to pay and whether the VCHA judgment would have priority in a foreclosure sale. Appellant attached financial disclosure forms to one of his e-mails and made a settlement offer.

In the penultimate e-mail exchange between the two attorneys, D.R. asserted that appellant was engaging in the unauthorized practice of law because he was not licensed in Minnesota. The final e-mail prior to D.R. filing an ethics complaint was a settlement proposal from appellant to D.R. on that same day. The Director received D.R.'s ethics complaint in October 2014. Approximately 2 months after filing the complaint, D.R. sent additional e-mails to appellant to determine whether the settlement offer was still available and whether appellant still represented his in-laws. Appellant did not respond to the subsequent e-mails and had no further involvement in the case.

Nothing in the record shows that appellant researched whether his activities constituted the unauthorized practice of law under the Minnesota Rules of Professional Conduct. When asked

Supreme Court of Minnesota, "In re Charges Unprofessional Conduct in Panel File No. 39302," 884 N.W.2d 661, 2016.

by the Panel at the evidentiary hearing whether he researched the rules in Minnesota, appellant said that he did not recall. Appellant admitted that he had not researched Minnesota law on foreclosure and how it would apply to his in-laws' case. Appellant also admitted that when he considered the relevant law and the rules of professional conduct, he was more familiar with the laws and rules in Colorado.

The Panel affirmed the Director's admonition, finding that clear and convincing evidence demonstrated a violation of Minn. R. Prof. Conduct 5.5(a). See Rule 9(j)(1)(iii), RLPR. The Panel found that appellant "is not licensed in Minnesota.... He is licensed in Colorado.... He was—although maybe not paid, he certainly has held out the fact that he represented clients, which regardless of whether they're related or not, he did represent them, admitted to representing them in a purely Minnesota case."

Pursuant to Rule 9(m), RLPR, appellant appealed the admonition to this court. Specifically, appellant challenges the Panel's determinations that he violated Minn. R. Prof. Conduct 5.5(a) and that his conduct did not fall within one of the exceptions in Minn. R. Prof. Conduct 5.5(c). We address each issue in turn.

II.

We turn first to appellant's claim regarding Rule 5.5(a). It states, in relevant part, that "[a] lawyer shall not practice law in a jurisdiction in violation of the regulation of the legal profession in that jurisdiction...." Minn. R. Prof. Conduct 5.5(a).

Appellant contends that he did not violate Rule 5.5(a) because he did not practice law in Minnesota. According to appellant, a lawyer practices in a jurisdiction in one of three ways: (1) by being physically present in the jurisdiction; (2) by establishing an office or other systematic and continuous presence in the jurisdiction; or (3) by entering an appearance in a matter through the filing of documents with a tribunal. Appellant argues that e-mail communication directed to a jurisdiction in which the lawyer is not admitted to practice does not fall within the definition of practicing law in a jurisdiction, and thus the Panel erred in its determination that he violated Rule 5.5(a).

[...]

Appellant concedes for the purpose of this appeal that he engaged in the practice of law, albeit in Colorado. Such a concession is consistent with our prior cases holding that negotiating the resolution of a claim on behalf of a client constitutes the practice of law. See In re Ray, 610 N.W.2d 342, 343, 346 (Minn.2000) (upholding the referee's finding that the attorney engaged in the unauthorized practice of law by negotiating with the county attorney on behalf of a client while the attorney was subject to a disciplinary suspension); In re Ray, 452 N.W.2d 689, 693 (Minn.1990) (holding that "the record support[ed] the referee's conclusion" that the attorney engaged in the unauthorized practice of law by attempting to negotiate settlements for two clients). Appellant maintains, however, that an attorney does not practice law in another jurisdiction merely by engaging in e-mail communications with individuals in that jurisdiction.

Whether an attorney engages in the practice of law in Minnesota by sending e-mails from another jurisdiction is a matter of first impression.

Rule 5.5(a) of the Minnesota Rules of Professional Conduct does not explicitly define what it means to practice law in a jurisdiction. Certainly, physical presence is one way to practice law in a jurisdiction. But, as we set forth below, it is not the only way.

Other courts have addressed the issue of whether an attorney practices law in a jurisdiction even though the attorney was not physically present in that jurisdiction. In Birbrower, Montalbano, Condon & Frank, P.C. v. Superior Court, 17 Cal.4th 119, 70 Cal.Rptr.2d 304, 949 P.2d 1, 5–6 (1998), the California Supreme Court analyzed what constituted the practice of law in a jurisdiction by looking at the nature of the legal representation in the jurisdiction, instead of focusing solely on physical presence. In determining what it means to practice law in California, the court considered whether the lawyer had "sufficient contact with the California client to render the nature of the legal services a clear legal representation" and whether the lawyers' contact with California was merely "fortuitous or attenuated." Id. , 70 Cal.Rptr.2d 304, 949 P.2d at 5. The court determined that a lawyer "may practice law in the state ... although not physically present here by advising a California client on California law in connection with a California legal dispute by telephone, fax, computer, or other modern technological means." Id. , 70 Cal.Rptr.2d 304, 949 P.2d at 5–6 ; see also In re Babies, 315 B.R. 785, 791–93 (Bankr.N.D.Ga.2004) (concluding that attorneys who were physically present in Illinois practiced law in Georgia by representing Georgia clients with respect to a bankruptcy, preparing documents related to that bankruptcy, and communicating with these clients via the telephone and mail).

The reasoning in Birbrower is persuasive. Based on that reasoning, we conclude that the Panel did not clearly err by finding that appellant practiced law in Minnesota, in violation of Minn. R. Prof. Conduct 5.5(a).1 Appellant contacted D.R., a Minnesota lawyer, and stated that he represented Minnesota clients in a Minnesota legal dispute. This legal dispute was not interjurisdictional; instead, it involved only Minnesota residents and a debt arising from a judgment entered by a Minnesota court. Appellant instructed D.R. to refer all future correspondence to him, and he continued to engage in correspondence and negotiations with D.R. over the course of several months. Appellant requested and received financial documents from his Minnesota clients and advised them on their legal options. By multiple e-mails sent over several months, appellant advised Minnesota clients on Minnesota law in connection with a Minnesota legal dispute and attempted to negotiate a resolution of that dispute with a Minnesota attorney. Appellant had a clear, ongoing attorney-client relationship with his Minnesota clients, and his contacts with Minnesota were not fortuitous or attenuated. Thus, there is ample support for the Panel's finding that appellant practiced law in Minnesota.

III.

Next, we turn to appellant's claim that even if the Panel did not err in determining that he was practicing law in Minnesota in violation of Minn. R. Prof. Conduct 5.5(a), his conduct was permitted under one of the exceptions in Minn. R. Prof. Conduct 5.5(c). Appellant argues that Rule 5.5(c)(2) authorized his conduct because he reasonably believed that he would be able to associate with local counsel and be admitted pro hac vice if necessary. Appellant further claims that Rule 5.5(c)(4) authorized his conduct because his in-laws reached out to him for assistance on a matter within his expertise; thus the matter "arose out of [Appellant's] law practice."2

Rule 5.5(c) permits an attorney to practice temporarily in a jurisdiction in which the attorney is not admitted. It states:

A lawyer admitted in another United States jurisdiction, and not disbarred or suspended from practice in any jurisdiction, may provide legal services on a temporary basis in this jurisdiction which:

....

(2) are in or reasonably related to a pending or potential proceeding before a tribunal in this or another jurisdiction, if the lawyer, or a person the lawyer is assisting, is authorized by law or order to appear in the proceeding or reasonably expects to be so authorized;

...

Or

(4) are not within paragraphs (c)(2) or (c)(3) and arise out of or are reasonably related to the lawyer's practice in a jurisdiction in which the lawyer is admitted to practice.

Minn. R. Prof. Conduct 5.5(c).

Under Minnesota Rules of Professional Conduct 5.5(c)(2), a lawyer admitted in another jurisdiction may provide legal services in Minnesota on a temporary basis if the lawyer's services are reasonably related to a pending or potential proceeding before a tribunal and the lawyer reasonably expects to be authorized by law to appear in the proceeding. Comment 10 explains that a lawyer rendering services in Minnesota on a temporary basis is permitted to engage in conduct in anticipation of a proceeding or hearing in which the lawyer reasonably expects to be admitted pro hac vice. Minn. R. Prof. Conduct 5.5(c)(2) cmt. 10.

Appellant suggests that there was a potential proceeding that could be brought on behalf of his in-laws. Because of this belief, appellant contends Rule 5.5(c)(2) protects him. The Director persuasively argues that appellant knew further litigation was unlikely because a court had already decided the underlying case involving his in-laws, and appellant was simply negotiating a potential debt resolution. In addition, Rule 5.5(c)(2), by its plain language, requires more than an attorney's speculation that the attorney can find local counsel and be admitted to practice pro hac vice. Appellant's e-mail correspondence does not indicate that he took steps to secure local counsel or investigate the possibility of pro hac vice admission. Thus, we conclude there is no support for appellant's claim that his conduct was authorized by Rule 5.5(c)(2).

Under Minnesota Rules of Professional Conduct 5.5(c)(4), a lawyer admitted in another jurisdiction may provide legal services in Minnesota on a temporary basis if the lawyer's services are not covered by paragraphs (c)(2) and (c)(3) and "arise out of or are reasonably related to the lawyer's practice in a jurisdiction in which the lawyer is admitted to practice." Appellant contends that his services arose out of or were reasonably related to his practice in Colorado because the clients are his relatives who "reached out to him for assistance" and appellant's environmental and personal-injury practice involves debt collection.

Comment 14 of Minnesota Rules of Professional Conduct 5.5 provides guidance on this issue. Specifically, comment 14 instructs that several factors may demonstrate that an attorney's temporary legal services in Minnesota reasonably relate to the lawyer's practice in a jurisdiction in which the lawyer is admitted to practice ("lawyer's home jurisdiction"), including: whether the client is a resident of or has substantial contacts with the lawyer's home jurisdiction; whether the client has previously been represented by the lawyer; whether a significant aspect of the matter involves the law of the lawyer's home jurisdiction; whether the client's activities or the legal issues involve multiple jurisdictions; or whether the services "draw on the lawyer's recognized expertise developed through the regular practice of law on behalf of clients in matters involving a particular body of federal, nationally-uniform, foreign, or international law." Minn. R. Prof. Conduct 5.5 cmt. 14; see also Restatement (Third) of the Law Governing Lawyers, § 3 cmt. e (Am. Law Inst.2000) (stating that a lawyer may provide legal services outside of a home jurisdiction if the services reasonably relate to the lawyer's practice in his or her home jurisdiction and listing factors similar to those in Minn. R. Prof. Conduct 5.5 cmt. 14 for determining if the services reasonably relate to the lawyer's practice in the home jurisdiction, including whether "the legal issues involved are primarily either multistate or federal in nature").

The legal services appellant provided to his in-laws were unrelated to his environmental and personal-injury practice in Colorado. The record establishes that appellant was involved in litigation in Colorado state court, including eight trials in the past 7 years in which collection issues arose,3 and that appellant negotiated the resolution of a debt with an out-of-state creditor on behalf of several Colorado residents. Although Rule 5.5(c) may permit appellant to negotiate with a Colorado client's out-of-state creditor because this representation is reasonably related to appellant's Colorado practice, the facts of this case are substantially different. Appellant's in-laws are not Colorado residents, and appellant had no prior attorney-client relationship with them.

Moreover, appellant's representation of his in-laws did not "arise out of" or "reasonably relate" to his practice in Colorado simply because his in-laws contacted him in Colorado or appellant has done collections work in Colorado. As the Director notes, appellant's in-laws were not long-standing clients; nor was there any connection between the in-laws' case and the state or laws of Colorado. And while appellant's Colorado practice may involve judgment collections work, nothing in the record establishes that this work was based on a body of federal or nationally uniform law.[4] To the contrary, appellant's clients were Minnesota residents with a debt that arose in Minnesota that they owed to a Minnesota resident and that was governed by Minnesota law. Accordingly, Rule 5.5(c)(4) does not apply to appellant's conduct.

IV.

Finally, we consider the appropriate discipline for appellant's misconduct. We give great weight to the recommendations of the Panel, but we have "the final responsibility for determining appropriate discipline for violations of the rules of professional conduct". Panel Case No. 23236, 728 N.W.2d at 258. We do not impose sanctions in attorney-discipline cases as punishment, but rather we impose sanctions "to protect the public, to protect the judicial system, and to deter future misconduct by the disciplined attorney [and] other attorneys." In re Rebeau, 787 N.W.2d 168, 173 (Minn.2010). We impose sanctions according to the unique facts of each case, and "when considering appropriate sanctions for misconduct, we weigh the following factors: (1) the nature of the misconduct, (2) the cumulative weight of the disciplinary violations, (3) the harm to the public, and (4) the harm to the legal profession." Panel Case No. 23236, 728 N.W.2d at 258 (citation omitted) (internal quotation marks omitted).

The nature of the misconduct in this case is non-serious. Appellant wrongly believed that he could negotiate a settlement in Minnesota without being licensed to practice law in the state. The cumulative weight of the misconduct is also minimal. Appellant engaged in a series of e-mail communications with one attorney in a single matter involving appellant's family members. In addition, the only harm appellant's clients suffered was a delay in the resolution of their debt because of appellant's actions. Accordingly, a private admonition is the appropriate discipline for appellant.

[...]

Do you agree with the Minnesota Supreme Court? Does this seem like too much regulation?

What Is Not UPL?

- Filling in the blanks on a particular form in accordance with information furnished by the parties.
- Acting as a scrivener to record the stated agreement of the parties to the transaction.
- When someone represents themselves in a legal proceeding (also known as pro se representation).

Maintaining the Integrity of the Profession

ABA Model Rule 8.4 serves as a general warning against attorney misconduct. It prohibits attorneys from inducing others from violating the rules of professional conduct. It also reminds lawyers that they should not engage in acts of dishonesty, fraud, deceit, misrepresentation, or other criminal activity. The ABA considers these actions as central concepts of conduct. Lawyers must not engage if respect for the legal profession and the proper administration of justice are not maintained.

Some examples include:

- Advising a client to offer a key witness in a real estate matter in exchange for favorable testimony in a criminal case.
- Advising a client to ignore a court order or subpoena.
- Advising a client to invent favorable evidence.

Most criminal conduct by a lawyer reflects a disregard for the law. While the above actions involved clients, what about acts by attorneys that trigger general concerns about honesty and fitness to practice law? For example, what if an attorney has a gambling addiction or falls asleep at the wheel and while driving home causes a major collision? Do activities that fall outside the practice of law concern a lawyer's character and fitness to practice law?

New Rule on Harassment and Discrimination

In 2018, the ABA added ABA Model Rule 8.4(g) to protect against harassment and discrimination. Lawyers challenged the rule for being broad and violating the First Amendment right to free speech and expression. The rule prohibits a lawyer from engaging in conduct related to the practice of law that the lawyer knows or reasonably should know is harassment or discrimination on the basis of various categories, including race, sex, religion, national origin, and sexual orientation. Whether the conduct violates the rule must be assessed using a standard of objective reasonableness, and only conduct that is found harmful will be grounds for discipline.[7]

We include ABA Model Rule 8.4 because it allows for and encourages important discussion. At the time of writing this book, we did not feel that ABA Model Rule 8.4 was in any way settled. We predict an ongoing discussion on attorney conduct, but also on any perceived restrictions on attorney conduct. As we said in the beginning of this chapter, once you are a lawyer, you are always a lawyer. Where does the oversight of ABA Model Rule 8.4 end on a person who is a member of the bar? As this is an ongoing discussion, we encourage you to seek guidance when necessary, from your local state bar ethics hotlines or the American Bar Association.

Bar	Contact
California State Bar Ethics Hotline	(415) 538-2148
New York State Bar Ethics Hotline	(212) 382-6663
American Bar Association Service Center Hotline	(800) 285-2221 International +1(312) 988-5000

---

7. ABA Formal Opinion 493

Key Takeaways

- Lawyer conduct is subject to a set of ethical rules (not moral rules).
- Most states follow the American Bar Association (ABA) Model Rules with some differences.
- This is a self-regulating field. A lawyer's conduct is always at issue—remember the general misconduct rule in ABA Model Rule 8.4.
- There is an obligation to report other attorney misconduct if reasonably certain that misconduct occurred.
- Lawyers must be licensed in a jurisdiction to practice law unless an exception for temporary practice or in-house counsel applies.

Ethics in Action

Read the following disciplinary action(s) where the state bar used the rules discussed in this chapter to bring disciplinary charges against an attorney.

- General Misconduct Rule (discipline for committing a crime that reflects poorly on one's honesty, trustworthiness, and fitness to practice law).
    - *In the Matter of Gordon R. Caplan* [two-year suspension]
      http://www.nycourts.gov/reporter/3dseries/2021/2021_01125.htm
    - *In the Matter of Robert V. Beltrani*
      http://www.nycourts.gov/reporter/3dseries/2021/2021_01004.htm
- Unauthorized Practice of Law [public reprimand]: *In the Matter of Heather Downs Russell*
  https://www.wicourts.gov/sc/opinion/DisplayDocument.pdf?content=pdf&seqNo=342084
- Rudy Giuliani Suspended from Practicing Law in New York by Appeals Court

---

Please refer to the interactive ebook in Cognella Active Learning for interactive/media content.

- Watch the following YouTube video on the differences between ethics, morality, and the law.

Please refer to the interactive ebook in Cognella Active Learning for interactive/media content.

End-of-Chapter Discussion Questions

1. Does your state have a code of conduct that regulates the practice of law? If yes, what is it?

2. If you are an LLM student, do you come from a country that had a code of conduct that regulates the practice of law? If your country does not have one, should they?
3. Based on where you are currently studying law, skim your state's rules of professional responsibility. Do they regulate non-lawyers? If so, how? Should non-lawyers be allowed to practice law? Why or why not? Read more about the steps California is taking to allow non-lawyers to practice law in a limited capacity. https://www.reuters.com/legal/legalindustry/a-very-big-deal-nonlaywer-licensing-plan-clears-hurdle-california-2021-09-24/

Additional Resources

Look Up a Lawyer example: http://www.calbar.ca.gov/
Sample Complaint Form: http://www.calbar.ca.gov/Portals/0/documents/forms/Attorney_Misconduct_Complaint.pdf

Image Credits

Fig. 1.3: Gallup, "Honesty/Ethics in Professions," https://news.gallup.com/poll/1654/honesty-ethics-professions.aspx. Copyright © 2020 by Gallup, Inc.

Fig. 1.4: The State Bar of California, "The State Bar of CA: What Happens After I File a Complaint Against an Attorney?" http://www.calbar.ca.gov/Public/Complaints-Claims/How-to-File-a-Complaint/After-You-File/File-Complaint-Against-Attorney. Copyright © by The State Bar of California.

CHAPTER 2

Establishing and Terminating the Attorney-Client Relationship

> Visit your interactive ebook to download the Chapter 2 Outline.

Learning Objectives

In this lesson, students will:

- Identify when the attorney-client relationship begins.
- Assess how technology has changed the attorney-client relationship.
- Evaluate the scope of representation.
- Identify scenarios where scope of representation might be limited.
- Examine an attorney's fiduciary duties.

Key Terms

- **Attorney-client relationship:** Relationship between attorney and client where attorney promises to provide legal services, usually for a fee.
- **Fiduciary duty:** Duty owed by attorney to client. Fiduciary means trust. Consequently, an attorney should act in the client's best interests. There are four fiduciary duties. They are confidentiality, candid communication, conflict of interest, competence.
- **Competence:** Legal knowledge, skill, thoroughness, and preparation reasonably necessary for representation.
- **Candid communication:** A requirement to reasonably communicate with the client at all times to ensure effective communication.
- **Confidentiality:** A duty not to disclose or use information about the client's representation.

- **Conflict of interest:** A duty of loyalty to the client by avoiding other lawyers', clients', or third-party interests.

Introduction: When Does the Attorney-Client Relationship Begin?

There will be many times during your legal career when someone finds out you are a lawyer and they quickly respond with, "Can I ask you question?" or "Can I get your take on something?" or even "Hey, I have a quick legal question ..." Now, you could just find a way to politely decline answering the question, but most of us will listen to the question and try to find a quick, responsible, and accurate way of answering the legal inquiry in front of us. The question then immediately becomes, has an attorney-client relationship been formed?

We often think of the attorney-client relationship as a formal, contract-based relationship. Something that started in the office, across a conference room table with signatures on an engagement letter (more on that below). That is the usual way a relationship would start. But what about the more informal inquiries? What happens then? Like when your cousin is involved in a car accident and needs legal advice or something more complicated, or perhaps if your parents want you to write up their will even though you have no experience in estate planning? Are you still the child helping your parents, or is there a formal attorney-client relationship pursuant to the ABA Model Rules or even pursuant to the rules of your particular state?

The ABA Model Rules do not provide a bright-line test on when an attorney-client relationship begins. Instead, they ask us to rely on relevant facts and circumstances.

Facts That Favor Formation of an Attorney-Client Relationship

Meeting at a law office, though not necessary.
Discussion of a legal problem.
Client expressly stating that they want to hire the attorney.
Signing of a retainer agreement or engagement letter, though not necessary. Attorney-client relationships can be implied or entered orally.

Fiduciary Relationship

The ABA Model Rules prescribe that once a formal attorney-client relationship is started, an attorney owes his or her client all the fiduciary duties that come with that relationship: competence, confidentiality, candid communication, and avoiding conflict of interest. These need to be in place not just at the start of the relationship but throughout the entire relationship and beyond. Thinking about the attorney-client relationship in terms of a fiduciary relationship is important. It requires lawyers to put their clients' interests before theirs. It requires acting in their best interests.

```
Understand what you are doing – both about the        Competence                              Confidentiality        Duty not to disclose client information as trust
law and the client.                                                                                                  is the hallmark of any relationship.

                                                          Fiduciary Duties

Give honest advice and keep the client informed.   Candid Communication              Loyalty/Avoid Conflicts of Interest    Put client's interests above all other interests.
```

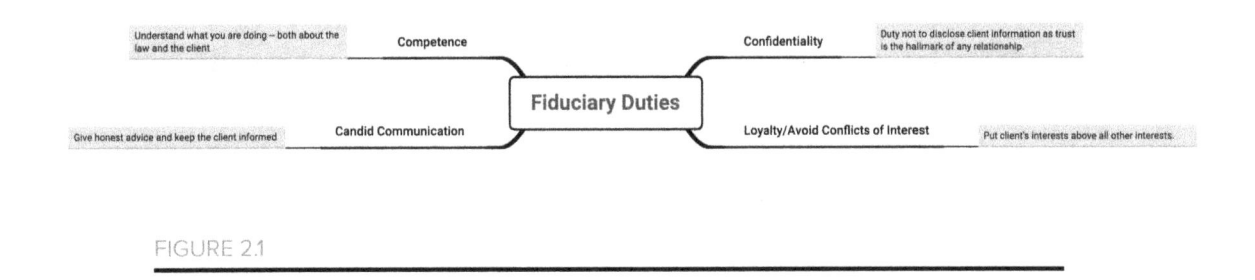

FIGURE 2.1

Identifying when the relationship starts is important for both the client and the attorney. Due to the duties that come into play once that relationship starts, it is important for the lawyer to know exactly when the relationship is defined and to make sure both parties are on the same page with the goals of that relationship. This also goes for when there is no start to the relationship, or the lawyer does not want to take on the client. It is important to communicate the same to the client and for the client to know that there is no attorney-client relationship. It is equally important to define the scope of the relationship, as attorney fees are usually collectible when the scope is absolutely clear.

Remember, the attorney-client relationship is never a casual relationship, and it should never be treated as one. Doing so can result in irreparable harm to both you and the client. It may be easy to answer a few casual legal questions from friends and family here and there. We often want to believe that we are immune from any consequences when it comes to bad advice to friends and family. But history has shown us that is not the case. The legal sector has seen many malpractice lawsuits from "casual legal questions" from friends and family. You want to help people, especially those you are closest to, but the reality of doing so when you are a lawyer requires you to take a step back and analyze the situation carefully. Doing so makes sure not only will your potential new client be protected, but so will you.

Do not be discouraged from helping friends and family during a time of legal need. Being able to help those we care for is one of the great rewards of the legal profession.

Section 14, The Restatement (Third) of the Law Governing Lawyers

As noted in the introduction to the chapter, the existence of the attorney-client relationship determines whether and what duties are owed to a client. Typically, attorney-client relationships are created by way of contract, either formal or informal, express or implied. The relationship can arise even without a formal agreement, exchange of money, or a formal fee agreement between the parties. Giving an attorney money for legal representation can be used to show intent—intent that the client was seeking legal representation. The restatement offers a helpful legal test to determine when an attorney-client relationship is formed.

SECTION 14, THE RESTATEMENT (THIRD) OF THE LAW GOVERNING LAWYERS

A relationship of client and lawyer arises when:

1. a person manifests to a lawyer the person's intent that the lawyer provide legal services for the person; and either

    (a) the lawyer manifests to the person consent to do so; or

    (b) the lawyer fails to manifest lack of consent to do so, and the lawyer knows or should know that the person reasonably relies on the lawyer to provide the services; or

2. a tribunal with power to do so appoints the lawyer to provide the services.

While this is the general rule for forming an attorney-client relationship, aspects of the relationship can be created at different times and manners. You could establish a relationship at a cocktail party, a barbecue, or a football game. It does not matter where you are, and relationships can be formed outside a law office. What matters is whether you are consulting a lawyer to either retain them as legal counsel or get advice from them in their capacity as a lawyer [emphasis added]. The courts will look at what the client believes.

A relationship can also be implied from actions. For example, in the absence of a formal agreement, a lawyer might prepare relevant court documents for a client, implying an attorney-client relationship.

Additionally, judges often have the power to appoint lawyers in cases where a client cannot afford legal services. This includes public defenders appointed to represent criminal defendants, attorneys appearing in juvenile dependency proceedings, attorneys appointed to represent children in abuse or neglect proceedings, etc.

LESSONS FROM *KURTENBACH* AND *TOGSTAD*

Case law is helpful in illustrating when attorney-client relationships begin. In *Kurtenbach v. TeKippe*,[1] the Iowa court made clear that neither a formal nor written agreement is required to establish an attorney-client relationship. Furthermore, in *Togstad v. Vesely*,[2] the court established that an individual could become a client by accident. Here, a prospective client consulted an attorney about a possible malpractice case. The attorney did not feel that the prospective client had a winnable case but wanted to consult his "partner" (an attorney at

---

1. 260 N.W. 2d, 53, 56 (Iowa 1977)
2. 291 N.W.2d 686 (1980)

another law firm), who was more familiar with medical practice cases. He never got back to the prospective client, and the statute of limitations passed. Was there an attorney-client relationship? The court said yes. At the very minimum, the lawyer should have reviewed the medical reports and reported back to the client before writing them off. From the client's perspective, she was seeking advice and the lawyer gave her said advice.

Togstad teaches an important lesson. Even if a lawyer does not intend a relationship, the courts can find one.

ABA Model Rule 1.18

As it relates to the client-lawyer relationship, the ABA defines this relationship in terms of a prospective client. That is, a person becomes a prospective client by consulting with a lawyer about the possibility of forming a client-lawyer relationship with respect to the matter [Comment 2 to ABA Model Rule 1.18].

Whether someone is a prospective client depends on facts and circumstances. If a person specifically requests legal services either in person or by responding to an advertisement, it's likely that they are a prospective client.

More importantly, even when no client-relationship results, a lawyer who has learned information from a prospective client shall not use or reveal that information unless an exception applies [ABA Model Rule 1.18 (b)].

For example, during a meeting with a prospective client, the attorney learns about the client's business, including an issue involving a recently fired employee who was accused of stealing from the employer. The prospective client does not ultimately hire the attorney. The attorney is obligated to keep information learned from the client meeting confidential.

HOW DOES AN ATTORNEY-CLIENT RELATIONSHIP FORM PRACTICALLY?

Step 1: Client contacts lawyer (either by way of a referral or otherwise)

Step 2: Lawyer screens client

Once contact is established, a law firm usually sends a consultation form or initial screening form to the client.

See Virginia Veteran Legal Services Client Intake Form

Here, the client provides basic information about their case. This information helps determine whether the lawyer wants to take the case and identify conflicts of interest.

Step 3: Interview

> If there are no conflicts, the lawyer sets up a time to meet with the client to learn more about the case. During the interview, the lawyer decides whether they would like to take the case, whether they are competent to take the case, and whether they have the time to do so.
>
> Lawyers also use this time to explain the scope and nature of representation and communicate what the representation entails. During this time, clients can also assess whether the lawyer is a good fit and if they want to move forward with the representation.
>
> **Note**: When a lawyer is associated with a law firm, a client of any lawyer is generally considered a client of all the lawyers in the law firm, at least as it relates to conflicts of interest. In accordance with ABA Model Rule 1.10 (Imputation of Conflicts of Interest: General Rule), while lawyers are associated in a firm, none of them shall knowingly represent a client when any one of them practicing alone would be prohibited from doing so by ABA Model Rules 1.7 or 1.9, save any exceptions.

HYPOTHETICAL 2.1: THE CASE OF A PARTY FOUL—IS THIS AN ATTORNEY-CLIENT RELATIONSHIP?

You are a new attorney and are attending a housewarming party for your new neighbor. Your neighbor's brother, Sam, comes up and makes small talk, and you tell him you are a lawyer. He then says, "Oh, that's great! Hey, can I pick your brain about a small matter?"

He then says, "My gardener, Eric, was working in my yard and fell off his ladder while he was trimming my tree. He immediately went to the hospital, and it turns out he has a broken arm."

"Eric wants me to pay for his medical expenses. The guy does not have medical insurance, and it is going to be expensive. Am I responsible for paying for his medical expenses?"

You then proceed to say, "Well, I do not really practice this kind of law, so I'm not sure what your responsibility would be."

Please refer to the interactive ebook in Cognella Active Learning for interactive/media content.

The Test:

- A person manifests the intent to employ the lawyer's legal services, and the lawyer consents thereto, OR the lawyer fails to manifest lack of consent thereto, and
- The lawyer knows or ought to have known that the person reasonably relies on the lawyer to provide legal services.

> Please refer to the interactive ebook in Cognella Active Learning for interactive/media content.

How Can We Avoid the Attorney-Client Relationship?

What can lawyers do if they do not want to represent a potential client? There is no obligation for lawyers to take on a client's case. We recommend reviewing the section on "how does this happen practically" in Section 14, The Restatement (Third) of the Law Governing Lawyers. If, after the initial consultation, the lawyer does not want to represent the client, they should send a nonengagement letter (or email) explaining their intent to decline representation. This type of letter will ensure that the client knows that they should obtain another attorney. The lawyer needs to alert the client promptly so that the client can find another lawyer.

For example:
David is at his college reunion when he sees his old roommate, Wayne. Wayne is a business attorney who primarily advises small businesses and entrepreneurs. David owns a pet clothing business.

During the reunion, David casually brings up to Wayne that he is dealing with a legal issue. One of his dog collars has three stripes on it, similar to the Adidas trademark. David received a cease-and-desist letter from Adidas asking him to stop selling the collars and hand over any revenue generated from its sales.

Wayne asks him to come over to the office the next day to review the letter. The next day, David emails the letter to Wayne. After reviewing the letter, Wayne decides that Adidas has a good case, and that David should stop selling the dog collar. On the other hand, David does not think his customers believe the collars have any affiliation with Adidas and wants to fight back. Wayne declines to take up the representation.

Should Wayne do anything else? Or is informing the client that he is not interested in the case enough?

Comments: Whenever an attorney or law firm decides not to represent a potential client after a discussion or client interview, they should send a nonengagement letter. This is true even if most of the conversation happened outside the attorney's office, over the phone, or elsewhere. In the nonengagement letter, the attorney should include a note about how the client should promptly seek advice from another attorney and remind the client about upcoming time limits (that is, the statute of limitations).

SAMPLE NONENGAGEMENT LETTER

Dear Mr. or Mrs. Smith:

It was nice to speak to you on September 14, 2011, in my office regarding the car accident you experienced in May 2011 on Highway 123. I am sorry for your accident and the injuries you experienced.

I understand from our conversation that you wish to file a lawsuit against other parties also

> involved in the same car accident. Unfortunately, this is not a lawsuit I can file on your behalf. This is not a case I am interested in taking on.
>
> I will not be your lawyer for this lawsuit, or any other claims, inquiries, or other matters stemming from the May 2011 accident. I advise that if you are interested in pursuing a claim or lawsuit that you immediately seek another lawyer. There may be time limits involved for you to file a lawsuit to seek recovery. Do not delay in retaining a lawyer.
>
> It was a pleasure meeting you.
>
> Best regards,
>
> Mickey Mouse

Review: What Should You Include in a Nonengagement Letter?

- Clearly state that you are not the client's attorney.
- Advise that there may be time limits to file a claim.
- Include that just because you do not want to pursue the claim, that does not mean other lawyers will not.

Revisiting ABA Model Rule 1.18

CASE ALERT: *FLATT V. SUPERIOR COURT*[3]

In this case, a prospective client (Daniel) met with an attorney (Flatt) about an issue involving his former lawyer (Hinkle). Hinkle happened to be an existing client of Flatt's law firm, albeit in an unrelated matter. Did Flatt have to inform Hinkle about the meeting with Daniel? What about Daniel?

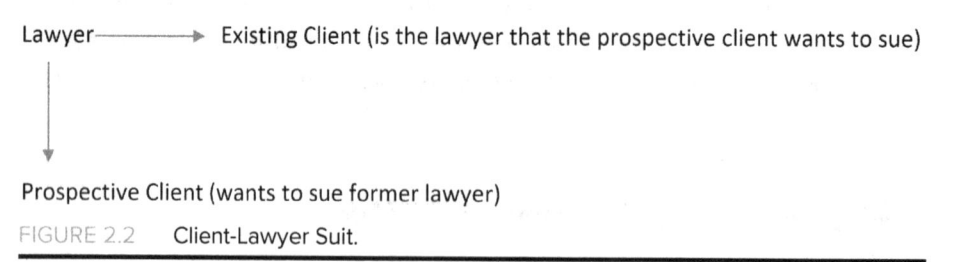

Lawyer ⟶ Existing Client (is the lawyer that the prospective client wants to sue)

⬇

Prospective Client (wants to sue former lawyer)

FIGURE 2.2   Client-Lawyer Suit.

In a narrow opinion, the California court held that the consulted lawyer had to maintain the

---

3. 9 Cal.4th 275

prospective client's confidentiality but did not have to tell the prospective client about any pending statute of limitations because of his duty to the existing client. Further, the court held that the lawyer has an unwaivable duty of loyalty not to represent the prospective client in light of an irremediable conflict with the existing client and should act promptly to terminate the relationship after learning about the client. As noted in the opinion, "[o]ne's loss ought not to be another's gain" and any advice given to Daniel would have been contrary to Hinkle's interests and the firm's duty to provide undivided loyalty to him.

Opinion

Arabian, J.

We granted review in this legal malpractice action to consider the scope of an attorney's duty to give advice when severing a relationship with a new or prospective client after learning that the representation-involving the filing of a lawsuit-would conflict irreconcilably with the duty of loyalty owed to an existing client, the target of the contemplated litigation. We conclude that the requirement of undivided loyalty to the first client negates any duty on the part of the attorney to inform the second client **[9 Cal. 4th 279]** of the statute of limitations applicable to the proposed lawsuit or even of the advisability of seeking alternative counsel, the two purported advisory duties that form the basis for this action for damages against the attorney by the second client.

Our holding is narrow, confined to the circumstances typified by this case -one in which the attorney is confronted with a mandatory and unwaivable duty not to represent the second client in light of an irremediable conflict with the existing client and acts promptly to terminate the relationship after learning of the conflict. We caution the bar that, in the absence of such an irreducible conflict and mandatory duty to withdraw, an attorney's duty to advise a new or even a "prospective" client, once the nonengagement decision has been taken, may well be more extensive; that, however, is a separate question, one not implicated by the principle of attorney loyalty that is the focus of our concern in this case.

I

[...]

William Daniel owned a two-thirds interest in a steel business and related assets acquired in a 1980 transaction structured by his then attorney, Donald Hinkle. On June 20, 1989, in the course of a marital dissolution proceeding, a superior court judge ruled that Daniel's wife had a community interest in the steel business and entered an interlocutory order to that effect. Unhappy with that result and believing it was the outcome of faulty lawyering by Hinkle in devising the 1980 acquisition, Daniel telephoned defendant Gail Flatt, an attorney with the defendant O'Brien law partnership, on July 20, 1989, one month after the decree was filed, and discussed his grievance. He arranged to meet personally with Flatt on July 27.

During an hour-long meeting on July 27, Daniel disclosed confidential information to Flatt concerning the conduct of Hinkle in structuring the 1980 transaction and turned over several documents bearing on that event. According to Daniel's subsequent declaration, filed in

Superior Court of Sonoma County, "Flatt v. Superior Court," 9 Cal.4th 275, 1994.

opposition to defendants' **[9 Cal. 4th 280]** motion for summary judgment, Flatt told him that he "definitely" had a claim for legal malpractice against Hinkle arising out of the dissolution proceeding and the antecedent purchase of the steel business.

In a letter dated August 3, a week after the July 27 meeting, Flatt returned Daniel's documents and advised him she could not represent him "in an action against [Hinkle]" because her firm "has a conflict ... in that we represent [Hinkle's firm] in an unrelated matter." At his deposition, Daniel later recalled that he understood Flatt's firm had declined to represent him and that he would need to continue his search for counsel ("[They said,] 'Hey, we can't represent you. We've got a conflict of interest.' Fine.... you can't represent me. So I've got to find somebody else"). He put off that search for a year and a half, however, because of other matters.

On June 3, 1991, almost two years after the July 27 meeting, Daniel filed this suit against the Hinkle firm (with respect to matters arising out of the 1980 business acquisition and the 1987 interlocutory decree) and Flatt and the other partners of her firm (collectively, Flatt). The latter claim alleged that Flatt had breached a duty to Daniel to advise him of the statute of limitations governing his claims against Hinkle and to seek other counsel in order to avoid having those claims time-barred; Daniel sought damages for legal malpractice against Flatt and her firm in the event that the court determined that the claims against Hinkle were barred by the statute of limitations.

Following discovery, Flatt moved for summary judgment on the ground that she owned no duty to advise Daniel as alleged in the complaint, because any advice concerning the statute of limitations governing the claim against Hinkle or to seek other counsel with respect to that matter would have been contrary to Hinkle's interests. The trial court declined to grant defendants' motion for summary judgment, reasoning that there were triable issues of fact material to the issue of whether an attorney-client relationship had arisen between Flatt and Daniel; Flatt then sought a writ of mandate from the Court of Appeal.

[...]

The majority's reasoning was confined entirely to the question of whether, as a result of the July 27 meeting and surrounding circumstances, Daniel had become a client of Flatt and her firm, and specifically whether issues of fact material to a resolution of that question remained for trial. After sifting through the record made by the **[9 Cal. 4th 281]** parties in the trial court and reviewing the case law governing the formation of the attorney-client relationship, the majority concluded that a professional relationship could have been formed under the version of the meeting alleged by Daniel; it therefore declined to disturb the trial court's ruling denying defendants' motion for summary judgment on the ground that facts material to that issue remained in dispute.

The dissenting justice reasoned that the dispositive issue was not whether Daniel had become a client of Flatt as a result of the July 27 meeting, but assuming he had, whether Flatt thereby owed a duty to advise him of the statute of limitations governing his contemplated malpractice claim against Hinkle and the advisability of retaining other counsel to pursue it. As will appear, we agree in part with the reasoning of the dissenting Court of Appeal justice. In our view, assuming that the circumstances of the July 27 meeting were sufficient to make Daniel a client of Flatt, her duty of loyalty to Hinkle, the firm's existing client, required her both to sever any professional relation with Daniel promptly upon learning of the conflict and, as a legal complement to that obligation, absolved her of a duty to provide any advice to Daniel adverse to the interests of Hinkle, including advice respecting the statute of limitations governing, and the advisability of engaging alternative counsel to pursue, the contemplated lawsuit against Hinkle claimed by Daniel to have been required of Flatt and breached in this case.

II

[...]

A

[1a] An attorney's duty of loyalty to a client is not one that is capable of being divided, at least under circumstances where the ethical obligation to withdraw from further representation of one of the parties is mandatory, rather than subject to disclosure and client consent. Although the principle upon which that conclusion rests is integral to the nature of an attorney's duty of loyalty itself, the result is also compelled by the highly practical dilemma that an advisory duty to the erstwhile client would impose on the attorney. In addition, our conclusion is motivated by an appreciation of the damage done to the existing client's sense of trust and security-features essential to the effective functioning of the fiduciary relationship-likely to follow from a conclusion that Flatt had a duty to advise Daniel under the facts of this case.

Neither the parties' research nor our own has unearthed case authority squarely in point. [2a] The dispositive principle, however, can be derived from the well established ethical stricture against attorney conflicts of interest embodied in rule 3-310 of our Rules of Professional Conduct (hereafter Rule 3-310). Subdivision (C)(2) of Rule 3-310-and its counterparts in the Model Code of Professional Responsibility and the Model Rules of Professional Conduct, both promulgated by the American Bar Association (ABA)-provides that an attorney "shall not ... [a]ccept or continue representation of more than one client in a matter in which the interests of the clients actually conflict ...."2 The practical administration of the rule has not been confined to what is perhaps the most egregious **[9 Cal. 4th 283]** example of its violation-simultaneously representing opposing parties in the same litigation. Rather, in parsing the effect of the ethical principle against attorney-client conflicts of interest in a variety of settings, the courts have identified two separate interests underlying the prohibition and formulated two distinct tests to determine the circumstances in which each applies.

Where the potential conflict is one that arises from the successive representation of clients with potentially adverse interests, the courts have recognized that the chief fiduciary value jeopardized is that of client confidentiality. [3a] Thus, where a former client seeks to have a previous attorney disqualified from serving as counsel to a successive client in litigation adverse to the interests of the first client, the governing test requires that the client demonstrate a "substantial relationship" between the subjects of the antecedent and current representations.

The "substantial relationship" test mediates between two interests that are in tension in such a context-the freedom of the subsequent client to counsel of choice, on the one hand, and the interest of the former client in ensuring the permanent confidentiality of matters disclosed to the attorney in the course of the prior representation, on the other. Where the requisite substantial relationship between the subjects of the prior and the current representations can be demonstrated, access to confidential information by the attorney in the course of the first representation (relevant, by definition, to the second representation) is presumed and disqualification of the attorney's representation of the second client is mandatory; indeed, the disqualification extends vicariously to the entire firm.

[...]

B

[2b] Both the interest implicated and the governing test are different, however, where an attorney's potentially conflicting representations are simultaneous. In such a situation-perhaps the classic case involving an attorney's interests in conflict with those of the client-the courts have discerned a distinctly separate professional value to be at risk by the attorney's adverse representations. The primary value at stake in cases of simultaneous or dual representation is the attorney's duty-and the client's legitimate expectation-of loyalty, rather than confidentiality. [3b] And because the substantial relationship test is founded on the need to protect against the improper use of client secrets-a concern that often is not implicated by the simultaneous representation of clients in unrelated matters -and applies "where the representation of a former client has been terminated and the parameters of such relationship ... fixed," such a test "does not set a sufficiently high standard by which the necessity for disqualification should be determined" in cases involving dual representation. (Cinema 5, Ltd. v. Cinerama, Inc. (2d Cir. 1976) 528 F.2d 1384, 1387.)

[4] In evaluating conflict claims in dual representation cases, the courts have accordingly imposed a test that is more stringent than that of demonstrating a substantial relationship between the subject matter of successive representations.3 Even though the simultaneous representations may have nothing in common, and there is no risk that confidences to which counsel is a party in the one case have any relation to the other matter, disqualification may nevertheless be required. Indeed, in all but a few instances, the rule of disqualification in simultaneous representation cases is a per se or "automatic" one. (See, e.g., Cinema 5, Ltd v. Cinerama, Inc., supra, 528 F.2d at p. 1387 ["Where the [attorney-client] relationship is a continuing one, **[9 Cal. 4th 285]** adverse representation is prima facie improper ...."]; Truck Ins. Exchange v. Fireman's Fund Ins. Co. (1992) 6 Cal. App. 4th 1050, 1056-1059 [8 Cal. Rptr. 2d 228] [discussing at p. 1057 whether "the automatic disqualification rule applicable to concurrent representation may be avoided by unilaterally converting a present client into a former client

...."]; Kelly v. Greason (1968) 23 N.Y.2d 368 [296 N.Y.S.2d 937, 943, 244 N.E.2d 456] ["[W]ith rare and conditional exceptions, the lawyer may not place himself in a position where a conflicting interest may, even inadvertently, affect, or give the appearance of affecting, the obligations of the professional relationship ...."]; Developments in the Law-Conflicts of Interest in the Legal Profession, supra, 94 Harv. L.Rev. at pp. 1296-1302 & accompanying fns.; cf. Rest., Law Governing Lawyers (Tent. Draft No. 4, supra) § 209, subd. (2).)

The reason for such a rule is evident, even (or perhaps especially) to the nonattorney. A client who learns that his or her lawyer is also representing a litigation adversary, even with respect to a matter wholly unrelated to the one for which counsel was retained, cannot long be expected to sustain the level of confidence and trust in counsel that is one of the foundations of the professional relationship. All legal technicalities aside, few if any clients would be willing to suffer the prospect of their attorney continuing to represent them under such circumstances. As one commentator on modern legal ethics has put it: "Something seems radically out of place if a lawyer sues one of the lawyer's own present clients in behalf of another client. Even if the representations have nothing to do with each other, so that no confidential information is apparently jeopardized, the client who is sued can obviously claim that the lawyer's sense of loyalty is askew." (Wolfram, Modern Legal Ethics (1986 ed.) § 7.3.2, p. 350, italics added.) It is for that reason, and not out of concerns rooted in the obligation of client confidentiality, that courts and ethical codes alike prohibit an attorney from simultaneously representing two client adversaries, even where the substance of the representations are unrelated.4 **[9 Cal. 4th 286]**

[...]

D

In California as well, our Court of Appeal, relying on some of the precedents discussed above, has reasoned that "[a] lay client is likely to doubt the loyalty of a lawyer who undertakes to oppose him in an unrelated matter. Hence the decisions condemn acceptance of employment adverse to a client even though the employment is unrelated to the existing representation." (Jeffry v. Pounds (1977) 67 Cal. App. 3d 6, 11 [136 Cal. Rptr. 373].) Jeffry v. Pounds arose as a suit for attorney fees brought by a lawyer who had represented Pounds in personal injury litigation following an automobile accident. While the personal injury case was pending, another partner in the same firm was retained by Pounds's wife to draw up papers in her divorce proceeding against her husband. When Pounds learned of this adverse representation, he instructed another lawyer to take over the personal injury matter. Following the settlement of the personal injury litigation, Pounds's original attorney-now representing his wife in the divorce proceeding- sought a share of the settlement proceeds as a fee.

Relying on then section 4-101 of our Rules of Professional Conduct, the trial court ruled in favor of the attorney-rejecting Pounds's claim that no fee was due because the lawyer had accepted employment hostile to his **[9 Cal. 4th 288]** interests by representing his wife-on the ground that no confidential financial information had passed to the attorneys which might have aided them in the divorce case. (67 Cal.App.3d. at pp. 8-9.) Reversing the judgment of the trial court, the Court of Appeal observed that "rule 4-101 [is] aimed to protect the confidential relationship between attorney and client. [Citations.] The strictures against dual representation of antagonistic interests are far broader; they arise without potential breaches of confidentiality. In California, these strictures are codified in rule 5-102 of the Rules of Professional Conduct.... [¶] The question here is whether a lawyer or law firm breaches rule 5-102(B), when, without the knowledge and consent of the current client, it undertakes to represent a third person in suing that client on an unrelated matter. We answer the question in the affirmative." (Id. at pp. 9-10, fn. omitted.)5

[5] So inviolate is the duty of loyalty to an existing client that not even by withdrawing from the relationship can an attorney evade it. Thus, in Truck Ins. Exchange v. Fireman's Fund Ins. Co., supra, 6 Cal. App. 4th 1050, the Court of Appeal discussed the aptly named "hot potato rule," that is, the bar on curing dual representation conflicts by the expedient of severing the relationship with the preexisting client. There, in a subrogation action by several insureds and their insurers against another carrier, a law firm representing plaintiff insurer A sought to avoid disqualification by withdrawing from a concurrent representation of a subsidiary of defendant insurer B in unrelated litigation. The court held that " '[t]he principle precluding representing an interest adverse to those of a current client is based not on any concern with the confidential relations between attorney and client but rather on the need to assure the attorney's undivided loyalty and commitment to the client. [Citations].' " (Id. at p. 1056.) The court went on to hold that the "automatic disqualification rule applicable to concurrent representation [cannot] be avoided by unilaterally converting a present client into a former client prior to hearing on the motion for disqualification[.]" (Id. at p. 1057; see also Civil Service Com. v. Superior Court (1984) 163 Cal. App. 3d 70, 78, fn. 1 [209 Cal. Rptr. 159] ["... an attorney may simply not undertake to represent an interest adverse to those of a current client without the client's approval. [Citations.].")

[...]

Flatt's decision not to represent Daniel in light of her firm's ongoing representation of the Hinkle firm thus placed her in an ethical dilemma: on severing-as she must-the relationship with Daniel, what if any duty did she have to advise him respecting his contemplated lawsuit, advice that would almost inevitably harm Hinkle's interests to some extent? We have no difficulty in concluding that under these circumstances any advice to Daniel regarding the statute of limitations governing his claim against Hinkle would have run counter to the interests of an existing client of Flatt and her firm and of their obligation of undivided loyalty to him. We therefore conclude that she had no duty to give Daniel any such advice.6

Not only would the advisory duty argued for by Daniel have been contrary to the principle of attorney loyalty, it would as a practical matter have placed both Hinkle and Flatt in an insupportably awkward position, one that was bound to damage Hinkle's relationship with the firm and hobble the firm's effectiveness in representing him. It is not difficult to imagine Hinkle's reaction on learning that, in the course of severing her professional relationship, however infant, with Daniel, Flatt had advised Hinkle's would-be adversary of the statute of limitations governing the timing of his lawsuit and that, Flatt having refused to take his case, it was prudent to seek alternative counsel lest Daniel's claim against Hinkle be barred by the passage of time.

Under such circumstances, we think any client-even an attorney such as Hinkle-would be entitled to wonder whether the law's sense of casuistry had gone seriously wrong. As noted, ante, at pages 284-285, several courts have mentioned these very practical effects on client morale and trust presented by the spectacle of an attorney simultaneously representing adverse parties, even as to matters that are unrelated. (See, e.g., Grievance Committee v. Rottner, supra, 203 A.2d at p. 84; Cinema 5, Ltd. v. Cinerama, Inc., supra, 528 F.2d at p. 1386; International Business Machines Corp. v. Levin, supra, 579 F.2d at p. 280 ["A serious effect on the attorney-client relationship may follow if the client discovers from a source other than the attorney that he is being sued in a different matter by the attorney. The fact that a deleterious result cannot be identified subsequently as having actually occurred does not refute the existence of a likelihood of its occurrence ...."]; Jeffry v. Pounds, 67 Cal.App.3d at p. 11; cf. Fried, The Lawyer as Friend: The Moral Foundations of the Lawyer-Client Relation (1976) 85 Yale **[9 Cal. 4th 291]** L. J. 1060, 1067 [portraying the attorney's relationship to the client as that of "one [who] has a special care for the interests of those accepted as clients, just as his friends, his family, and he himself have a very general claim to his special concern."].)

E

Neither, we conclude, did Flatt have a duty under the circumstances to advise Daniel that it was prudent to seek other counsel promptly. Having sought an attorney to plead his case against Hinkle and having been turned down by Flatt, Daniel obviously knew that he had to continue the search for representation if he intended to pursue the claim. He admitted as much at his deposition. (See, ante, fn. 1, at p. 282.) Although, as Justice Phelan pointed out in his dissent from the majority Court of Appeal opinion, it is prudent for any attorney not facing a conflict in representation like that here to routinely advise a client or potential client not to delay in finding alternative representation (see, e.g., Mallen & Smith, Legal Malpractice (3d ed. 1989) § 2.11, at pp. 114-115), we cannot hold Flatt liable for not having done so. Not only is the average client's understanding of the practical realities of obtaining representation to defend or vindicate interests adequate to protect against the risks at stake, but the insoluble ethical dilemma raised by imposing on a fiduciary a duty to provide advice that is against the interests of an existing client argues conclusively against a contrary holding.

Conclusion

Using an optical metaphor, the dissent twice describes the majority opinion as "myopic." We agree that the utility of a judicial opinion often lies in its choice of focal point. While one ponders the outline of a single tree, another may discern, across a boundless forest, the path of the law. We choose to take the latter road. The judgment of the Court of Appeal is reversed and the cause is remanded with directions to order that defendants' motion for summary judgment be granted.

Lucas, C. J., Baxter, J., and George, J., concurred.

[…]

Another Scenario

CASE ALERT: *PEOPLE V. GIONIS*[4]

In this case, the attorney went to the defendant's house after being asked by the defendant (who was the attorney's friend) to come over. The defendant had just been served divorce papers and was upset. The attorney made clear that he would not be willing to have any involvement in the divorce and that he was there as a friend. The defendant shared more about the circumstances of the separation and a legal document regarding "venue" for the divorce. Defendant also expressed that he "had no idea how easy it would be for him to pay somebody to take care of her." Were these exchanges and statements subject to the attorney-client privilege?

The court concluded that the attorney spoke to the defendant as a friend after the attorney refused representation, supporting the conclusion that the attorney-client privilege did not protect the defendant's incriminating remarks. Thus, these statements were not subject to the attorney-client privilege.

Please refer to the interactive ebook in Cognella Active Learning for interactive/media content.

How Has Technology Changed the Attorney-Client Relationship?

Technology has made it easier for prospective clients to communicate with lawyers. One such way is through direct messaging or live chat. For example:

- Visit https://www.kbarneslaw.com/.

4. 9 Cal.4th 1196

- Scroll down to the section titled "Contact Us For Aggressive Representation."
- Review the contact form and read the disclaimer.

By filling out the form, has an attorney-client relationship formed? The answer is likely in the disclaimer! It should be noted that using a disclaimer may not prevent the formation of an attorney-client relationship if the parties' subsequent conduct is inconsistent with the disclaimer.

Besides, law firm websites, instant messages, blogs, and social media platforms (like Facebook, Reddit, and LinkedIn) have changed the way attorneys interact with prospective clients. For example, visit the subreddit, /r/legal advice. Here, Reddit users post legal questions hoping another user (usually a practicing attorney) responds. By responding to a question posted on a public forum, has an attorney-client relationship formed?

For example:

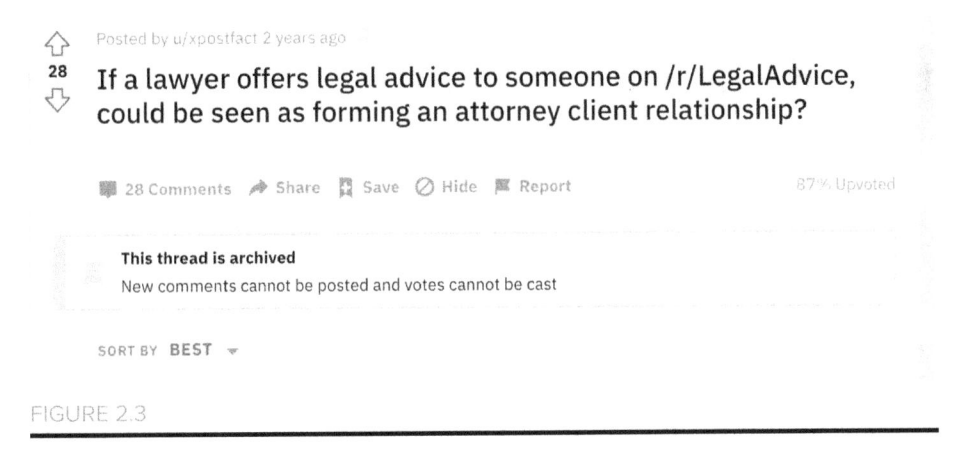

> Posted by u/xpostfact 2 years ago
> **28**
> If a lawyer offers legal advice to someone on /r/LegalAdvice, could be seen as forming an attorney client relationship?
>
> 28 Comments Share Save Hide Report   87% Upvoted
>
> **This thread is archived**
> New comments cannot be posted and votes cannot be cast
>
> SORT BY BEST

FIGURE 2.3

See the full post and comment thread here: https://www.reddit.com/r/legaladviceofftopic/comments/7ke427/if_a_lawyer_offers_legal_advice_to_someone_on/.

Comments: Probably not. Recall Section 14, The Restatement (Third) of the Law Governing Lawyers. Courts will look at the relationship from the prospective client's vantage point and ask whether the client is seeking legal advice. More specifically,

- Does the client consult the lawyer to retain the lawyer or to secure legal services or advice from the lawyer in their professional capacity?
- Determine whether the attorney agrees to provide legal services or the advice being sought.

Here, although a person is looking to get free advice or guidance on their issue, they know that the responses are usually in the form of general advice or information. No one on reading a reddit post would reasonably think that "the lawyer just agreed to provide me with legal services." Furthermore, internet forums usually have disclaimers where lawyers specifically state that responding to a post does not amount to an attorney-client relationship.

Another consideration is, what exactly is legal advice? The DC bar has this to say:

Providing legal information involves discussion of legal principles, trends, and considerations—the kind of information one might give in a speech or newspaper article, for example. Providing legal advice, on the other hand, involves offering recommendations tailored to the unique facts of a particular person's circumstances. Thus, in discussing legal information, lawyers should be careful to emphasize that it is intended as general information only, which may or may not be applicable to an individual's specific situation. (D.C. Bar Ass'n Comm. on Prof'l Ethics, Op. 316)

Before moving to the next section, think about the following: Would your answer to the scenarios presented above change if a friend or friend of a friend emailed you with details about their case?

Remember that advising someone on an internet forum is risky. You do not know to whom you are speaking and whether you are giving advice to someone in another state. This could very easily venture into the territory of unauthorized practice of law.

Ending the Relationship

Please refer to the interactive ebook in Cognella Active Learning for interactive/media content.

Like a non-engagement letter, a lawyer might consider sending written communication about the lawyer-client relationship ending. Read the following guide (pages 10–16) from the Minnesota Lawyers Mutual Insurance Company for sample termination language:
https://www.mlmins.com/Library/Terminating%20Representation%20Guide.pdf.

Scope of Representation

Once an attorney-client relationship is established, the next step is to determine the scope of that representation. Generally, attorneys are free to limit the scope of their representation to specific tasks or areas of laws. In other words, limited-scope representation is when the client and lawyer agree that the lawyer will handle some parts of the case, while the client will handle others. Limited-scope representation is also referred to as "unbundling."

ABA Model Rule 1.2(c) allows a lawyer to limit the scope of the representation if the limitation is reasonable under the circumstances and the client gives informed consent.

Why would an attorney limit the scope of representation?

- Lacks expertise

- Presence of potential conflicts of interest

- Time constraints

- Client with a limited budget

- Unpleasant client who is difficult to work with

EXAMPLES

1. Litigation: Represent in trial but not in appeal.
2. Transactional: Represent newly formed legal entity and not the principal individuals.
3. Client with cost constraints: Provide short consultation or oversee work prepared by client.
4. Associate with co-counsel and divide work: Two firms taking on different aspects of a matter.

Key Takeaways

- General theme—communicate early, often, and clearly.
- Remember the 4Cs: competence, candid communication, confidentiality, and conflict of interest.
- Client relationships can be deliberate or accidental.
- Forming an attorney-client relationship usually depends on the facts and circumstances of each interaction. The courts usually look at whether the client believes there is a relationship.
- Ending a relationship that has started can be difficult. It's not impossible. The courts recognize mandatory and permissive ways to withdraw.

Ethics in Action

Read the following disciplinary action(s) in which the state bar used the rules discussed in this chapter to bring disciplinary charges against an attorney.

- Acting without an attorney-client relationship [six-month suspension]: *Disciplinary Counsel v. Mamich* https://casetext.com/case/disciplinary-counsel-v-mamich-2011

End-of-Chapter Discussion Questions

1. Does the duty of confidentiality apply if a client has not hired the lawyer yet?
2. Is a written agreement needed to form an attorney-client relationship?
3. How can a lawyer avoid the unintended client?
4. Claimant emails lawyer describing a medical malpractice suit that claimant wishes to bring and asking lawyer to represent claimant. Lawyer does not respond to the email. A year later, the statute of limitations applicable to the lawsuit passes. Claimant sues lawyers for malpractice for not having filed the suit on time. Was there an attorney-client relationship?

Image Credits

Fig. 2.2: Source: https://www.reddit.com/r/legaladviceofftopic/comments/7ke427/if_a_lawyer_offers_legal_advice_to_someone_on/.

CHAPTER 3

Competency and Diligence

Visit your interactive ebook to download the Chapter 3 Outline.

Learning Objectives

In this lesson, students will:

- Define competence and diligence.
- Identify attorney fiduciary duties.
- Evaluate when an attorney can be disciplined for incompetence.
- Understand the relationship between competence and negligence vis-à-vis malpractice.

Key Terms

- **Competence:** Having the legal knowledge, skills, and thoroughness to represent a client. In some states, this also includes having the mental, emotional, and physical ability to perform legal services.
- **Incompetence:** Acting without competence.
- **Diligence:** Devoting adequate care and attention to each client's matter.
- **Negligence:** When an attorney makes a mistake that causes "damages" to a client, which a reasonable attorney in a similar situation would not have made.
- **Malpractice:** A lawsuit filed by a client against an attorney (or any professional for that matter) for damages. Malpractice lawsuits occur due to improper or negligent conduct by an attorney.

Introduction

As a general proposition, remember that most of the ethical rules and guidelines under the ABA Model Rules of Professional Conduct are in place to protect the public or your future client. The rules were created to foster a relationship of trust between attorney and client. Lawyering requires dealing with someone else's sensitive information or helping a client through a difficult time (some would even say crisis). It requires "looking out" for a client, often when dealing with monetary issues, or even issues of personal freedoms in criminal matters. How can this type of relationship possibly endure without some type of trust relationship? The notion of competency is no different. It was created to aid in building trust.

It is not uncommon for a non-lawyer to meet a lawyer and think they can handle a wide array of legal matters. Most people do not know (and really, why should they?) that there are specializations within the law. For example, a prospective client might think a corporate lawyer, can handle a personal injury dispute, not knowing that the lawyer may not know the ins and outs of personal injury or tort law. It's incumbent on the lawyer to clarify that the client might be better off with a lawyer competent in tort law. In short, lawyers need to recognize what they know and what they do not know so they can advise potential clients.

It seems like a simple thing ... if you cannot adequately handle a case, do not take it on. In other words, if you are incompetent to handle a matter for a client, let it go. Unfortunately, in practice, that idea does not always work. Lawyers take on matters all the time where they do not have enough expertise, experience, or even time to properly handle a matter. Any or all of these reasons can deem an attorney incompetent. Worse yet, it can harm a client, sometimes irreparably.

Pause here and ask yourself, why would an attorney take a case even when they do not have the expertise? A simple answer might be economics. It's much harder for a solo attorney or a small firm to reject a case that could eventually bring in revenue. Other reasons might be to get experience, work with a particular client to build their portfolio, or elevate their profile or reputation, especially if it's a well-known client.

The concept of competence was introduced to give lawyers guidelines to ensure they were capable to take on a matter. These guidelines are not only for when an attorney takes on a matter but requires that competency must continue during the representation, and even after it ends. An attorney is responsible for ensuring their competence throughout the representation.

The ABA Model Rules allow room for interpretation. The rule for competency is no exception. Just because you are not competent does not mean you cannot become competent to take on a matter. In fact, the rules specifically allow lawyers to become competent to take on a matter, even during the representation. This is even if it's your first day lawyering! Why? Well, for two reasons:

1. **The ABA Model Rules allow lawyers to take on new and different cases and clients**—Lawyering is a service-based industry. Your product is your legal competency in exchange for money.

Legal Competency ↔ Money

If we did not allow for lawyers to become competent to take on different types of cases, their ability to earn money would be greatly limited, especially if they are in a niche area or start practicing in an area that becomes more of a short-term "trend" rather than a long-term one. For example, let's say we had a deeply knowledgeable lawyer in the science and litigation of asbestos-related injuries and cases, but they were in a jurisdiction where there were not many asbestos-related case filings. They would have two choices:

(i) **Move to a jurisdiction that had more asbestos-related cases**. This may not be the most realistic option for many lawyers. This could mean a move to a different state. Uprooting oneself, practice, or even family can be difficult for several reasons. It can be expensive, hard on the family, unfamiliar, and the lawyer may be moving to a jurisdiction where they may have to take the state's bar exam to obtain a license to practice law. Doing all this and then establishing a new practice to be part of the asbestos cases can be risky.

(ii) **Pivot the lawyer's litigation skills to other practice areas**. The better option may be to use the litigation skills learned to work on more readily available cases in the current jurisdiction. Skills such as motion and pleading writing, depositions, and trial work can transfer into many areas of law. They would work to become competent to handle other types of cases. A prime example of this was in 2020 when law firms had to rethink how they practiced law with the spread of COVID-19. Law firms reorganized their practice areas to focus more on legal issues in demand, like debt collection, contract disputes, business interruption insurance, etc.

2. **The ABA Model Rules allow for more access to lawyers for the public**—Allowing lawyers to become competent in more than one area of practice means a wider range of lawyers available to more people for dispute resolution.

Let's think about this for a minute. If you are involved in a lawsuit involving a claim of medical malpractice against your doctor, who are your choices for a lawyer? Maybe the lawyer who has successfully handled a number of medical malpractice cases against doctors? They are well known for their success. This could mean the lawyer is busy or expensive (a good reputation usually means higher legal fees). Or you could ask your cousin who graduated from law school two years ago. Your cousin has some trial experience, but no medical malpractice experience. She is willing to charge you a fraction of an experienced medical malpractice lawyer and she says she will try to become competent to handle the case. You trust her. She did well in law school, and you know she will do her best to work hard for you. Okay, this works! Now, how can she become competent to handle this case? And is what she does enough for her to become competent?

Elements of Competence

ABA Model Rule 1.1 defines competence for the legal profession. Specifically, it states that the formation of an attorney-client relationship must start with a competent attorney. You cannot have an attorney-client relationship without a competent attorney.

> ABA Model Rule 1.1: A lawyer shall provide competent representation to a client. Competent representation requires the legal knowledge, skill, thoroughness and preparation reasonably necessary for the representation.

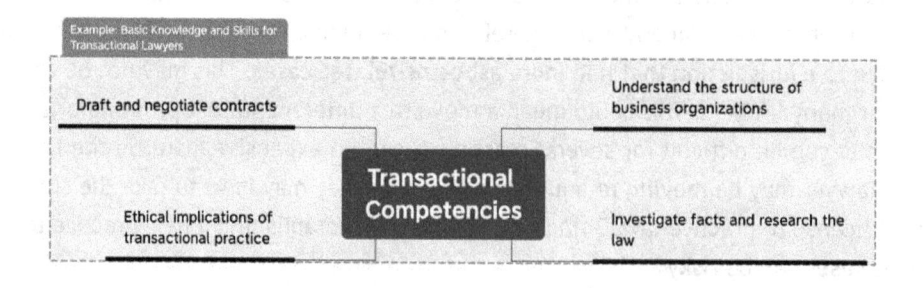

FIGURE 3.1

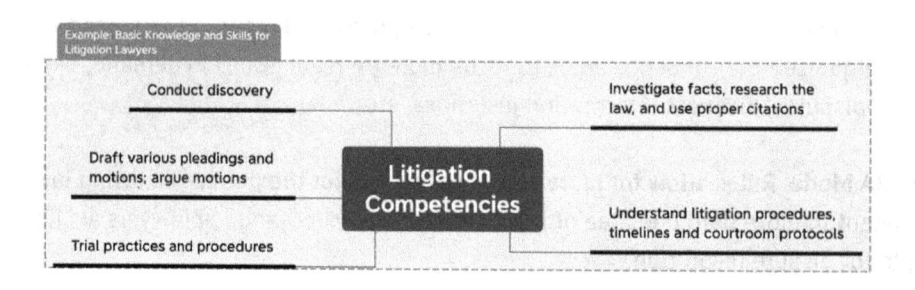

FIGURE 3.2

California Exception: Read the following "Ethics in Brief" from the San Diego County Bar Association and then answer the following questions. https://www.sdcba.org/index.cfm?pg=Ethics-in-Brief-2018-06-18

- What state of mind is needed to violate the rule on competence in California?
- Why do you think California includes mental, emotional, and physical abilities as part of its competency definition?

Relevant Factors of Competence

Comment 2 to ABA Model Rule 1.1 uses various factors to determine competency. These include the following:

- the complexity of the matter,
- the lawyer's experience and training,
- the preparation and study the lawyer can give to the matter, and
- whether it is feasible to refer the matter to or associate with a lawyer of established competence in the field in question.

Thus, the amount of legal knowledge and skill a lawyer would need for each representation varies. The more complex the representation, the more competence one would need.

HYPOTHETICAL 3.1: CAUSING AN UNFORCED ERROR—IS SAM COMPETENT?

Sam Cook has been practicing law for ten years. His practice includes mostly representing doctors whom patients have sued for medical malpractice for a variety of reasons.

Sam is an avid tennis player. He meets with other tennis enthusiasts at a country club where he is a member. One such member is Bobby Bright, who has become Sam's favorite tennis partner. They often play doubles together as teammates. Over the years they have become not only a great doubles team, but good friends!

Knowing that Sam is a lawyer, Bobby asks Sam to represent him in a boating accident. Bobby was operating his own boat when an electrical malfunction occurred. Investigations confirm that the wiring that powers up the boat was not properly configured by the manufacturer to industry safety and performance standards. The electrical malfunction caused a massive fire to Bobby's boat and caused injury to Bobby and his family who were on the boat at the time of the malfunction. Bobby wants Sam to sue the boat manufacturer on his behalf.

Sam has never argued a boating accident case, let alone done plaintiff-side work. His only experience is in defending doctors who are sued for malpractice, which often involves, among other things, presenting complex medical evidence to the court, selecting a jury, and cross-examining witnesses.

Would it be ethical for Sam to keep the case? Is he competent?

Please refer to the interactive ebook in Cognella Active Learning for interactive/media content.

Once you have had a chance to think about these questions, consider the chart below. It outlines the type of legal knowledge, skills, and other issues that Sam needs to consider before keeping the case. This type of analysis is key to assessing competence.

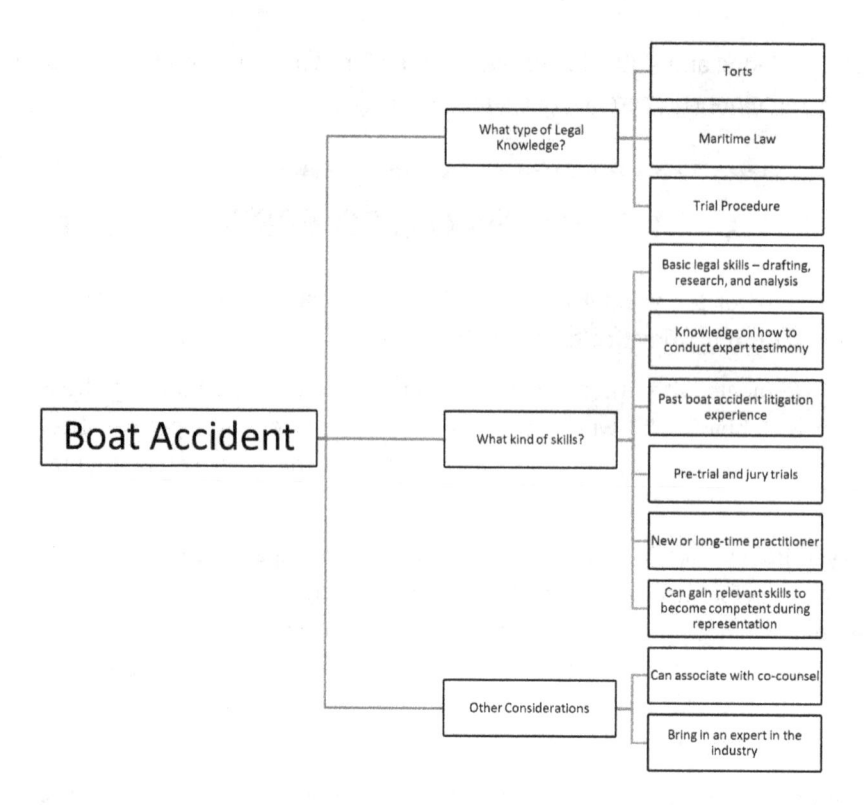

```
                                              ┌── Torts
                          ┌─ What type of Legal┤
                          │      Knowledge?    ├── Maritime Law
                          │                    │
                          │                    └── Trial Procedure
                          │
                          │                    ┌── Basic legal skills – drafting,
                          │                    │   research, and analysis
                          │                    │
                          │                    ├── Knowledge on how to
                          │                    │   conduct expert testimony
                          │                    │
                          │                    ├── Past boat accident litigation
Boat Accident ────────────┼─ What kind of skills?   experience
                          │                    │
                          │                    ├── Pre-trial and jury trials
                          │                    │
                          │                    ├── New or long-time practitioner
                          │                    │
                          │                    └── Can gain relevant skills to
                          │                        become competent during
                          │                        representation
                          │
                          │                    ┌── Can associate with co-counsel
                          └─ Other Considerations
                                               └── Bring in an expert in the
                                                   industry
```

FIGURE 3.3   Sam's considerations when deciding whether or not to keep the case.

As noted in the chart, Sam has to have a working knowledge of torts, the rules and protocols for bringing a case to trial (i.e., civil procedure), and basic legal skills related to drafting motions, discovery requests, and other court documents. He must also know how to conduct legal research and present analysis to support any arguments made in court. Sam needs to know how to conduct discovery before trial as well as present evidence during a trial. It would be helpful if Sam has experience litigating boat accidents, as he will know what to expect in future trials. Lastly, he needs to know when and what amount to settle for should such a situation arise.

It should be noted that knowledge of general torts may not apply in a maritime case (such as a boating accident) that has unique doctrines. Depending on the complexity of the case, the novel issues involved, and other related legal issues, Sam might need to know maritime law. In such a case, he should associate with a maritime specialist to ensure competence.

As with the current hypothetical involving Sam, lawyers need to analyze competency at each stage—that is, at the start, during, and throughout representation.

Key Considerations

Skill Set

The most fundamental skill consists of determining what kind of legal problem or issue a situation may involve. This does not require any specialized knowledge but rather an understanding of how to identify and spot legal issues. An attorney must know how to analyze precedent, evaluate evidence, draft legal documents and identify legal issues and problems [Comment 2, ABA Model Rule 1.1].

In some instances, even experienced attorneys will need to consult outside experts. For example, an attorney's obligations under the ethical duty of competency evolve as new technologies develop and become integrated with the practice of law. Competency may require even a highly experienced lawyer to seek assistance in some litigation matters involving electronically stored information (ESI).

Can Competence Be Achieved During Representation?

Yes, the ABA in Model Rule 1.1 carves out an important provision stating that a lawyer may become competent during representation in one of two ways.

1. **Through reasonable preparation.** This means an attorney is willing to dedicate time, energy, and study to learning about the case. This includes, but is not limited to, legal research (like reading case law and other publications) and consulting with attorneys who possess expertise in the representation.
2. **By associating with an attorney who is competent (referred to as "co-counsel").** That is, someone who has more experience or knowledge on the subject. Before entering into an agreement with co-counsel, an attorney must first seek client consent.

Thus, it is permissible for, say, an employment lawyer to take a criminal law case for the first time, and vice versa.

What about New Lawyers?

A newly admitted lawyer can be just as competent as a seasoned practitioner (Comment 2 to ABA Model Rule 1.1). Although one of the factors used to determine legal knowledge and skill relates to experience, it should be noted that the level of competency required is that of a general practitioner and not a specialist. In certain instances, like in extremely complex situations (think corporate taxation of an international enterprise), expertise or specialization is required.

How Do Lawyers Stay Competent?

Like other professions, lawyers are required to "engage in continuing study and education and comply with all legal education requirements to which the lawyer is subject" [Comment 8 to ABA Model Rule 1.1].

Lawyers are required to complete continuing legal education trainings, commonly known as CLEs, to keep up with changes in law and practice. These training hours are reported to the state bar and are required to ensure lawyer competence.

Can Clients Waive Competence?

An incompetent attorney might want to waive competence by asking clients to enter into agreements that ask them not to sue for malpractice due to incompetence. However, an attorney's competency is non-waivable. This applies even to pro bono and public defender services, where clients do not generally pay for the attorney's services.

States like California have made this point clear by prohibiting lawyers from entering into contracts with clients that prospectively limit the lawyer's liability for professional malpractice (see California Rule 1.8.8).

What about Technology Competence?

Included in the definition of competence is technology competence. ABA Model Rule 1.1 requires that a lawyer "maintain the requisite knowledge and skill … including the benefits and risks associated with relevant technology …"

What does this really mean?

- A working knowledge of the infrastructure that supports storing and retaining client data in a safe way. This goes to confidentiality and the requirement that lawyers keep client data (especially that which is stored electronically) safe when using technology such as email, text messages, cloud storage, client portals, etc.
- Using electronic discovery.
- Leveraging technology to deliver legal services such as automated document assembly.
- Knowing how to conduct basic internet searches to help investigate a case.
- Knowing how to use technology to organize, present, and explain information in a courtroom. Many attorneys use technology while presenting to a jury.

ABA Model Rule 1.1, Comment 8 requires that an attorney's duty of competence includes keeping "abreast of changes in the law and its practice, including the benefits and risks associated with relevant technology." Attorneys must implement cybersecurity measures to protect client data and understand how to conduct discovery of electronically stored information (ESI) as part of their duties of competence, confidentiality and diligence. Consequently, a lack of technological knowledge will not serve as a defense (California State Bar Formal Opinion No. 2015-193) in disciplinary action.

Attorneys should take appropriate steps to ensure client information remains protected against unauthorized disclosure. This includes but is not limited to: taking proper safeguards, such as using strong user names and passwords, restricting file permissions, using malware protection or firewalls, and encrypting sensitive information before transmission. All law firm personnel should be instructed and trained in client confidentiality. Furthermore, with increasing regulation being implemented around the world on data privacy (ranging from the General Data Protection Regulation (GDPR) to the California Consumer Privacy Act (CCPA)), attorneys not only face liability to state bar rules, but they also have to remain compliant with new data privacy statutes.

Consequences for Incompetence

Breach of Standard of Conduct

Violating the ethical rule for competence can result in discipline by the state bar. For example, in *In re Dominic G. Vorv*, 172 A.3d 911, the DC Board on Professional Responsibility found an attorney incompetent for several missteps made in representing a burglary client. Notably, the court found that the attorney did not provide competent representation when he failed to warn his client about possible immigration consequences for pleading guilty to felony burglary.

CASE ALERT: IN RE DOMINIC G. VORV, 172 A.3D 911

In this disciplinary matter, the District of Columbia Court of Appeals Board on Professional Responsibility Ad Hoc Hearing Committee (the Committee) recommends approval of a petition for negotiated attorney discipline. The violations stem from respondent Dominic G. Vorv's professional misconduct arising from acts or omissions during the course of his representation of one client in post-conviction and immigration proceedings. In brief, after the client had pleaded guilty and been convicted of burglary in the Circuit Court of Fairfax County, Virginia, the United States Department of Homeland Security instituted proceedings for his removal on the premise that he had been convicted of an "aggravated felony" as defined by the Immigration and Nationality Act, see 8 U.S.C. § 1101 (a)(43)(G). In attempting to forestall his client's removal, respondent made several missteps that jeopardized his client's rights. First, respondent petitioned the Virginia Circuit Court to vacate his client's conviction and guilty plea based on the mistaken claim that the court had failed to advise his client about the potential immigration consequences of the conviction. Thereafter, without consulting his client, respondent dismissed the petition, conceded removability before the Immigration Court, and did not seek to challenge or delay his client's deportation on any other ground. Ultimately, the client retained new counsel who successfully argued against removal on the ground that the burglary offense for which he had been convicted was not an "aggravated felony" within the meaning of the Immigration and Nationality Act.

Respondent acknowledged that he (1) failed to provide competent representation and serve his client with skill and care; (2) failed to explain a matter to the client; and (3) engaged in conduct that seriously interfered with the administration of justice, thereby violating Rules 1.1 (a) & (b), 1.4 (b) and 8.4 (d) of the District of Columbia Rules of Professional Conduct.

District of Columbia Court of Appeals, "In re Dominic G. Vorv," 172 A.3d 911, 2017.

In mitigation, the Committee considered the fact that respondent knowingly and voluntarily acknowledged the facts and misconduct and does not have a prior history of discipline. As a result, Disciplinary Counsel and respondent negotiated the imposition of discipline in the form of a thirty-day suspension, stayed, and one year of probation during which respondent must (1) contact the District of Columbia Bar's Practice Management Advisory Service (PMAS) within thirty days of the commencement of the probationary period and schedule and obtain an assessment; (2) implement any PMAS recommendations; (3) provide PMAS with a signed release waiving confidentiality so Disciplinary Counsel can verify respondent obtained an assessment; (4) join the American Immigration Lawyers' Association (AILA), or an equivalent organization; (5) enroll in and attend ten CLE hours pertaining to immigration law; (6) submit proof of both his enrollment in AILA, or an equivalent organization, and his completion of ten CLE hours pertaining to immigration law; and (7) not be found to have engaged in any ethical misconduct. After reviewing the amended petition for negotiated discipline, considering a supporting affidavit, conducting a limited hearing, reviewing Disciplinary Counsel's files and records, and holding an ex parte meeting with Disciplinary Counsel, the Committee concluded that the petition for negotiated discipline should be approved.

In accordance with our procedures in uncontested disciplinary cases, we agree this case is appropriate for negotiated discipline. We accept the Committee's recommendation because the Committee properly applied D.C. Bar R. XI, § 12.1 (c), and we find no error in the Committee's determination. Based upon the record before the court, the negotiated discipline of a thirty-day suspension from the practice of law, stayed, and one year of probation with the conditions set forth above is not unduly lenient considering the discipline imposed by this court for similar actions.

Accordingly, it is ORDERED that Dominic G. Vorv is hereby suspended from the practice of law in the District of Columbia for thirty days, stayed, and is placed on one year of supervised probation during which respondent must (1) contact PMAS within thirty days of the commencement of the probationary period and schedule and obtain an assessment; (2) implement any PMAS recommendations; (3) provide PMAS with a signed release waiving confidentiality so Disciplinary Counsel can verify respondent obtained an assessment; (4) join AILA or an equivalent organization; (5) enroll in and attend ten CLE hours pertaining to immigration law; (6) submit proof of both his enrollment in AILA, or an equivalent organization, and his completion of ten CLE hours pertaining to immigration law; and (7) not be found to have engaged in any ethical misconduct.

So ordered.

After reading the case, ask yourself: is understanding the immigration consequences of pleading guilty to a crime knowledge that every attorney has? Is it knowledge an attorney <u>should</u> have?

Negligence

What happens if the lack of competence is so great that it amounts to negligence? Negligence occurs when there is a tortious breach of a duty of care and there is monetary harm to the client. The client has lost money or can prove that they would have received a different (better) damages amount due to the attorney's incompetence. Causation between loss and any incompetence must be proven here to prevail on an allegation of negligence.

Review the state bar complaint against a California attorney who missed several court appearances for a dog bite case for the client. During a final settlement conference, the attorney accepted the settlement offer without consulting his client. In fact, the attorney made false statements about his client's approval of the settlement, knowing them to be false. Consequently, the attorney was given a one-year stayed suspension with 30 days of actual suspension and two years' probation.

Ineffective Assistance of Counsel

Ineffective assistance of counsel is a claim asserted by a criminal defendant that the defense attorney failed to perform in a reasonably competent manner. The heart of the claim comes from the US Constitution—namely, the Sixth Amendment—which guarantees the right to counsel for one's defense. The right to counsel is the right to the effective assistance of counsel.[1]

For a claim to be successful, the court must determine that: (i) defense counsel's performance fell "below an objective standard of reasonableness" and (ii) "but for counsel's unprofessional errors, the result of the proceeding would have been different."[2] This is a difficult test to prove, as it is easy for judges on review to say that they think a judge or jury would have come to the same conclusion anyway. Justice Marshall in his dissent in *Strickland* noted:

> I object to the prejudice standard adopted by the Court for two independent reasons. First, it is often very difficult to tell whether a defendant convicted after a trial in which he was ineffectively represented would have fared better if his lawyer had been competent. Seemingly impregnable cases can sometimes be dismantled by good defense counsel. On the basis of a cold record, it may be impossible for a reviewing court confidently to ascertain how the government's evidence and arguments would have stood up against rebuttal and cross-examination by a shrewd, well-prepared lawyer.[3]

Thus, although frequently filed, very few ineffective assistance of counsel claims are successful. However, the reader should consider that such a claim relates to competent lawyering.

---

1. *McMann v. Richardson*, 397 U.S. 759
2. *Strickland v. Washington*, 466 U.S. 668 (1984)
3. Ibid. at 710 (Marshall, J., dissenting)

Diligence

Rule 1.3 is the shortest rule with one sentence—A lawyer shall act with reasonable diligence and promptness in representing a client. Of course, the use of the word "reasonable" is noteworthy, as the lawyer has some discretion when it comes to how a matter is pursued. The rules do not require a lawyer to press for every advantage (Comment 1). In other words, the lawyer does not have to use offensive or uncourteous tactics to pursue the client's objectives. It does, however, require that the lawyer act with commitment and dedication to the interests of the client.

Consider the boating accident example discussed earlier. The attorney will want to promptly ascertain the basic facts, including the location of the accident, identification and citizenship of the parties, and whether any documents govern the case—like a passenger contract. Each of these could affect where and when the case needs to be filed. If you do not do this soon enough, it might become too late to actually file the case in the correct court and harming the client's ability to recover.

An important aspect of diligence is about controlling workload so that lawyers can give proper attention to each client's matter (Comment 2). This issue can be particularly problematic at public defender and legal aid clinics where resources are limited. Even large law firms are not immune to this issue during a busy period, such as a trial where more resources than usual are allocated to a single case. They can be short-staffed and may not be able to hire lawyers quickly enough for cases coming in. Sometimes, the business logistics of law firms can impede diligence. It is an important reminder that diligence is not about the lawyer's singular abilities but also many other factors.

Additionally, neglect and procrastination are generally frowned upon, as it undermines the client's confidence in the lawyer's trustworthiness. When lawyers miss important deadlines, it can change the client's legal position or advantage.

Despite its brevity, diligence is one of the most important rules for lawyers, as it is linked with client communication. Neglect of a client matter can lead to discipline, even when the client did not suffer an injury or obtained the desired result.

Although competence and diligence go hand in hand, they are different. For example, competence requires lawyers to know how to determine the applicable statute of limitations. In contrast, diligence requires being aware of the period of limitations and ensuring legal claims are brought within that time.

Ethics vs. Malpractice

In closing, the reader should consider the differences between a violation of the ethical rules and a lawsuit for malpractice. The Preamble to the ABA Model Rules states that they are not designed to be a basis for civil liability. A violation of the ethical rules does not automatically result in a winning malpractice lawsuit. A client will need to show a violation of the duty of care to the client, causation, and damages for a successful malpractice claim. The duty of care is usually judged against the skills, knowledge, and thoroughness that other members of the profession commonly possess.

For example, fulfilling the ethical duty of competence in elder law can be challenging. Lawyers must know estate planning, probate law, property law, and understand the basics of planning for incapacity (including the powers of attorney and conservatorships). When the elderly client suffers an impairment, the lawyer must determine whether the client still has the legal capacity to execute legal documents. All of these issues require a level of care that satisfies each of these practice areas, the absence of which could result in possible malpractice exposure.

Lawyers try to avoid malpractice in several ways. First, they usually prefer that attorney-client communication be documented and in writing. Next, they have malpractice insurance, which is helpful should a lawyer need to defend themselves. Lastly, they limit the scope of their representation, such that they are not advising clients about matters that are outside their expertise or comfort level. For instance, a transactional attorney will limit their scope of representation such that they are not doing litigation work if a dispute arises.

Key Takeaways

- The key component of an attorney's job is competency.
- An attorney can take on a matter even if not competent because the rules let attorneys become competent through reasonable preparation or by associating with someone who is competent.
- Clients cannot waive competence.
- If it turns out an attorney is not competent, an attorney can be disciplined or sued for malpractice. Malpractice only works if all elements are satisfied: duty, breach, causation, and damages.
- Most attorneys have malpractice insurance.
- In a criminal case, use competency as a standard for ineffective assistance of counsel.
- Technology competence is just as important.

Ethics in Action

Read the following disciplinary action(s) in which the state bar used the rules discussed in this chapter to bring disciplinary charges against an attorney.

- Neglecting a client [six-month suspension]: *Matter of Wallace* https://law.justia.com/cases/new-jersey/supreme-court/1986/104-n-j-589-1.html

End-of-Chapter Discussion Questions

1. Does the bar exam do enough to ensure attorney competence?
2. What steps can new lawyers take to become competent?
3. What steps can international LLMs take to become competent?
4. What role does a supervising attorney play in lawyer competency?
5. What if an emergency situation comes up, but a lawyer is not deemed competent under ABA Model Rule 1.1? For example, your neighbor knocks on your door asking for help as police officers are at her house asking questions. You are not a criminal lawyer, but you would still like to help your neighbor. Can you?

CHAPTER 4

Attorney Fees

> Visit your interactive ebook to download the Chapter 4 Outline.

Learning Objectives

- Recognize types of attorney fees.
- Understand what goes into a fee agreement.
- Know when referral fees may be given.

Key Terms

- **Contingency fees:** A sum of money, usually a previously set percentage, that a lawyer receives for a fee only if the matter is successful.
- **Flat or fixed fees:** A fixed amount paid to a lawyer irrespective of the number of hours spent on the case.
- **Retainer:** An advance or deposit against future work.
- **Hourly fees:** A set hourly rate a lawyer will receive for legal service throughout the legal representation.
- **Hybrid-hourly contingency:** A mixture of the hourly rate and contingency fee models, it involves the attorney being paid a guaranteed hourly fee and then being paid a bonus fee if the client's claim receives strong recovery.
- **Statutory fees:** Fees in some cases may be set by statute or a court may set and approve a fee. Often seen in probate, bankruptcy, or other proceedings.
- **Consultation fees:** Though rare, a lawyer may charge an hourly or fixed amount at an initial meeting where both the lawyer and potential client determine whether the lawyer can assist the client on the matter.
- **Referral fees:** A lawyer who refers a matter to another lawyer for a portion of the total

fees paid for the case, usually one-third.
- **Alternative Fee Arrangements (AFA):** An AFA is any fee agreement in which a client pays an attorney something other than a standard hourly rate for the legal work performed. Sometimes, AFAs are rereferred to as "value-based billing." Here, a lawyer is paid for the value delivered rather than the time taken to provide the service.

Authors' Note: In this chapter, we heavily discuss the California Rules of Professional Conduct when discussing fees. We do this for two main reasons: 1) the authors are California-based practitioners who know the jurisdiction well, and we felt a discussion of the California Rules provided a good contrast and comparison to the ABA Model Rules, and 2) the authors wanted to highlight the creativity that the ABA Model Rules and jurisdictions like California allow when it comes to fee arrangements between clients and lawyers.

Introduction

HYPOTHETICAL 4.1: WHEN A THIRD PARTY PAYS YOUR BILL

Can someone else pay your legal fees if you cannot afford a lawyer? Could it interfere with how the lawyer interacts with you (the nonpaying client)? What happens if you agree to a portion of your recovery to the lawsuit funder as reimbursement for the legal fees paid? These questions and more are addressed in State Bar of California Standing Committee Formal Opinion No.14-0002.

Please refer to the interactive ebook in Cognella Active Learning for interactive/media content.

Pause for Reflection

Attorneys have an obligation to understand how any agreement where a nonclient is paying for legal fees (also called a funding agreement) impacts the litigation and advise a client accordingly. ABA Model Rule 1.7 prohibits a lawyer from representing a client if there is a significant risk that the representation will be materially limited by the lawyer's relationship with a third person or the lawyer's own interest without informed written consent, or in other words, does it create a conflict of interest? ABA Model Rule 1.7 (d) further requires that the lawyer must reasonably believe that they can provide diligent and competent representation, notwithstanding the potential relationship with a third party. The most important aspect of litigation funding is that the lawyer's independent professional judgment should not impair their ability to maintain the fiduciary duties of care, loyalty, and confidentiality to the client.

After reviewing the opinion, what concerns do you have with litigation funding? If proper safeguards were in place, is it possible to maintain confidentiality?

> Please refer to the interactive ebook in Cognella Active Learning for interactive/media content.

The ABA Model Rules require lawyers to serve their clients with competence, diligence, and loyalty. These duties are balanced against the business side of every attorney-client relationship, where the attorney is paid for services rendered. Even though the ABA and many other state rules allow for creativity when it comes to fee agreements between clients and lawyers, we cannot overlook the fact that every fee agreement creates the potential for conflict. For this reason, the ABA Model Rules have created clear guidelines on how fees should be set.

Standard for Fees

Reasonableness

As we established in Chapter 1, lawyers are not generally regarded by the public as ethical. One major contributor is lawyer billing practices. Many lawsuits and state bar complaints arise because clients disagree with the total fees payable for lawyer services. The very factors that make attorney's services valuable—their knowledge of the law and specialized training—lead to special scrutiny of fee agreements. The attorney-client relationship is a fiduciary relationship wherein the attorney must put the client's interests before their own financial interests.

The ABA has established guidelines for lawyers to follow when setting fees. The lawyer must provide the basis for the fees and clearly outline how fees are established. ABA Model Rule 1.5 requires that fees (whether hourly, fixed or contingent) must be reasonable.

The word *reasonable* is an inherently ambiguous term, which is why the ABA provides eight factors for assessing reasonableness. In practice, fees can be much more complex than what the rules set them out to be.

It is important to note that fee arrangements should be established at the commencement of the attorney-client relationship. However, the analysis pertaining to reasonableness applies throughout the representation.

Although the ABA does not require non-contingency fee agreements to be in writing, the authors of this textbook strongly recommend that all fee agreements be in writing. Attorneys should take special care to make sure that their client understands, and agrees to, the fee agreement. This is especially important if your client speaks a different language, may have diminished mental capacity, or is a minor. You must make sure there is an agreement as to the fees.

Factors

ABA Model Rule 1.5(a) provides a variety of factors in determining the reasonableness of a fee. They are:

- Time and labor required.
- Novelty and difficulty of the questions involved.
- The skill required to handle the problems presented.
- The lawyer's experience, ability, and reputation.
- The amount involved and benefit resulting to the client from the services.
- The customary fee charged in the locality for similar services.
- The time limitations imposed by the client or by the circumstances.
- Whether the fee is fixed or contingent.

This is by no means an exclusive list, and not all factors have to be present when evaluating the reasonableness of the fee. Whether an attorney has violated ABA Model Rule 1.5 depends on the facts and circumstances of each specific situation as determined when the fee agreement is initiated and throughout representation. Generally, the more time and labor a lawyer invests, the higher the fee is likely to be. Similarly, if a lawyer is handling a complex legal issue that requires a certain level of expertise, they can charge a higher fee. Lawyers who have a certain reputation and experience level can charge a higher fee and will have clients who are willing to pay for this higher fee.

PRACTICE PROBLEM: IS THIS FEE REASONABLE?
Apply the eight factors above and decide which lawyer you would choose.

You are driving alone in your car. It is a relatively new car—only about a year old, about 9,500 miles on it, and in good condition. You have been fairly good about maintaining the service on the car, although you have missed the last service appointment about 200 miles ago because you have just been busy. As you are driving along, your brakes fail. You crash into a storefront causing substantial damage to the store and to your car. You are severely injured and spend months in the hospital.

The store and the hospital have filed a lawsuit against you for damages. In the lawsuit, the store and hospital estimate actual damages for this case are almost $2 million. You are worried about the missing service appointment and the brake failure. Are the two related? Is this your fault, or the fault of the manufacturer of the car or the brakes? You interview two lawyers who are willing to take on your case:

1. Jessica Hart—She is a lawyer who has been practicing for 10 years who is considered a "bulldog" in car accident cases and knows the ins and outs of car mechanisms. Her reputation precedes her, and her trial track record is impressive. Some cases are known to settle just because she is the lawyer on the case. She

assures you she can "pin" this on the manufacturer of the car and the brakes (does not matter which one!) and make them pay! She has a car and brake expert she works with regularly that she will bring into this case, but you will have to pay for their expertise. Her strategy seems hard to beat. She is also brash, arrogant, and not the nicest or most nurturing person in the world. You do not necessarily feel soothed around her. Her **hourly fee** is $850, and she requires a $50,000 retainer upfront.

2. Bill Ward—He is also a lawyer who has been practicing for 10 years. He has handled plenty of auto accident cases and does not see this one as much different from other normal car accident cases. He thinks you should try to settle early in the case, and he does not seem interested in negotiating down what the hospital and store are asking for. But he also says if the parties are not open to settlement, "let us do some discovery and flesh out the issues and go from there." He does not really have a strategy, but you feel comfortable around him. He has a great "bedside manner" and is friendly. His hourly fee is $350.

Which lawyer do you choose and why? Which lawyer are you willing to pay the hourly fee for and why?

CASE ALERT: IN CRUZ V. SEWARD PARK HOUS. CORP.

In Cruz v. Seward Park Hous. Corp., a New York judge called the fee request of Greenberg Traurig (a well-known New York law firm) "highway robbery without the six-gun." In this case, five shareholders brought a lawsuit rejecting the Seward Park board's decision to switch from self-parking to valet parking. The court dismissed the case, describing it as a "relatively straightforward" proceeding. Greenberg Traurig, who helped the shareholders win this lawsuit, requested $235,000 in attorney fees for all work, including pre-hearing letter briefs and preparing for the hearing, up to, but not including, the one-day hearing before a special referee. Seward Park challenged the fee as unreasonable.

After reviewing the case, what do you think? Is this a reasonable fee?

In another case, *In re Fordham* (1997),[1] the court said that even though a lawyer had done work for the client, he should not have spent $50,022 worth of time clearing an accused drunken driver. The court found that Mr. Fordham, a trial lawyer, violated the state's ethics rules by charging $50,002 for 227 hours of billable work by his firm. They found the fee excessive, even though the lawyer came up with a novel theory to suppress the breathalyzer results. The average fee for drunken driving cases typically ranges from $1,500 to $10,000.

---

1. 423 Mass. 481

Expert witnesses testified the hours were excessive and no unusual circumstances required such excessive work. This case was a "standard operating under the influence" matter. There was no way to justify these hours with reference to any novelty or difficulty in question. Defense experts for Fordham claimed the matter to be "extremely tough" and that the breathalyzer argument took time because of its novelty. The court agreed that the novelty of the breathalyzer suppression argument was novel and impressive. Still, such efforts could not justify the ultimate fee of $50,000 in a case usually amounting to one-third of that fee. Inexperience in criminal matters cannot justify an excessive fee, and a lawyer should generally avoid employment in an area of the law they are unfamiliar with. Fordham departed substantially from the obligation of professional responsibility owed to his clients. Fordham received a public reprimand for charging excessive fees.

Opinion
O'Connor, J.

This is an appeal from the Board of Bar Overseers' (board's) dismissal of a petition for discipline filed by bar counsel against attorney Laurence S. Fordham. On March 11, 1992, bar counsel served Fordham with a petition for discipline alleging that Fordham had charged a clearly excessive fee in violation of S.J.C. Rule 3:07, DR 2-106, as appearing in 382 Mass. 772 (1981), for defending Timothy Clark (Timothy) in the District Court against a charge that he operated a motor vehicle while under the influence of intoxicating liquor (OUI) and against other related charges. Fordham moved that the board dismiss the petition and the board chair recommended that that be done. Bar counsel appealed from the chair's decision to the full board, and the board referred the matter to a hearing committee.

After five days of hearings, and with "serious reservations," the hearing committee concluded that Fordham's fee was not substantially in excess of a reasonable fee and that, therefore, the committee recommended against bar discipline. Bar counsel appealed from that determination to the board. By a vote of six to five, with one abstention, the board accepted the recommendation of the hearing committee and dismissed the petition for discipline. Bar counsel then filed in the Supreme Judicial Court for Suffolk County (county court) a claim of appeal from the board's action.

Fordham moved in the county court for a dismissal of bar counsel's appeal. A single justice denied Fordham's motion and reported the case to the full court. We conclude that the single justice correctly denied Fordham's motion to dismiss bar counsel's appeal. We conclude, also, that the board erred in dismissing bar counsel's petition for discipline. We direct a judgment ordering public censure be entered in the county court.

We summarize the hearing committee's findings. On March 4, 1989, the Acton police department arrested Timothy, then twenty-one years old, and charged him with OUI, operating a motor vehicle after suspension, speeding, and operating an unregistered motor vehicle. At the time of the arrest, the police discovered a partially full quart of vodka in the vehicle. After failing

Supreme Judicial Court of Massachusetts, Suffolk, "In Re Fordham," 668 N.E.2d 816, 1997.

a field sobriety test, Timothy was taken to the Acton police station where he submitted to two breathalyzer tests which registered .10 and .12 respectively.

Subsequent to Timothy's arraignment, he and his father, Laurence Clark (Clark) consulted with three lawyers, who offered to represent Timothy for fees between $3,000 and $10,000. Shortly after the arrest, Clark went to Fordham's home to service an alarm system which he had installed several years before. While there, Clark discussed Timothy's arrest with Fordham's wife who invited Clark to discuss the case with Fordham. Fordham then met with Clark and Timothy.

At this meeting, Timothy described the incidents leading to his arrest and the charges against him. Fordham, whom the hearing committee described as a "very experienced senior trial attorney with impressive credentials," told Clark and Timothy that he had never represented a client in a driving while under the influence case or in any criminal matter, and he had never tried a case in the District Court. The hearing committee found that "Fordham explained that although he lacked experience in this area, he was a knowledgeable and hard-working attorney and that he believed he could competently represent Timothy. Fordham described himself as 'efficient and economic in the use of [his] time.'...

"Towards the end of the meeting, Fordham told the Clarks that he worked on [a] time charge basis and that he billed monthly. . . . In other words, Fordham would calculate the amount of hours he and others in the firm worked on a matter each month and multiply it by the respective hourly rates. He also told the Clarks that he would engage others in his firm to prepare the case. Clark had indicated that he would pay Timothy's legal fees." After the meeting, Clark hired Fordham to represent Timothy.

According to the hearing committee's findings, Fordham filed four pretrial motions on Timothy's behalf, two of which were allowed. One motion, entitled "Motion in Limine to Suppress Results of Breathalyzer Tests," was based on the theory that, although two breathalyzer tests were exactly .02 apart, they were not "within" .02 of one another as the regulations require. See 501 Code Mass. Regs. § 2.56(2) (1994). The hearing committee characterized the motion and its rationale as "a creative, if not novel, approach to suppression of breathalyzer results." Although the original trial date was June 20, 1989, the trial, which was before a judge without jury, was held on October 10 and October 19, 1989. The judge found Timothy not guilty of driving while under the influence.

Fordham sent the following bills to Clark:

"1. April 19, 1989, $3,250 for services rendered in March, 1989.

"2. May 15, 1989, $9,850 for services rendered in April, 1989.

"3. June 19, 1989, $3,950 for services rendered in May, 1989.

"4. July 13, 1989, $13,300 for services rendered in June, 1989.

"5. October 13, 1989, $35,022.25 revised bill for services rendered from March 19 to June 30, 1989.

"6. November 7, 1989, $15,000 for services rendered from July 1, 1989 to October 19, 1989."

The bills totaled $50,022.25, reflecting 227 hours of billed time, 153 hours of which were expended by Fordham and seventy-four of which were his associates' time. Clark did not pay the first two bills when they became due and expressed to Fordham his concern about their amount. Clark paid Fordham $10,000 on June 20, 1989. At that time, Fordham assured Clark that most of the work had been completed "other than taking [the case] to trial." Clark did not make any subsequent payments. Fordham requested Clark to sign a promissory note evidencing his debt to Fordham and, on October 7, 1989, Clark did so. In the October 13, 1989, bill, Fordham added a charge of $5,000 as a "retroactive increase" in fees. On November 7, 1989, after the case was completed, Fordham sent Clark a bill for $15,000.

Bar counsel and Fordham have stipulated that all the work billed by Fordham was actually done and that Fordham and his associates spent the time they claim to have spent. They also have stipulated that Fordham acted conscientiously, diligently, and in good faith in representing Timothy and in his billing in this case.

[...]

Bar counsel contends that the board's decision to dismiss the petition for discipline is erroneous on three grounds: First, "[t]he hearing committee and the Board committed error by analyzing only three of the factors set out in DR 2-106(B) (1) – (8), and their findings with regard to these criteria do not support their conclusion that the fee in this case was not clearly excessive"; second, the board "misinterpreted [DR 2-106'S] prohibition against charging a clearly excessive fee by reading into the rule a 'safe harbor' provision"; and third, "by allowing client acquiescence as a complete defense."

[...]

The first factor listed in DR 2-106(B) requires examining "[t]he time and labor required, the novelty and difficulty of the questions involved, and the skill requisite to perform the legal service properly." Although the hearing committee determined that Fordham "spent a large number of hours on [the] matter, in essence learning from scratch what others . . . already know," it "[did] not credit Bar Counsel's argument that Fordham violated DR 2-106 by spending too many hours." The hearing committee reasoned that even if the number of hours Fordham "spent [were] wholly out of proportion" to the number of hours that a lawyer with experience in the trying of OUI cases would require, the committee was not required to conclude that the fee based on time spent was "clearly excessive." It was enough, the hearing committee concluded, that Clark instructed Fordham to pursue the case to trial, Fordham did so zealously and, as stipulated, Fordham spent the hours he billed in good faith and diligence. We disagree.

Four witnesses testified before the hearing committee as experts on OUI cases. One of the experts, testifying on behalf of bar counsel, opined that "the amount of time spent in this case is clearly excessive." He testified that there were no unusual circumstances in the OUI charge against Timothy and that it was a "standard operating under the influence case." The witness did agree that Fordham's argument for suppression of the breathalyzer test results, which was successful, was novel and would have justified additional time and labor. He also acknowledged that the acquittal was a good result; even with the suppression of the breathalyzer tests, he testified, the chances of an acquittal would have been "[n]ot likely at a bench trial." The witness estimated that it would have been necessary, for thorough preparation of the case including the novel breathalyzer suppression argument, to have billed twenty to thirty hours for preparation, not including trial time.

A second expert, testifying on behalf of bar counsel, expressed his belief that the issues presented in this case were not particularly difficult, nor novel, and that "[t]he degree of skill required to defend a case such as this. . . was not that high." He did recognize, however, that the theory that Fordham utilized to suppress the breathalyzer tests was impressive and one of which he had previously never heard. Nonetheless, the witness concluded that "clearly there is no way that [he] could justify these kind of hours to do this kind of work." He estimated that an OUI case involving these types of issues would require sixteen hours of trial preparation and approximately fifteen hours of trial time. He testified that he had once spent ninety hours in connection with an OUI charge against a client that had resulted in a plea. The witness explained, however, that that case had involved a second offense OUI and that it was a case of first impression in 1987, concerning new breathalyzer equipment and comparative breathalyzer tests.

An expert called by Fordham testified that the facts of Timothy's case presented a challenge and that without the suppression of the breathalyzer test results it would have been "an almost impossible situation in terms of prevailing on the trier of fact." He further stated that, based on the particulars in Timothy's case, he believed that Fordham's hours were not excessive and, in fact, he, the witness, would have spent a comparable amount of time. The witness later admitted, however, that within the past five years, the OUI cases which he had brought to trial required no more than a total of forty billed hours, which encompassed all preparation and court appearances. He explained that, although he had not charged more than forty hours to prepare an OUI case, in comparison to Fordham's more than 200 expended hours, Fordham nonetheless had spent a reasonable number of hours on the case in light of the continuance and the subsequent need to reprepare, as well as the "very ingenious" breathalyzer suppression argument, and the Clarks' insistence on trial. In addition, the witness testified that, although the field sobriety test, breathalyzer tests, and the presence of a half-empty liquor bottle in the car placed Fordham at a serious disadvantage in being able to prevail on the OUI charge, those circumstances were not unusual and in fact agreed that they were "[n]ormal circumstances."

The fourth expert witness, called by Fordham, testified that she believed the case was "extremely tough" and that the breathalyzer suppression theory was novel. She testified that, although the time and labor consumed on the case was more than usual in defending an OUI charge, the hours were not excessive. They were not excessive, she explained, because the case was particularly difficult due to the "stakes [and] the evidence." She conceded, however, that legal issues in defending OUI charges are "pretty standard" and that the issues presented in this case were not unusual. Furthermore, the witness testified that challenging the breathalyzer test due to the .02 discrepancy was not unusual, but the theory on which Fordham proceeded was novel. Finally, she stated that she thought she may have known of one person who might have spent close to one hundred hours on a difficult OUI case; she was not sure; but she had never heard of a fee in excess of $10,000 for a bench trial.

In considering whether a fee is "clearly excessive" within the meaning of S.J.C. Rule 3:07, DR 2-106(B), the first factor to be considered pursuant to that rule is "the novelty and difficulty of the questions involved, and the skill requisite to perform the legal service properly." DR 2-106(B)(1). That standard is similar to the familiar standard of reasonableness traditionally applied in civil fee disputes. See *Society of Jesus of New England v. Boston Landmarks Comm'n*, 411 Mass. 754, 759 n. 10 (1992)(reasonable hours, when calculating fees pursuant to 42 U.S.C. § 1988, requires consideration as to "whether that time was reasonable in light of the difficulty of the case and the results achieved"). See also Restatement (Third) of the Law Governing Lawyers § 46 comment f (Proposed Final Draft 1996)("The standards that apply when fees are challenged as unreasonable in fee disputes are also relevant in the discipline of lawyers for charging unreasonably high fees"). Based on the testimony of the four experts, the number of hours devoted to Timothy's OUI case by Fordham and his associates was substantially in excess of the hours that a prudent experienced lawyer would have spent. According to the evidence, the number of hours spent was several times the amount of time any of the witnesses had ever spent on a similar case. We are not unmindful of the novel and successful motion to suppress the breathalyzer test results, but that effort cannot justify a $50,000 fee in a type of case in which the usual fee is less than one-third of that amount.

The board determined that "[b]ecause [Fordham] had never tried an OUI case or appeared in the district court, [Fordham] spent over 200 hours preparing the case, in part to educate himself in the relevant substantive law and court procedures." Fordham's inexperience in criminal defense work and OUI cases in particular cannot justify the extraordinarily high fee. It cannot be that an inexperienced lawyer is entitled to charge three or four times as much as an experienced lawyer for the same service. A client "should not be expected to pay for the education of a lawyer when he spends excessive amounts of time on tasks which, with reasonable experience, become matters of routine." *Matter of the Estate of Larson*, 103 Wn.2d 517, 531 (1985). "While the licensing of a lawyer is evidence that he has met the standards then prevailing for admission to the bar, a lawyer generally should not accept employment in any area of the law in which he is not qualified. However, he may accept such employment if in good faith he expects to become qualified through study and investigation, as long as such preparation would not result in unreasonable delay or expense to his client." Model Code of Professional Responsibility

EC 6-3 (1982). Although the ethical considerations set forth in the ABA Code of Professional Responsibility and Canons of Judicial Ethics are not binding, they nonetheless serve as a guiding principle. See SJ.C. Rule 3:07, as appearing in 382 Mass. 768 (1981) (Ethical Considerations "are not adopted as a rule of this court, but those Ethical Considerations form a body of principles upon which the Canons of Ethics and Disciplinary Rules, as herein adopted, are to be interpreted").

DR 2-106(B) provides that the third factor to be considered in ascertaining the reasonableness of a fee is its comparability to "[t]he fee customarily charged in the locality for similar legal services." The hearing committee made no finding as to the comparability of Fordham's fee with the fees customarily charged in the locality for similar services. However, one of bar counsel's expert witnesses testified that he had never heard of a fee in excess of $15,000 to defend a first OUI charge, and the customary flat fee in an OUI case, including trial, "runs from $1,000 to $7,500." Bar counsel's other expert testified that he had never heard of a fee in excess of $10,000 for a bench trial. In his view, the customary charge for a case similar to Timothy's would vary between $1,500 and $5,000. One of Fordham's experts testified that she considered a $40,000 or $50,000 fee for defending an OUI charge "unusual and certainly higher by far than any I've ever seen before." The witness had never charged a fee of more than $3,500 for representing a client at a bench trial to defend a first offense OUI charge. She further testified that she believed an "average OUI in the bench session is two thousand [dollars] and sometimes less." Finally, that witness testified that she had "heard a rumor" that one attorney charged $10,000 for a bench trial involving an OUI charge; this fee represented the highest fee of which she was aware. The other expert witness called by Fordham testified that he had heard of a $35,000 fee for defending OUI charges, but he had never charged more than $12,000 (less than twenty-five per cent of Fordham's fee).

Although finding that Fordham's fee was "much higher than the fee charged by many attorneys with more experience litigating driving under the influence cases," the hearing committee nevertheless determined that the fee charged by Fordham was not clearly excessive because Clark "went into the relationship with Fordham with open eyes," Fordham's fee fell within a "safe harbor," and Clark acquiesced in Fordham's fee by not strenuously objecting to his bills. The board accepted the hearing committee's analysis apart from the committee's reliance on the "safe harbor" rule.

The finding that Clark had entered into the fee agreement "with open eyes" was based on the finding that Clark hired Fordham after being fully apprised that he lacked any type of experience in defending an OUI charge and after interviewing other lawyers who were experts in defending OUI charges. Furthermore, the hearing committee and the board relied on testimony which revealed that the fee arrangement had been fully disclosed to Clark including the fact that Fordham "would have to become familiar with the law in that area." It is also significant, however, that the hearing committee found that "[d]espite Fordham's disclaimers concerning his experience, Clark did not appear to have understood in any real sense the implications of choosing Fordham to represent Timothy. Fordham did not give Clark any estimate of the total expected fee or the number of $200 hours that would be required." The express finding of the hearing committee that Clark "did not appear to have understood in any real sense the implications of choosing Fordham to represent Timothy" directly militates against the finding that Clark entered into the agreement "with open eyes."

That brings us to the hearing committee's finding that Fordham's fee fell within a "safe harbor." The hearing committee reasoned that as long as an agreement existed between a client and an attorney to bill a reasonable rate multiplied by the number of hours actually worked, the attorney's fee was within a "safe harbor" and thus protected from a challenge that the fee was clearly excessive. The board, however, in reviewing the hearing committee's decision, correctly rejected the notion "that a lawyer may always escape discipline with billings based on accurate time charges for work honestly performed."

The "safe harbor" formula would not be an appropriate rationale in this case because the amount of time Fordham spent to educate himself and represent Timothy was clearly excessive despite his good faith and diligence. Disciplinary Rule 2-106(B)'s mandate that "[a] fee is clearly excessive when, after a review of the facts, a lawyer of ordinary prudence, experienced in the area of the law involved, would be left with a definite and firm conviction that the fee is substantially in excess of a reasonable fee," creates explicitly an objective standard by which attorneys' fees are to be judged. We are not persuaded by Fordham's argument that "unless it can be shown that the 'excessive' work for which the attorney has charged goes beyond mere matters of professional judgment and can be proven, either directly or by reasonable inference, to have involved dishonesty, bad faith or overreaching of the client, no case for discipline has been established." Disciplinary Rule 2-106 plainly does not require an inquiry into whether the clearly excessive fee was charged to the client under fraudulent circumstances, and we shall not write such a meaning into the disciplinary rule. See *Private Reprimand PR-87-14*, 5 Mass. Att'y Discipline Rep. 501, 502 (1987) (violation of DR 2-106 [A] and [B], as appearing in 382 Mass. 772 found even where "no evidence of bad faith on the part of respondent"); *Matter of the Discipline of an Attorney*, 2 Mass. Att'y Discipline Rep. 115, 117 (1980) (violation of DR 2-106 [A] and [C], as appearing in 382 Mass. 772 even though no "overreaching or improper motivation").

Finally, bar counsel challenges the hearing committee's finding that "if Clark objected to the numbers of hours being spent by Fordham, he could have spoken up with some force when he began receiving bills." Bar counsel notes, and we agree, that "[t]he test as stated in the DR 2-106(A) is whether the fee 'charged' is clearly excessive, not whether the fee is accepted as valid or acquiesced in by the client." Therefore, we conclude that the hearing committee and the board erred in not concluding that Fordham's fee was clearly excessive.

Fordham argues that our imposition of discipline would offend his right to due process. A disciplinary sanction constitutes "a punishment or penalty" levied against the respondent, and therefore the respondent is entitled to procedural due process. *In re Ruffalo*, 390 U.S. 544, 550

(1968). *Matter of Kenney*, 399 Mass. 431, 436 (1987) ("attorney has a substantial property right in his license to practice law"). Fordham contends that the bar and, therefore, he, have not been given fair notice through prior decisions of this court or the express language of DR 2-106 that discipline may be imposed for billing excessive hours that were nonetheless spent diligently and in good faith. *Commonwealth v. Sefranka* 382 Mass. 108, 110 (1980), quoting *Connally v. General Constr. Co.*, 269 U.S. 385, 391 (1926) ("An essential principle of due process is that a statute may not proscribe conduct 'in terms so vague that men of common intelligence must necessarily guess at its meaning'"). It is true, as Fordham asserts, that there is a dearth of case law in the Commonwealth meting out discipline for an attorney's billing of a clearly excessive fee. There is, however, as we have noted above, case law which specifically addresses what constitutes an unreasonable attorney's fee employing virtually the identical factors contained within DR 2-106. See *Mulhern v. Roach*, 398 Mass. 18, 25-30 (1986); *McLaughlin v. Old Colony Trust Co.*, 313 Mass. 329, 335 (1943); *Cummings v. National Shawmut Bank*, 284 Mass. 563, 569 (1933). See also *Beatty v. NP Corp.*, 31 Mass. App. Ct. 606, 611 (1991) ("factors . . . to be considered in determining whether a lawyer's fee is fair and reasonable have been amply discussed in the cases"). More importantly, the general prohibition in DR 2-106(A) that "[a] lawyer shall not enter into an agreement for, charge, or collect an illegal or clearly excessive fee," is followed by eight specific, and clearly expressed, factors, to be evaluated by the standard of "a lawyer of ordinary prudence," in determining the propriety of the fee. Contrast *Gentile v. State Bar of Nev.*, 501 U.S. 1030, 1049 (1991), quoting *Grayned v. Rockford*, 408 U.S. 104, 112 (1972) (grammatical structure of attorney disciplinary rule and lack of clarifying interpretation by State court forced attorney to "guess at [the rule's] contours" thus failing to "provide 'fair notice to those to whom [it] is directed'"). In addition, nothing contained within the disciplinary rule nor within any pertinent case law indicates in any manner that a clearly excessive fee does not warrant discipline whenever the time spent during the representation was spent in good faith. The fact that this court has not previously had occasion to discipline an attorney in the circumstances of this case does not suggest that the imposition of discipline in this case offends due process. See *Commonwealth v. Twitchell*, 416 Mass. 114, 123, 125 n. 13 (1993) (defendants not deprived of "fair warning" that particular conduct was proscribed by penal statute where criminal liability depended on "degree" of conduct); *Matter of Saab*, 406 Mass. 315, 324 n. 13 (1989) (absence of codified standards to govern attorney discipline proceedings does not offend due process). We reject Fordham's due process argument.

In charging a clearly excessive fee, Fordham departed substantially from the obligation of professional responsibility that he owed to his client. The ABA Model Standards for Imposing Lawyer Sanctions § 7.3 (1992) endorses a public reprimand as the appropriate sanction for charging a clearly excessive fee. We deem such a sanction appropriate in this case. Accordingly, a judgment is to be entered in the county court imposing a public censure. The record in this case is to be unimpounded.

So ordered.

After reviewing the case, what do you think? Was the right decision made?

Client Trust Account

ABA Model Rule 1.15 requires a client's lawyers to hold client property in an account separate from the lawyer's personal property. The client's property includes client fees. Since the lawyer is a fiduciary with respect to the funds, they should be placed in a separate account until earned.

- Lawyers should be incredibly careful against the commingling of client funds with their own personal funds and also with other client funds. Absolute accurate accounting is a must!
- Exception: Government lawyers and in-house counsel do not have to maintain trust accounts.

Are Fees Refundable?

Unearned fees are refundable. In other words, any fees paid, whether in advance of representation or after, remain client property until services are rendered. Once services are rendered, these fees become the lawyer's property. Thus, if a lawyer withdraws before representation, any unearned fees must be returned to the client.

Exception

A pure retainer fee is a fee paid to secure the lawyer's availability during a specific time or for a specified matter. Think of it as a situation where the lawyer needs to drop everything when the client calls because the client has essentially paid for the lawyer's availability. These are rarely used anymore, as finding a lawyer is easier today than before. Today, a retainer is understood in the context of a "security" retainer, which is a fee paid to secure future services that the lawyer is expected to perform. When the lawyer performs these services, the deposit goes towards their payment.

Different Fee Arrangements

The three most common types of fee agreements are hourly, fixed, and **contingency fee** agreements. Lawyers can also enter into mixed agreements, also called alternative fee agreements—part fixed, part contingency.

Type of Fee Agreement	Description	Formula to Remember	Example
Hourly	Lawyer charges client per hour spent on a case, regardless of whether the client's claim or defense succeeds.	$+$+$	Common in litigation or transactional law
Fixed or Flat Fee	Lawyer charges client one amount irrespective of the number of hours spent on client's case.	$	Common in family law or criminal law

Contingency	Client pays a percentage of the total recovery; requires the lawyer to win the case. This fee arrangement can only be used when there is a substantial risk that the attorney gets no fee if the plaintiff loses.	% of $	Common for personal injury cases
Hybrid-Hourly Contingency	A mixture of the hourly rate and contingency fee model, it involves the attorney being paid a guaranteed (but relatively low) hourly fee and then being paid a bonus fee if the client's claim receives strong recovery.	$+% of $	Used for litigation
Statutory Fees	Statutory fees in some cases may be set by statute or a court may set and approve a fee that you pay. The reasoning behind scheduled fees is that any additional or unique legal services or time will not be required for that particular service.		These types of fees appear more often in probate or bankruptcy proceedings.

While these are the most common types of fee arrangements used, other variations of fee arrangements are used by parties, popularly referred to as Alternative Fee Agreements (AFAs). Examples include reverse contingency, success fees, blended rate, holdback with success bonus, and hybrid agreements.

Regardless of the type of fee arrangement you have with your client, it is important always to lay out the formal start of your relationship in an engagement letter. An attorney-client engagement letter should include the scope of the relationship, lawyer and client duties, and conflict waivers. Most importantly, they should be in plain English. They will also contain the basis of the fee, costs, and expenses associated with the matter and usually provide a way out of the relationship.

Sample Fee Agreements/Engagement Letters

Below are links to two sample fee engagement letters and language for you to consider.

- California Sample Fee Agreement Forms: http://www.calbar.ca.gov/Portals/0/documents/publicComment/2019/Sample-Fee-Agreement-Forms-for-Public-Comment-(03-15-19).pdf
- Simple Hourly Engagement Letter—Continuing Education of the Bar (CEB)

Please refer to the interactive ebook in Cognella Active Learning for interactive/media content.

Referral Fees: When Do Referral Fees Come into Play?

Referral fees are those fees that lawyers can collect from other lawyers simply for referring a case over to a different lawyer. Both the ABA and California Rules allow for referral fees between lawyers not of the same law firm. The practice encourages less experienced or competent lawyers not to handle matters that may be too complex for them, simply to earn a fee. This practice is often used at the time of trial. A less experienced trial lawyer may work up the case all the way through trial and then refer the case to an attorney who has more experience in trial practice. This practice is also useful when you have a case that becomes more complex as the discovery and investigation unfold. Suppose more complex legal issues come up, or it becomes clear that the case is now more high profile. In that case, referring the case to a more high-profile lawyer or a lawyer who has handled the type of complex issues you see can be beneficial to the case and the client.

The ABA, California Rules, and the courts in many jurisdictions are agreed that referral to an outside lawyer must still be done with the consent of the client.[2] Comment 6 to ABA Model Rule 1.1: Competence states that "Before a lawyer retains or contracts with other lawyers outside the lawyer's own firm to provide or assist in the provision of legal services to a client, the lawyer should ordinarily obtain informed consent from the client and must reasonably believe that the other lawyers' services will contribute to the competent and ethical representation of the client."

Referral Fees: *ABA v. California*

Both the ABA Model Rules and California Rules allow for the use of referral fees in practice. There is some difference in the ongoing requirement of the referring lawyer as highlighted below. In short, California allows pure referral fees, while the ABA does not. The ABA and California rules both use the term "sharing" or "dividing" fees when referencing referral fees.

---

2. Samuel v. Druckman & Sinel, LLP (2008 NY Slip Op 03073) (nycourts.gov)

ABA	CA
• A lawyer can share fees with a lawyer at another law firm only if: (1) the division is proportional to each lawyer's work or if each lawyer assumes joint responsibility (2) the client agrees to the division of fees, including the share each lawyer will receive, in writing and (3) the total fee is reasonable (ABA Model Rule 1.5(e)). For Example, Attorney A works up a case in preparation for trial. Attorney B, a reputable trial attorney, takes the case from Attorney A and handles the case completely through the completion of trial. Client agrees to this hand-off and agrees, in writing, that Attorney A will be paid for all work done prior to trial and Attorney B will be paid for all work done through completion of trial. The total fees are reasonable. • ABA Model Rule 1.5(e), division of fees between lawyers not in the same firm, is subject to the conflicts rules in ABA Model Rule 1.7—if a conflict under 1.7 exists the referring lawyer can only accept the fee and continue to take responsibility for the client in the referred matter if the requirements of 1.7(b) are met.	• Unlike the ABA Model Rules, California does not require ongoing responsibility to the client by the referring attorney. This means the referring attorney does not have to be involved in any part of the case once the referral is complete. Legal fees may be divided if (1) the client consents in writing after full disclosure and (2) total fee charged by all lawyers is not increased solely by reason of the provision for division of fees and (3) is not unconscionable (California Rule of Professional Conduct 1.5.1).

Attorney Fees: Does the Losing Side Have to Pay?

Unlike certain other countries, the losing party does not automatically pay the other side's attorney fees in the US. Generally, each side will bear its own attorney fees and costs. Many states do have individual statutes allowing for the recovery of attorney fees in specific instances. One such example is for malicious prosecution in civil or criminal matters. A defendant can bring a malicious prosecution action alleging that a party knowingly and maliciously initiated a baseless action against a defendant. Parties who prevail on malicious prosecution actions can recover their attorney fees spent in the underlying matter. They may even be able to recover other costs associated with the defense of an action that turned out to be deemed frivolous or harassment.

In other cases, if the parties are litigating a contract and the contract has a provision that the losing side pay attorney fees, such contracts can be held valid. The best practice is to understand how your specific jurisdiction handles attorney fees.

Sharing Fees with Nonlawyers

Can lawyers share legal fees with nonlawyers? Under ABA Model Rule 5.4, lawyers shall not share legal fees with nonlawyers. More recently, some states have started exploring the possible inclusion of nonlawyers as shareholders in law firms and allowing nonlawyers to practice law in a limited capacity. With this change, the rules could be amended to enable sharing of fees with nonlawyers.

Non-sharing of fees discourages nonlawyers from practicing law. It prevents those who are not equipped or competent to handle legal matters for clients from somehow coming into the picture and doing so. It prevents "too busy" lawyers from relying on their staff too much and blurring the lines from staff support to the staff practicing law.

We bring this up because we have seen examples of incredible staff, who after years of experience in law firms or the legal industry, are more than equipped to practice law, handle complex legal matters, and understand legal arguments. But the rules are clear. While this experience and expertise greatly help support lawyers, it cannot cross over into practice.

Please refer to the interactive ebook in Cognella Active Learning for interactive/media content.

When Can Lawyers Accept Stock/Equity for Services?

You would be surprised by how often this question gets asked. Often, early-stage companies want to pay attorneys in stock in lieu of all or a portion of the legal fees to be received. When doing so, several ethical questions present themselves.

- How do we determine the "reasonableness" of stock ownership vis-à-vis ABA Model Rule 1.5?
- What happens when the attorney-client relationship ends?
- Could there be a conflict of interest?
- What happens if the attorney-client relationship ends abruptly? Would the lawyer have to return a part of the stock?

ABA Model Rule 1.8(a) is a good starting point in assessing the answers to these questions. It treats stock ownership as a business transaction with a client and requires three things:

1. the transaction and terms in which the lawyer acquires the interest are fair and reasonable to the client and are fully disclosed and transmitted in writing to the client in a manner which can be reasonably understood by the client;
2. the client is given a reasonable opportunity to seek the advice of independent counsel in the transaction;
3. the client consents in writing.

Note: ABA Model Rule 1.8(a) does not apply when the lawyer acquires the stock in an open-market purchase. For example, lawyer buys 100 shares of Apple off the stock exchange, even though he represents a subsidiary of Apple.

Similar to the reasonableness factors in ABA Model Rule 1.5, ABA Model Rule 1.8(a)(1) requires that the terms of the transaction be fair and reasonable. The factors highlighted in ABA Model Rule 1.5 (and discussed above) would apply here. In addition to providing clear terms in writing, it's incumbent on the lawyer to explain how the business arrangement might affect the attorney-client relationship. For example, if owning such stock would give the lawyer voting rights that affect the status of the client corporation, it could impact the attorney-client relationship.

In terms of conflicts of interest, a lawyer should inform the client that a stock acquisition could lead to a conflict between the lawyer's exercise of independent judgment as a lawyer on behalf of the corporate client and the lawyer's desire to protect his stock value. If the conflict prevents the lawyer from acting in the client's best interest, the lawyer may have to withdraw.

In sum, it's not uncommon for lawyers to receive stock as fees. However, several ethical rules govern this relationship.

Third-Party Litigation Funding

Can someone else pay your legal fees if you cannot afford a lawyer? Could it interfere with how the lawyer interacts with you (the nonpaying client)? What happens if you agree to a portion of your recovery to the lawsuit funder? All of these questions and more are addressed in State Bar of California Standing Committee Formal Opinion No.14-0002.

After reviewing the opinion, what concerns do you have with litigation funding? If proper safeguards were in place, is it possible to maintain confidentiality?

Suggested Answer: The answer is yes. The key is maintaining independent professional judgment at all times. If the funder could interfere with the lawyer's judgment, the lawyer should advise the client about the impact of such interference. Similarly, before sharing any relevant client information and documents, the lawyer should get client consent. Funders look for high-value claims. These include contract disputes, antitrust claims, trade secret and misappropriation claims, insurance coverage cases, and intellectual property matters.[3]

Fee Disputes

What happens when you have a fee dispute? The first place to look is the fee agreement itself. Generally, lawyers will include dispute resolution clauses in their fee agreement. This clause usually requires parties to either arbitrate or mediate their disputes outside of court. The dispute resolution clause should go beyond just fee disputes.

---

3. Validity Finance is a litigation finance company that has committed nearly $300 million in more than 40 investments.

SAMPLE LANGUAGE

"Any dispute, claim or controversy arising out of or relating to this Agreement or the breach, termination, enforcement, interpretation or validity thereof, including the determination of the scope or applicability of this agreement to arbitrate, shall be determined by arbitration in [insert the desired place of arbitration] before [one/three] arbitrator(s). The arbitration shall be administered by JAMS pursuant to its Comprehensive Arbitration Rules and Procedures [and in accordance with the Expedited Procedures in those Rules] [or pursuant to JAMS' Streamlined Arbitration Rules and Procedures]. Judgment on the Award may be entered in any court having jurisdiction. This clause shall not preclude parties from seeking provisional remedies in aid of arbitration from a court of appropriate jurisdiction."[4]

California Exception: Mandatory Arbitration

In many states, including California, fee disputes are subject to mandatory arbitration. That is, a client has a right to settle the dispute through arbitration. When a client disputes a fee or fails to pay the lawyer, the lawyer must provide notice of the client's right to fee arbitration.

Sample Notice:

http://www.calbar.ca.gov/Portals/0/documents/forms/mfa/2013_NoticeofClientsRightstoArb-Mar2013.pdf

You will use the local bar counsel's arbitration rules and procedures. How do you determine which local bar counsel to use? Look for the county where the lawyer's office or law firm is located. At the end of the chapter is a link to all approved programs in California.

In the absence of an approved program, the state bar will fill in or look at the attorney-client contract to determine what was agreed upon.

Loans to Clients

Although loans to clients fall outside the scope of fee agreements, we felt that including a section on other types of lawyer-client agreements was worth including in this chapter. As a starting point, we want to distinguish lending money to a current client to help fund his or her litigation from other types of loans.

1. There is a **general exception** to loaning money to clients for litigation in ABA Model Rule 1.8(e). Lawyers can lend money to clients in two situations:

---

4. JAMS. (n.d.). *ADR Clause Workbook: JAMS Mediation, Arbitration, ADR Services.* ADR Clause Workbook | JAMS Mediation, Arbitration, ADR Services. https://www.jamsadr.com/clauses/#Standard.

- in the case of indigent clients; or
- where there is a contingency fee agreement, and the lawyer is paying for court costs.

2. **Why have this restriction**? We do not want the client to feel pressured by the obligation to repay the loan. Also, the idea that a lawyer is lending money could encourage unnecessary litigation. We want clients to pick lawyers for their competence and diligence, not because they can fund a lawsuit.

Generally, a lawyer does not want to advance any living expenses to a client either—like rent, medical fees, or costs to obtain evidence. See Comment 10 to ABA Model Rule 1.8. Some states even prohibit small gifts like paying for gas.

Another Situation

For non-litigation clients and where the money is not being used to fund a lawsuit or has any connection to a client's representation, a lawyer can (but probably should not) loan money to a client. If they do, the loan is subject ABA Model Rule 1.8(a) on business transactions.

Let's say you have a client for whom you are providing contract review services. You then decide to enter into a real estate transaction with the client where you (the lawyer) will buy a property to be held jointly by the lawyer and the client. You agree that you will pay for all upfront costs like the down payment for the property with the understanding that the client will repay you. This transaction is subject to the business transaction rules. Although unrelated to the legal representation, there is a fear that the lawyer's superior knowledge and position could put the client in a disadvantageous situation.

Key Takeaways

- Fee agreements do not have to be in writing. A written fee agreement is strongly encouraged.
- Fees are measured against the standard of reasonableness. Several factors influence reasonableness.
- Lawyers can enter into unique fee agreements, provided they are reasonable.
- If accepting stock, a lawyer must follow the business transaction rules.
- If funded by a third party, a lawyer must not let their independent judgment be compromised in any way.
- Referral fees are okay, provided lawyers follow ABA Model Rule 1.5(e).
- Sharing fees with nonlawyers is prohibited.

Ethics in Action

Read the following disciplinary action(s) in which the state bar used the rules discussed in this chapter to bring disciplinary charges against an attorney.

- Excessive Fees: *In re Robert Michael Griffin* https://lawprofessors.typepad.com/legal_profession/2021/03/the-massachusetts-imposed-a-public-reprimand-for-an-attorneys-fee-sharing-and-failure-to-have-a-writing-setting-forth-the-rat.html

End-of-Chapter Discussion Questions

1. Why have contingency fees? What purpose do they serve? Does it help promote access to justice?
2. High legal fees and costs are some of the largest obstacles to the access to justice. What are some ways that you can think of to curb this high cost?
3. Should the ABA Model Rules allow lawyers to share fees with nonlawyers (like accountants, insurance agents, friends, etc.)? What issues do you anticipate with this type of arrangement?
4. California Attorney Abigail refers a case to Attorney Tom. The client consents in writing after full disclosure, the total fees charged by all lawyers are not increased by the provision for division of fees, and the agreement is not unconscionable. What is Attorney Abigail's obligation after the referral?

Additional Resource

Mandatory Fee Arbitration Approved Programs: http://www.calbar.ca.gov/Attorneys/Attorney-Regulation/Mandatory-Fee-Arbitration/Approved-Programs

CHAPTER 5

Communication, Confidentiality, and Privilege

Visit your interactive ebook to download the Chapter 5 Outline.

Learning Objectives

In this lesson, students will:

- Explain the duty of confidentiality.
- Evaluate when the exceptions to confidentiality apply.
- Distinguish the evidentiary rule of privilege from confidentiality.
- Apply the rule to the lawyer's duty to keep up with technological advancements.

Key Terms

- **Confidentiality:** Information that cannot be disclosed because of the attorney-client relationship.
- **Secrets:** Things that are kept from the knowledge of others or shared only with those concerned. Usually, information shared as a course of the professional relationship.
- **Communication:** The exchange of information by speech, writing, gesture, conduct, or other means.
- **Privilege:** (Generally) A special legal right, exemption, or immunity granted.
- **Consent:** (Generally) Agreement, approval, or permission.
- **Waive:** To surrender, abandon, or give up.
- **Objection:** Opposition, legal reason for disapproval.

An Introduction to Confidentiality: The Buried Bodies Podcast

A short warning before we begin: *Please note that the following podcast raises murder and sexual violence and therefore contains sensitive or potentially triggering content. The authors of the textbook believe that the podcast helps explore the duty of confidentiality from an extreme vantage point. For these reasons, they decided to start the chapter on confidentiality with Robert Garrow's story and his attorneys, Frank Armani and Francis Belge.*

Listen to Radiolab's episode titled, "The Buried Bodies Case" (2016) before starting this chapter. After listening to the podcast, consider these questions:

1. Should the confidentiality rules be different for those accused of a crime versus those who have not been accused of a crime? Does the heinousness of the crime matter?
2. Would you be able to keep the secret that Frank Armani and Francis Belge kept?
3. The rule of confidentiality continues after the death of the client. In a situation like this one, let's say the bodies were not found, and Belge did not reveal the victim's location. Should the attorneys reveal the information after the client's death?
4. In the final segment of the podcast, a journalist interviews Susan Petz's mother, one of the murdered women whose body was missing. She explains that she's horrified that the case is taught in law schools as the right way to handle confidentiality, and she feels that Frank Armani lied to her husband when he went to visit Armani back when the case was awaiting trial. Do you agree?

An Expanded Introduction

When you think about attorney-client communication, you cannot help but also think about confidentiality. The idea is that all communications between an attorney and a client, whether they are a potential, former, or current client, is completely secret—or better put, guarded. Attorneys are the guardians of their clients' communications. This duty to guard our clients' secrets is absolute unless:

1. There is an exception to the confidentiality; or
2. The client **waives** confidentiality.

That's it. Attorney-client confidential communication is the hallmark of the attorney-client relationship. Without confidential communications, the relationship does not, and cannot, exist.

Why Have a Policy?

Potential clients usually come seeking legal advice at some vulnerable times in their lives. Maybe they are going through a divorce, were just fired, or were involved in a car accident. All these events can lead to legal issues, and all can take a heavy emotional, financial, and even physical toll on a person. People need help with such issues, and sometimes that is in the form of legal help from a lawyer.

During these difficult times, we are asking our clients to:

1. Be honest with us and give us candid communication. We need our clients to tell us all relevant facts, both good and bad, so we can help them however we can. This may also mean explaining to them that we may not help them in the way they want.
2. Be vulnerable with us. Dealing with emotions, financial difficulties, or even physical pain while dealing with legal issues is hard. We need our clients to be vulnerable with us, so that we can best help them.

How can we expect our clients to do this if we do not promise to keep their secrets? Lawyers must show that they respect the difficulties that potential clients are dealing with, and they are willing and capable of guarding these difficulties. Would you tell a secret if you knew it would be made public?

HYPOTHETICAL 5.1: PUT YOURSELF IN THEIR SHOES—THE CASE OF THE PEEPING TOM

We ask you to put yourself in your client's shoes in the below scenario.

Your landlord secretly installed cameras in the vents in the bathroom in your apartment. They have been recording you for months. Recently, you've started to hear a strange noise in the vent, so you stand on a chair with a flashlight to investigate. You immediately find the camera. Confused, you call your landlord, who confesses that they have been recording everything you have done in the bathroom. They then threaten you and tell you that if you go to the police or tell anyone, your landlord will release all the recordings to a revenge pornographic website site for all the world to see.

You are scared and even more confused about what to do. You cannot break the lease because you cannot afford to move or pay the penalty for breaking the lease. You decide to see a lawyer.

A good friend recommends Robert. You go and see Robert and, through lots of tears and with difficulty, quickly relay your story. It is clear that Robert needs more information to understand the legal issues involved here, so he asks the following questions:

1. Do you bathe or shower in this bathroom?
2. How long per day do you spend in this bathroom? How long in that time are you either naked or partially naked?
3. Give me some examples of things you have done there that you would consider embarrassing if anyone ever found out.

You answer his questions. You feel sick to your stomach, realizing even more now all the things that could be on those recordings. Robert listens, takes some notes, and tells you that he wants to think about this case a little bit and do some research. He will call you tomorrow. You thank him for his time and leave. You feel somewhat relieved about having shared the horror and violation of what happened to you and feel a little better that you are taking action. You go home and sleep.

A few days go by, and you have not heard from Robert. But a friend calls you. They found your videos online. Livid, you call your landlord. They tell you that they uploaded all the videos because you told a lawyer about what happened.

It turns out Robert and some of the other lawyers from his firm went out for happy hour that evening. During happy hour, Robert shared the story of how you came to see him and all that you told him. Your landlord was also at the same restaurant and overheard.

How would you feel if Robert did this to you?

Any Secret

In certain jurisdictions, attorneys are required to keep confidential whatever their clients want them to keep confidential. For example, the California Rules of Professional Conduct do not ask attorneys to make judgments on their client's secrets.[1] It is simply an attorney's duty in such jurisdictions to guard their client's secrets, regardless of what they are. If your client wants you to keep confidential that they were wearing a green shirt the day they came in to see you, then you must keep that confidential. Be careful making judgments on your clients' lives. Especially because they might be at their most vulnerable when they come to see you.

The Flip Side

We ask that you go into this chapter with some empathy for potential clients, but also think about the potential secrets that lawyers must hear and hold on to. Think about the brutal and gut-wrenching secret that Frank Armani and his co-counsel held on to for so long. While we consider the rule of confidentiality, the narrow exceptions, and when clients waive the confidences, we must also think of the lawyer, not just the client. Sometimes following these rules can take a toll on the carriers of these secrets—the legal profession. How can we also help lawyers so that they can continue to carry their clients' confidentialities? Who should be helping lawyers? You cannot discuss confidentiality without also delving into these questions.

> **SUMMARY**
> Confidentiality includes:
>
> - Information gained during or relating to the representation, including information from documents or witnesses.

---

1. Rule 1.6 Confidential Information of a Client. Comment [1] "To maintain inviolate the confidence, and at every peril to himself or herself to preserve the secrets, of his or her client."

- In some jurisdictions, information likely to be embarrassing or detrimental to the client (secrets).
- Information that the client has requested to keep confidential.

What Is the Rule on Confidentiality? What Exceptions Apply?

Please refer to the interactive ebook in Cognella Active Learning for interactive/media content.

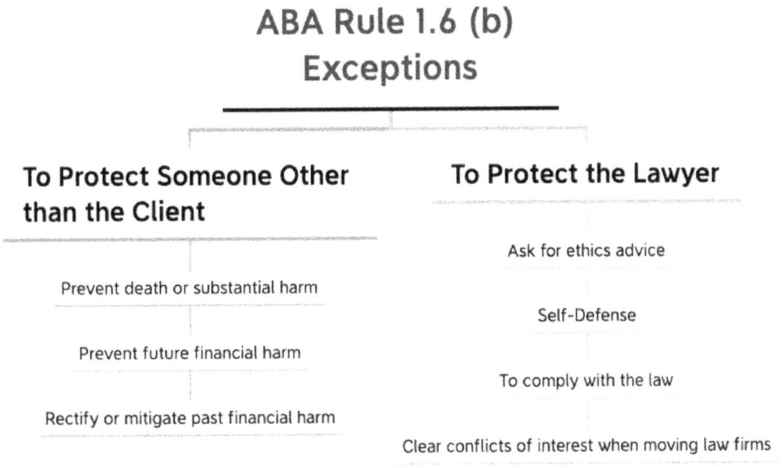

ABA Rule 1.6 (b) Exceptions

To Protect Someone Other than the Client
- Prevent death or substantial harm
- Prevent future financial harm
- Rectify or mitigate past financial harm

To Protect the Lawyer
- Ask for ethics advice
- Self-Defense
- To comply with the law
- Clear conflicts of interest when moving law firms

FIGURE 5.1

HYPOTHETICAL 5.2: WHAT DO YOU DO WHEN A CLIENT ASKS YOU TO KEEP PHYSICAL EVIDENCE THAT IS PART OF AN ONGOING INVESTIGATION?

We ask you to put yourself in your client's shoes in the below scenario.

Every year, Kim participates in CES, an annual technology show in Las Vegas, Nevada. Here, new products and technologies are displayed. On day 2 of CES, she finds a brand-new tablet in the lounge area that is not yet on the market. CES is huge and it is hard to determine where the tablet originally came from or why it ended up in the lounge area. Kim decides to take a closer look at it. The tablet is made by Kim's favorite search engine company, Google. She posts a picture of the tablet to her personal Twitter account. Since she does not know where it belongs, she put it in her bag to keep it safe. But, in the chaos of the rest of the show and travel back home, Kim forgets she has the tablet. Since finding the tablet, and posting the picture on Twitter, Kim has received several offers to review the tablet for publication and sell it. Kim does not know what to do. She asks her company lawyer, Samantha, to keep the tablet with her.

Google catches wind of the missing tablet and knows that Kim has received offers to review it. They file a police report noting that it is stolen. Police successfully secure a warrant to search Kim's apartment for the tablet. The search of the apartment comes up empty.

Does Samantha need to turn over the tablet? If she does, will she be violating her duty of confidentiality?

Please refer to the interactive ebook in Cognella Active Learning for interactive/media content.

Recap

Privilege

The attorney-client privilege "is the oldest of the privilege for confidential communications known to the common law." *Upjohn v. United States*, 449 U.S. 383, 389 (1981)

The *Upjohn* decision (discussed below) is a hallmark case on the issue of attorney-client privilege. The Supreme Court, in a unanimous decision, expanded the existing definition of the attorney-client privilege and held that communications of non-management employees were protected under the attorney-client privilege.

Confidentiality and the Attorney-Client Privilege

The concept of the attorney-client privilege is "[a] client's right to refuse to disclose and to prevent any other person from disclosing confidential communications between the client and the attorney."[2] It is a privilege assured by the United States Supreme Court to promote honest, accurate, and full disclosures between the attorney and the client. Without such assurances, effective representation of clients would not be possible.

---

2. "Attorney-client privilege," *Black's Law Dictionary*, p. 1391, col. 2 (Bryan A. Garner, 10th ed., 2014).

In order for there to be a concrete attorney-client privilege, there are certain elements that must be met:

- The communication must be between the attorney, or a representative of the attorney, such as a paralegal, associate, or other legal staff, and the client only. Any other individual present during the communication will break the privilege. If you are married, but you represent that person individually in a litigation, having the person's spouse in the room during a communication would break attorney-client communication.
- The communication was made as a part of seeking legal advice.

The "communication" applies to any form of communication: verbal, electronic, and/or written communication. The privilege is absolute.

Many attorneys treat attorney-client privilege and confidentiality as identical concepts. They are not. First, confidentiality is an affirmative duty placed on the attorney, while privilege is an exemption from a duty to disclose information. Second, confidentiality is broader as it applies to virtually every interaction between the lawyer and client. On the other hand, privilege only applies to communications given for the purpose of getting legal advice. For example, a client tells the attorney something embarrassing and tells the attorney to keep it confidential. The attorney is required to keep it confidential. However, if the information is not shared with the attorney as part of communication seeking legal advice, one cannot claim attorney-client privilege over it. If a judge asks, the attorney or the other side about the thing client asked the attorney to keep confidential, what is the attorney to do? Is it clear to you what the attorney's obligations are in that instance?

CASE ALERT: UPJOHN CO. V. US

Opinion

Justice Rehnquist

We granted certiorari in this case to address important questions concerning the scope of the attorney-client privilege in the corporate context and the applicability of the work product doctrine in proceedings to enforce tax summonses. 445 U.S. 925. [...]

I

Petitioner Upjohn Co. manufactures and sells pharmaceuticals here and abroad. In January, 1976, independent accountants conducting an audit of one of Upjohn's foreign subsidiaries discovered that the subsidiary made payments to or for the benefit of foreign government officials in order to secure government business. The accountants so informed petitioner Mr. Gerard Thomas, Upjohn's Vice President, Secretary, and General Counsel. Thomas is a member of the Michigan and New York Bars, and has been Upjohn's General Counsel for 20 years. He consulted with outside counsel and R. T. Parfet, Jr., Upjohn's Chairman of the Board. It was decided that the

US Supreme Court, "Upjohn Co. v. US ," 449 U.S. 383, 1981.

company would conduct an internal investigation of what were termed "questionable payments." As part of this investigation, the attorneys prepared a letter containing a questionnaire which was sent to "All Foreign General and Area Managers" over the Chairman's signature. The letter began by noting recent disclosures that several American companies made "possibly illegal" payments to foreign government officials, and emphasized that the management needed full information concerning any such payments made by Upjohn. The letter indicated that the Chairman had asked Thomas, identified as "the company's General Counsel,"

to conduct an investigation for the purpose of determining the nature and magnitude of any payments made by the Upjohn Company or any of its subsidiaries to any employee or official of a foreign government.

The questionnaire sought detailed information concerning such payments. Managers were instructed to treat the investigation as "highly confidential" and not to discuss it with anyone other than Upjohn employees who might be helpful in providing the requested information. Responses were to be sent directly to Thomas. Thomas and outside counsel also interviewed the recipients of the questionnaire and some 33 other Upjohn officers or employees as part of the investigation.

On March 26, 1976, the company voluntarily submitted a preliminary report to the Securities and Exchange Commission on Form 8-K disclosing certain questionable payments. A copy of the report was simultaneously submitted to the Internal Revenue Service, which immediately began an investigation to determine the tax consequences of the payments. Special agents conducting the investigation were given lists by Upjohn of all those interviewed and all who had responded to the questionnaire. On November 23, 1976, the Service issued a summons pursuant to 26 U.S.C. § 7602 demanding production of:

All files relative to the investigation conducted under the supervision of Gerard Thomas to identify payments to employees of foreign governments and any political contributions made by the Upjohn Company or any of its affiliates since January 1, 1971, and to determine whether any funds of the Upjohn Company had been improperly accounted for on the corporate books during the same period.

The records should include but not be limited to written questionnaires sent to managers of the Upjohn Company's foreign affiliates, and memorandums or notes of the interviews conducted in the United States and abroad with officers and employees of the Upjohn Company and its subsidiaries.

App. 17a-18a. The company declined to produce the documents specified in the second paragraph on the grounds that they were protected from disclosure by the attorney-client privilege and constituted the work product of attorneys prepared in anticipation of litigation. On August 31, 1977, the United States filed a petition seeking enforcement of the summons under 26 U.S.C. § 7402(b) and 7604(a) in the United States District Court for the Western District of Michigan. That court adopted the recommendation of a Magistrate who concluded that the summons should be enforced. Petitioners appealed to the Court of Appeals for the Sixth Circuit, which rejected the Magistrate's finding of a waiver of the attorney-client privilege, 600 F.2d 1223, 1227, n. 12, but agreed that the privilege did not apply

[t]o the extent that the communications were made by officers and agents not responsible for directing Upjohn's actions in response to legal advice..., for the simple reason that the communications were not the 'client's.'

Id. at 1225. The court reasoned that accepting petitioners' claim for a broader application of the privilege would encourage upper-echelon management to ignore unpleasant facts and create too broad a "zone of silence." Noting that Upjohn's counsel had interviewed officials such as the Chairman and President, the Court of Appeals remanded to the District Court so that a determination of who was within the "control group" could be made. In a concluding footnote, the court stated that the work product doctrine "is not applicable to administrative summonses issued under 26 U.S.C. § 7602." *Id.* at 1228, n. 13.

II

Federal Rule of Evidence 501 provides that

the privilege of a witness . . . shall be governed by the principles of the common law as they may be interpreted by the courts of the United States in light of reason and experience.

The attorney-client privilege is the oldest of the privileges for confidential communications known to the common law. 8 J. Wigmore, Evidence § 2290 (McNaughton rev.1961). Its purpose is to encourage full and frank communication between attorneys and their clients, and thereby promote broader public interests in the observance of law and administration of justice. The privilege recognizes that sound legal advice or advocacy serves public ends and that such advice or advocacy depends upon the lawyer's being fully informed by the client. As we stated last Term in *Trammel v. United States*, 445 U. S. 40, 445 U. S. 51 (1980):

The lawyer-client privilege rests on the need for the advocate and counselor to know all that relates to the client's reasons for seeking representation if the professional mission is to be carried out.

And in *Fisher v. United States*, 425 U. S. 391, 425 U. S. 403 (1976), we recognized the purpose of the privilege to be "to encourage clients to make full disclosure to their attorneys." This rationale for the privilege has long been recognized by the Court, *see Hunt v. Blackburn*, 128 U. S. 464, 128 U. S. 470 (1888) (privilege "is founded upon the necessity, in the interest and administration of justice, of the aid of persons having knowledge of the law and skilled in its practice, which assistance can only be safely and readily availed of when free from the consequences or the apprehension of disclosure"). Admittedly complications in the application of the privilege arise when the client is a corporation, which, in theory, is an artificial creature of the law, and not an individual; but this Court has assumed that the privilege applies when the client is a corporation, *United States v. Louisville Nashville R. Co.*, 236 U. S. 318, 236 U. S. 336 (1915), and the Government does not contest the general proposition.

The Court of Appeals, however, considered the application of the privilege in the corporate context to present a "different problem," since the client was an inanimate entity, and

only the senior management, guiding and integrating the several operations, . . . can be said to possess an identity analogous to the corporation as a whole.

600 F.2d at 1226. The first case to articulate the so-called "control group test" adopted by the court below, *Philadelphia v. Westinghouse Electric Corp.*, 210 F. Supp. 483, 485 (ED Pa.), *petition for mandamus and prohibition denied sub nom. General Electric Co. v. Kirkpatrick*, 312 F.2d 742 (CA3 1962), *cert. denied*, 372 U.S. 943 (1963), reflected a similar conceptual approach:

Keeping in mind that the question is, is it the corporation which is seeking the lawyer's advice when the asserted privileged communication is made?, the most satisfactory solution, I think, is that, if the employee making the communication, of whatever rank he may be, is in a position to control or even to take a substantial part in a decision about any action which the corporation may take upon the advice of the attorney, . . . then, in effect, *he is (or personifies) the corporation* when he makes his disclosure to the lawyer, and the privilege would apply.

(Emphasis supplied.) Such a view, we think, overlooks the fact that the privilege exists to protect not only the giving of professional advice to those who can act on it, but also the giving of information to the lawyer to enable him to give sound and informed advice. *See Trammel, supra* at 445 U. S. 51; *Fisher, supra* at 425 U. S. 403. The first step in the resolution of any legal problem is ascertaining the factual background and sifting through the facts with an eye to the legally relevant. *See* ABA Code of Professional Responsibility, Ethical Consideration 4-1:

A lawyer should be fully informed of all the facts of the matter he is handling in order for his client to obtain the full advantage of our legal system. It is for the lawyer in the exercise of his independent professional judgment to separate the relevant and important from the irrelevant and unimportant. The observance of the ethical obligation of a lawyer to hold inviolate the confidences and secrets of his client not only facilitates the full development of facts essential to proper representation of the client, but also encourages laymen to seek early legal assistance.

See also Hickman v. Taylor, 329 U. S. 495, 329 U. S. 511 (1947).

In the case of the individual client, the provider of information and the person who acts on the lawyer's advice are one and the same. In the corporate context, however, it will frequently be employees beyond the control group as defined by the court below — "officers and agents . . . responsible for directing [the company's] actions in response to legal advice" — who will possess the information needed by the corporation's lawyers. Middle-level — and indeed lower-level employees can, by actions within the scope of their employment, embroil the corporation in serious legal difficulties, and it is only natural that these employees would have the relevant information needed by corporate counsel if he is adequately to advise the client with respect to such actual or potential difficulties. This fact was noted in *Diversified Industries, Inc. v. Meredith*, 572 F.2d 596 (CA8 1978) (en banc):

In a corporation, it may be necessary to glean information relevant to a legal problem from middle management or non-management personnel as well as from top executives. The attorney dealing with a complex legal problem is thus faced with a 'Hobson's choice.' If he interviews employees not having 'the very highest authority,' their communications to him will not be privileged. If, on the other hand, he interviews only those employees with 'the very highest authority,' he may find it extremely difficult, if not impossible, to determine what happened.

Id. at 608-609 (quoting Weinschel, Corporate Employee Interviews and the Attorney-Client Privilege, 12 B.C.Ind. & Com.L.Rev. 873, 876 (1971)). The control group test adopted by the court below thus frustrates the very purpose of the privilege by discouraging the communication of relevant information by employees of the client to attorneys seeking to render legal advice to the client corporation. The attorney's advice will also frequently be more significant to noncontrol group members than to those who officially sanction the advice, and the control group test makes it more difficult to convey full and frank legal advice to the employees who will put into effect the client corporation's policy. *See, e.g., Duplan Corp. v. Deering Milliken*, Inc., 397 F. Supp. 1146, 1164 (SC 1974) ("After the lawyer forms his or her opinion, it is of no immediate benefit to the Chairman of the Board or the President. It must be given to the corporate personnel who will apply it").

The narrow scope given the attorney-client privilege by the court below not only makes it difficult for corporate attorneys to formulate sound advice when their client is faced with a specific legal problem, but also threatens to limit the valuable efforts of corporate counsel to ensure their client's compliance with the law. In light of the vast and complicated array of regulatory legislation confronting the modern corporation, corporations, unlike most individuals, "constantly go to lawyers to find out how to obey the law," Burnham, The Attorney-Client Privilege in the Corporate Arena, 24 Bus.Law. 901, 913 (1969), particularly since compliance with the law in this area is hardly an instinctive matter, see, e.g., *United States v. United States Gypsum Co.*, 438 U. S. 422, 438 U. S. 440-441 (1978) ("the behavior proscribed by the [Sherman] Act is often difficult to distinguish from the gray zone of socially acceptable and economically justifiable business conduct"). The test adopted by the court below is difficult to apply in practice, though no abstractly formulated and unvarying "test" will necessarily enable courts to decide questions such as this with mathematical precision. But if the purpose of the attorney-client privilege is to be served, the attorney and client must be able to predict with some degree of certainty whether particular discussions will be protected. An uncertain privilege, or one which purports to be certain but results in widely varying applications by the courts, is little better than no privilege at all. The very terms of the test adopted by the court below suggest the unpredictability of its application. The test restricts the availability of the privilege to those officers who play a "substantial role" in deciding and directing a corporation's legal response. Disparate decisions in cases applying this test illustrate its unpredictability. *Compare, e.g., Hogan v. Zletz*, 43 F.R.D. 308, 315-316 (ND Okla.1967), *aff'd in part sub nom. Natta v. Hogan*, 392 F.2d 686 (CA10 1968) (control group includes managers and assistant managers of patent division and research and development department), *with Congoleum Industries, Inc. v. GAF Corp.*, 49 F.R.D. 82, 83-85 (ED Pa.1969), *aff'd*, 478 F.2d 1398 (CA3 1973) (control group includes only division and corporate vice-presidents, and not two directors of research and vice-president for production and research).

The communications at issue were made by Upjohn employees to counsel for Upjohn, acting as such, at the direction of corporate superiors in order to secure legal advice from counsel. As the Magistrate found,

Mr. Thomas consulted with the Chairman of the Board and outside counsel, and thereafter conducted a factual investigation to determine the nature and extent of the questionable payments *and to be in a position to give legal advice to the company with respect to the payments.*

(Emphasis supplied.) 78-1 USTC 9277, pp. 83,598, 83,599. Information, not available from upper-echelon management, was needed to supply a basis for legal advice concerning compliance with securities and tax laws, foreign laws, currency regulations, duties to shareholders, and potential litigation in each of these areas. The communications concerned matters within the scope of the employees' corporate duties, and the employees themselves were sufficiently aware that they were being questioned in order that the corporation could obtain legal advice. The questionnaire identified Thomas as "the company's General Counsel" and referred in its opening sentence to the possible illegality of payments such as the ones on which information was sought. App. 40a. A statement of policy accompanying the questionnaire clearly indicated the legal implications of the investigation. The policy statement was issued "in order that there be no uncertainty in the future as to the policy with respect to the practices which are the subject of this investigation."

It began "Upjohn will comply with all laws and regulations," and stated that commissions or payments "will not be used as a subterfuge for bribes or illegal payments" and that all payments must be "proper and legal." Any future agreements with foreign distributors or agents were to be approved "by a company attorney," and any questions concerning the policy were to be referred "to the company's General Counsel." *Id.* at 165a-166a. This statement was issued to Upjohn employees worldwide, so that even those interviewees not receiving a questionnaire were aware of the legal implications of the interviews. Pursuant to explicit instructions from the Chairman of the Board, the communications were considered "highly confidential" when made, *id.* at 39a, 43a, and have been kept confidential by the company. Consistent with the underlying purposes of the attorney-client privilege, these communications must be protected against compelled disclosure.

The Court of Appeals declined to extend the attorney-client privilege beyond the limits of the control group test for fear that doing so would entail severe burdens on discovery and create a broad "zone of silence" over corporate affairs. Application of the attorney-client privilege to communications such as those involved here, however, puts the adversary in no worse position than if the communications had never taken place. The privilege only protects disclosure of communications; it does not protect disclosure of the underlying facts by those who communicated with the attorney:

> [T]he protection of the privilege extends only to *communications*, and not to facts. A fact is one thing and a communication concerning that fact is an entirely different thing. The client cannot be compelled to answer the question, 'What did you say or write to the attorney?' but may not refuse to disclose any relevant fact within his knowledge merely because he incorporated a statement of such fact into his communication to his attorney.

Philadelphia v. Westinghouse Electric Corp., 205 F. Supp. 830, 831 (ED Pa.1962). *See also Diversified Industries*, 572 F.2d at 611; *State ex rel. Dudek v. Circuit Court*, 34 Wis.2d 559, 580, 150 N.W.2d 387, 399 (1967) ("the courts have noted that a party cannot conceal a fact merely by revealing it to his lawyer"). Here, the Government was free to question the employees who communicated with Thomas and outside counsel. Upjohn has provided the IRS with a list of such employees, and the IRS has already interviewed some 25 of them. While it would probably be more convenient for the Government to secure the results of petitioner's internal investigation by simply subpoenaing the questionnaires and notes taken by petitioner's attorneys, such considerations of convenience do not overcome the policies served by the attorney-client privilege. As Justice Jackson noted in his concurring opinion in *Hickman v. Taylor*, 329 U.S. at 329 U. S. 516: "Discovery was hardly intended to enable a learned profession to perform its functions . . . on wits borrowed from the adversary."

[...]

Accordingly, the judgment of the Court of Appeals is reversed, and the case remanded for further proceedings.

It is so ordered.

[...]

Upjohn manufactures and sells pharmaceuticals in the United States and abroad. Independent accountants conducted an audit and discovered that one of their foreign subsidiaries engaged in "questionable payments" or bribes to secure government business. As a result, the general counsel for Upjohn sent an internal questionnaire to all foreign managers of Upjohn asking for information related to the bribes. The questionnaire acknowledged that possible illegal payments were made and that the managers needed to answer the questionnaire truthfully. Upjohn voluntarily submitted a report about the payments to the Internal Revenue Service (IRS).

The IRS requested access to this questionnaire, but Upjohn refused, claiming that attorney-client privilege protected it. The district court and appeals court held that the attorney-client privilege did not apply to corporate employees that were not directly responsible for directing Upjohn's actions in response to legal advice. The Supreme Court granted review.

The issue in this case was whether attorney-client privilege extended to lower-level or non-management employees. The court ruled that attorney-client privilege applies to all employees, including lower-level employees, who give factual information to an attorney representing the company to provide appropriate legal advice. If the privilege did not extend to lower-level employees, communication between these employees and the company attorney would be discouraged, hindering the attorney's ability to give appropriate legal advice to their client (that is, the company). Furthermore, as lower-level employees are involved in areas of the attorneys' concerns, the privilege should extend to them. Thus, the communication is privileged when it is made by employees, at the direction of corporate superiors, to corporate counsel to secure legal advice. Here, the questionnaire concerned matters within the scope of their employment, and the employees knew they were responding to it at the direction of their corporate superiors to secure legal advice. Thus, the communication was privileged. The judgment was reversed.

Key Takeaways:

- The attorney-client privilege applies to communications between company/general counsel and employees if the significant purpose of the communication is to obtain or provide legal advice.
- The communication must be made within the scope of the employee's duties and the employee must be sufficiently aware that he is being questioned so the company can obtain legal advice.

Inadvertent Disclosures

An inadvertent disclosure is defined as an unintentional revelation of materials or information otherwise protected by the duty of confidentiality. It is one of the most common ways attorneys break confidentiality.

Attorneys must ensure client confidentiality is constantly intact, which can be difficult. We all like to talk, share what is going on in our lives, and be social. This includes what we are working on. Being aware of your surroundings and recognizing and understanding that lawyers cannot share the stories of their work like other professions get to do is important. Any of the below innocent actions can break confidentiality:

- Returning a phone call to a client while waiting in line for coffee at your local Starbucks and then talking to your client about the case.
- Talking to your fellow law partner about a difficult case while sitting on a busy outside patio watching the people walk by on the sidewalk a mere few feet away.
- Advising your client during a break during a deposition or mediation while in a full elevator on the way down to get some fresh air.
- Sending an email to a client to a computer you know to be shared by other people within the client's family.
- Sending a written correspondence via US mail to your client, knowing that the mail is customarily opened by another individual in the residence.
- Communicating with both spouses about an ongoing case rather than just the one spouse that is

your client. Even though they both may be concerned about a legal issue, and we often think of couples as a "single unit," doing this would break confidentiality.

These examples are all day-to-day happenings that do not seem consequential, yet in an attorney-client relationship they can have dire consequences.

So, what happens if there is inadvertent disclosure? It largely depends on the nature of the information that is disclosed. Some examples of questions that would need to be examined to determine what, if any, consequences there would be are:

- Would the information be something that would otherwise be discoverable or general knowledge? Or is it truly something that is "secret?"
- Who heard the disclosure? Was it someone who had no idea what you were talking about, or was it opposing counsel?

Depending on the nature of the information, the attorney may be disciplined for failure to maintain the confidentiality.

CASE ALERT: RICO V. MITSUBISHI MOTORS CORP.[3]

Zerle Rico sued Mitsubishi after they were injured in an accident where their sports utility vehicle rolled over. A Mitsubishi employee left notes he took during a meeting with Mitsubishi's attorneys when he went to the restroom, and Raymond Johnson (Zerle Rico's counsel) obtained those notes. Johnson claimed that the court reporter gave the notes to him because she believed it was an exhibit, though Johnson knew "within a minute or two" that it was not meant to be produced as an exhibit. However, he still made copies of the notes, discussed them with other lawyers and experts, and used the notes as part of a deposition. Mitsubishi's attorneys moved to disqualify Johnson as counsel. The trial court granted the motion, finding that although Johnson received the notes inadvertently, he acted unethically by examining and using the notes. The appeals court confirmed the ruling, and the California Supreme Court granted review.

In this case, the issue is whether an attorney who inadvertently receives privileged documents must immediately notify opposing counsel once it becomes apparent to the attorney that the documents are privileged. The California Supreme Court held that yes, the attorney must immediately notify opposing counsel because inadvertent disclosure does not waive the privilege. The attorney who receives the documents may only read as much of the document as necessary to determine that it is privileged. Once the attorney notifies the opposing counsel, they can mutually agree on what to do next or go to court for guidance. Johnson was correctly disqualified because he

3. 42 Cal. 4th 807

did not immediately notify opposing counsel but instead made copies of the document and used it for his own benefit. Therefore, the judgment was affirmed.

Please refer to the interactive ebook in Cognella Active Learning for interactive/media content.

MCDERMOTT WILL & EMERY LLP V. SUPERIOR COURT (2017)[4]

In a malpractice case, a plaintiff inadvertently forwarded a confidential email he received from his personal attorney to his sister-in-law from his smartphone. He was not aware that he forwarded the email until a year later. The sister-in-law forwarded it to her husband, who shared it with four other individuals, including the defendant's attorney.

The issues, in this case, were whether the client waived his attorney-client privilege by disclosing the email to third parties and whether the law firm should be disqualified for failing to notify the client or his attorney that the firm had obtained a copy of this communication and proceeding to use the communication in the lawsuit. The court found that the plaintiff did not waive attorney-client privilege because he inadvertently and unknowingly forwarded the email from his smartphone and did not have the intent to waive the privilege, given that he was elderly, had reduced dexterity due to multiple sclerosis, and never communicated with his sister-in-law explaining why he forwarded it. The sister-in-law and her husband also did not waive the privilege because they do not hold the privilege, and the client did not consent to the disclosures, given that he did not know about them (or even his own disclosure) until after it happened. The trial court ordered the defendants to seal or return all copies of the email and the relevant portions of the deposition transcripts. The court also disqualified the law firm that represented defendants from representing them in this suit to prevent future harm to the client since the firm could use it to their advantage in the case. The firm violated its duty by using the emails in depositions, interrogatories, and motions. The appeals court affirmed.

Please refer to the interactive ebook in Cognella Active Learning for interactive/media content.

---

4. 10 Cal.App.5th 1083

It is important to remember that it is always the client that holds the attorney-client privilege. This is an important distinction. As we noted earlier in the book, clients often come to attorneys during some of the most vulnerable times in their lives. They need help, counseling, and legal services. It can be difficult to be vulnerable, especially if your lawyer is someone whom you just met and are establishing a relationship with. The attorney-client privilege allows for some comfort in that relationship and allows the client to be vulnerable so that the attorney can best help them. As the client is the holder of the privilege, the client can also break the attorney-client confidentiality if they so choose.

Confidentiality and the Attorney Work-Product Privilege

The policies of confidentiality also govern the attorney work-product privilege. The attorney work-product doctrine protects tangible material or its intangible equivalent that is collected or prepared in anticipation of litigation. Such material is not discoverable.[5]

This privilege allows attorneys to investigate, interview, strategize, and prepare to help their clients without the fear of the opposing side ever obtaining their notes, documents, photographs, scribbles, diagrams, recordings, or research, to name a few examples. It allows attorneys the freedom to explore theories to help their clients without having to share the information with anyone other than their clients. The attorney work-product doctrine is now recognized as a rule within the broader scope of attorney-client confidentiality.

OBJECTION!

What happens if an opposing party asks for work-product documents during the course of discovery during litigation? This happens almost all of the time. Attorneys can make appropriate attorney work-product privilege objections to protect the information. This can be during deposition, interrogatory requests, or other discovery requests, motions, or even during formal hearings. The objection may be worded as such:

- Objection. Plaintiff objects to this interrogatory on the grounds that this interrogatory calls for information which is privileged within the attorney-client privilege and that it seeks information which is in the attorney's work product.
- Objection. Plaintiff objects because this request calls for the disclosure of attorney work product prepared in anticipation of litigation or for trial. Moreover, the defendant has failed to demonstrate a substantial need and the substantial equivalent of which the defendant would be unable to obtain by other means without due hardship.
- Objection. Defendant objects to this request as being ambiguous, overbroad, and

---

5. *Hickman v. Taylor*, 329 U.S. 495 (1947)

inclusive of documents protected by attorney-client and/or work-product privileges.

Even if, for example a document was found to contain information that was partially attorney work product and information that was not work product, most courts would allow the information that was not work product to be discovered, while redacting the privileged information.

Similarly, if an attorney claims privilege, they will be asked to submit a privilege log, which is a document that describes documents or other items that are withheld from production under a claim that the documents are subject to privilege or attorney work-product.

SAMPLE PRIVILEGE LOG

Note: Some courts will order the information to be listed in a Privilege Log. If they do not, provide only the information necessary for the court to examine why the document or evidence is considered privileged. It is important not to provide unnecessary confidential information. Most courts will ask for additional information if necessary.

	Bates No.	Document Type	Date of Document	Author/ Holder of Document	Recipient(s)	Custody/ Persons with Historical Access	Subject Matter	Privilege Applied	Notes	Court Ruling
1.	ABC00001	Letter	10/01/ 2005	Santa Claus	Mrs. Claus	Master Elf John Smith, Asst. Elf Joe John	Naughty List	Trade Secret, Attorney/ Client Privilege		
2.	ABC00005	Email	10/18/ 2005	Mrs. Claus	The Grinch	Mrs. Claus	Litigation	Attorney/ Client Privilege		
3.	ABC00108	Email	11/27/ 2005	Albert Sony, Esq.	Mr. & Mrs. Claus	Albert Sony, Mr. & Mrs. Claus	Litigation, Deposition Summaries	Attorney Work Product, Attorney/ Client Privilege		
4.	ABC00124	Contract	12/08/ 2006	Albert Sony, Esq.	Mr. & Mrs. Claus	Albert Sony, Mr. & Mrs. Claus	Scope of Work	Litigation	Document created by Mr. Sony for clients Mr. & Mrs. Claus for Scope of Work for 3rd-party document review company.	

Information should include the following:
- Title/description
- Subject matter in the document
- The purpose of why it was created
- Any privileges claimed
- Any additional notes
- A place for the court to rule on each document as Privileged or Not Privileged

Technology and Confidentiality

Does an attorney violate their duty of confidentiality by using technology to transmit or store information that may be susceptible to unauthorized access by third parties? The answer is maybe, depending on whether the attorney takes reasonable steps/efforts to protect that information. What constitutes reasonable efforts? The *ABA Cybersecurity Handbook* explains that reasonable effort is a fact-specific inquiry. It looks at a few factors; namely, the sensitivity of the information, the risk of disclosure without additional precautions, the cost of extra measures, the difficulty of adding safeguards, and whether more safeguards adversely affect the lawyer's ability to represent the client.

FIGURE 5.2   The more sensitive the information, the more protective measures are needed.

The practice of law includes technology (like email, cloud storage, public Wi-Fi, etc.). Often, lawyers take their work laptops home to conduct research and email clients from their personal Wi-Fi. Whenever data is transmitted (without proper safeguards like firewalls, secure username/password, encryption, etc.), it can be intercepted and read. (Think Russia hacking US government emails.) If intercepted, lawyers risk violating their duty of confidentiality. The rules require that they take "reasonable steps" to protect against disclosure/interception. For example: encrypting email may be a reasonable step for an attorney to take to ensure confidentiality. Similarly, requiring law firm associates, partners, and staff to use password-protected mobile phones, laptops, and other devices to access confidential information is a reasonable step.

Additionally, lawyers include email disclaimers regarding the confidentiality of information. This helps ensure that the receiver is aware of its confidentiality and protects attorney-client privilege. For example,

> *This message contains information that may be confidential. Unless you are the addressee (or authorized to receive emails for the addressee), you may not use, copy, or disclose to anyone this message or any information contained in this message. If you have received this message in error, please advise the sender by reply email and delete the message. Thank you.*

Besides taking reasonable steps, lawyers should also consider:

ABA Model Rule 1.4 requires lawyers to inform clients about inherent risks associated with "highly sensitive confidential client information." This includes letting clients know that information is subject to cyber threats and that extra measures are needed for protection.[6]

In order to provide Client with efficient and convenient legal services, Attorney will frequently communicate and transmit documents using e-mail. Because e-mail continues to evolve, there may be risks communicating in this manner, including risks related to confidentiality and security. By entering into this Agreement, Client is consenting to such e-mail transmissions with Client and Client's representatives and agents.

In addition, Attorney uses a cloud computing service with servers located in a facility other than Attorney's office. Most of Attorney's electronic data, including e-mails and documents, are stored in this manner. By entering into this Agreement, Client understands and consents to having communications, documents and information pertinent to the Client's matter stored through such a cloud-based service.

 (i) If a breach occurs, promptly stop the breach and mitigate damages resulting from the breach. This is popularly known as an incident response plan.

 (ii) Incorporating a firm-wide policy that addresses the proper use of technology and client information.

Note: ABA Model Rule 1.1, Comment 8 requires lawyers "to maintain the requisite knowledge and skill, a lawyer should keep abreast of changes in the law and its practice, including the benefits and risks associated with relevant technology …" Thus, confidentiality and competence go hand in hand. Lawyers must understand everything that goes with using technology—positive and negative. We can see a good example of this from the recent COVID-19 pandemic. Remote trial proceedings require both judges and litigators to refresh their technical skills and learn new ways to communicate. Lawyers who use Zoom, Skype, Google Meet or other conferencing software must remind everyone that the conversation is confidential. They should not record the meeting without consent and should lock the meeting once it's begun. Further, suppose lawyers share their homes with other people. In that case, they need to ensure that they are not interrupted during the meetings, as in some cases, even the client's identity can be confidential.

---

6. Engagement letters usually contain a consent to use of email and cloud services clause; e.g., the California State Bar provides the following sample language as guidance.

What about Social Media and Blogs?

The rules on confidentiality apply. Read the following cases and assess whether the right decision was made.

CASE ALERT: IN RE PESHE

In re Peshek, Kristine Peshek, an Illinois public defender, published a blog on various topics. Included in her blog were articles about current cases. She never used the clients' full names, instead referring to them by their first name or case number. Peshek was suspended from practice for 60 days, both in Illinois and Wisconsin (where she was also licensed).

> Please refer to the interactive ebook in Cognella Active Learning for interactive/media content.

CASE ALERT: *HUNTER V. VIRGINIA STATE BAR*

In *Hunter v. Virginia State Bar* the Virginia Supreme Court found that the duty of confidentiality did not apply to Hunter's blog as all the cases mentioned were no longer pending. They also reasoned that this information was public information and thus would have been public speech had the media or a news outlet shared it. They balanced Hunter's First Amendment rights to free speech with the duty of confidentiality. They treated Hunter like a citizen journalist since he was commenting on cases that were no longer pending.

> Please refer to the interactive ebook in Cognella Active Learning for interactive/media content.

What about Organizations?

Confidentiality extends to organizations. Communications about legal matters related to an organization are protected under the duty of confidentiality. Thus, if a company's CEO discloses information relating to an ongoing investigation to his lawyer, that is protected. If the CEO reveals information about his golf game, ABA Model Rule 1.6 will not protect this information.

ABA Model Rule 1.13 addresses when an organization is a client. It says that a lawyer employed or retained by an organization represents the organization acting through its duly authorized constituent(s). Since an organization can only act through a person, it is important to make this distinction. For example, the following individuals are considered constituents in a corporation: officers, directors, shareholders, and in some cases, employees. The lawyer represents the corporation, not the constituents addressed herein. These officers, directors, or shareholders speak on behalf of the corporation (because obviously, a corporation cannot speak!). Therefore, the attorney-client confidentiality is maintained when one or more of these designated individuals speak on behalf of the corporation to the attorney. There may be situations where the lawyer represents both the corporation and its constituents (a board member) if their interests are aligned. Here, there is no conflict of interest.

The lawyer should take appropriate steps in informing clients about possible conflicts of interest issues. As is true with any other client, the lawyer must act in the organization's best interest.

In the case of organizational representation, the lawyer owes confidentiality to the organization. There can be confusion as to the types of information that is confidential. Generally, information that an employee shares in their duly authorized capacity is confidential.

What Happens If the Lawyer Learns Something That Could Harm the Organization?

Suppose an organizational actor (officer, director, or employee) is doing something (like a treasurer stealing from the organization) or intends to do something that could harm the organization or whose actions could be imputed to the organization. In that case, the lawyer may disclose confidential information to protect the organization. ABA Model Rule 1.13(b) allows the lawyer to refer the matter to a _higher authority_ in the organization. For example, a lawyer learns that a factory manager belonging to the organization is discharging toxic waste into a waterway that feeds into a local town. The lawyer may disclose this information, as it will likely result in substantial injury to the organization.

Who is the higher or highest authority in an organization? It's usually the board of directors or higher-level officers like the CEO and CFO. That way, the board can take remedial measures to prevent further injury.

What Happens If the Board Refuses to Act?

If the misconduct is clearly a violation of the law, the lawyer _may_ disclose confidential information by reporting it out, usually to a state or federal administrative agency. For example, a lawyer learns that the chief regulatory officer for the company has been filing false environmental reports to the Environmental Protection Agency (EPA). In this case, the lawyer may report out if reporting within the organization fails.

Note and recall the section on withdrawal. The lawyer should consider withdrawing if the organization refuses to act.

Key Takeaways

- Confidentiality is broad. It includes all information relating to the representation, regardless of

form or source.
- The rule does not classify confidential or non-confidential information. All information that relates to the representation of a client is required to be kept confidential.
- The broad definition of confidentiality is constrained by numerous exceptions (permissive). These include consent, implied authorization, and situations relating to preventing death, harm, or financial injury.
- Any disclosure of confidential information is not open ended. A lawyer may reveal information to the extent the lawyer reasonably believes necessary to prevent whatever harm the exception is designed to avoid.
- Confidentiality is not the same as the attorney-client privilege. The duty of confidentiality is broader.
- Confidentiality has a long timeline. It continues even after death.
- Lawyers should make reasonable efforts in protecting client information, especially if storing or transmitting information electronically.
- Lawyers owe confidentiality to organizations. They may report out internally or externally if there is a violation of law that would cause substantial injury to the organization.

Ethics in Action

Read the following disciplinary action(s) in which the state bar used the rules discussed in this chapter to bring disciplinary charges against an attorney.

- Improperly disclosing client confidential information [six-month suspension]: *Disciplinary Counsel v. Holmes and Kerr* http://www.supremecourt.ohio.gov/rod/docs/pdf/0/2018/2018-Ohio-4308.pdf
- Improperly disclosing client confidential information [private admonition]: *Bar Counsel v. Frank Arthur Smith* https://bbopublic.blob.core.windows.net/web/f/pr19-16.pdf

End-of-Chapter Discussion Questions

1. Should confidentiality apply to cases involving prospective clients? Why or why not? If the client never signs with the lawyer, would it make a difference?
2. Should lawyers be allowed to discuss closed cases on podcasts, in editorial articles, or as examples while discussing a case with a client (who is dealing with a similar matter)?
3. Should lawyers ever be allowed to speak to the media about a case?
4. We are using technology more and more as a means of communicating. Social media, email, text messages, and other forms of messaging have replaced phone conversations. How do we maintain confidentiality with our increasing use of technology?
5. How do we maintain confidentiality when technology such as video chats have taken over in-person meetings? Should the duty to maintain confidentiality include a duty to prevent hackers?
6. Should there be an instance where lawyers should be criminally prosecuted for failure to maintain confidentiality? What do you think that threshold should be? What should the punishment be?

CHAPTER 6

Conflict of Interest [Part 1]

Visit your interactive ebook to download the Chapter 6a Outline.

Learning Objectives

In this lesson, students will:

- Identify conflict of interest situations involving multiple clients.
- Assess the relationship between confidentiality and conflict of interest.
- Distinguish actual and potential conflicts of interest.
- Develop an effective conflict waiver.

Key Terms

- **Concurrent conflicts:** Conflict between two current clients with adverse/opposing interests.
- **Successive conflicts:** Conflict between a former client and a current client.
- **Actual conflicts:** Conflicts that have materialized.
- **Potential conflicts:** Conflicts that could arise in the future but have not yet materialized.
- **Informed consent:** The process of getting permission from a client after providing them with information about the conflict and an explanation of risks and alternatives.
- **Conflict waiver:** Agreement to proceed in light of a conflict after informed consent is provided.
- **Screening for conflicts:** The process of checking for actual or potential conflicts before taking on a client or legal matter.

Authors' Note: Welcome to the chapter on conflict of interest! We have divided Chapter 6 into two parts because conflicts are an extraordinarily complicated and rule-heavy topic. However, it is one of the most important–both for the MPRE exam or your respective state bar exam, and in terms of actual practice. Please be patient while you further explore the rules on conflicts, as even seasoned practitioners struggle with this topic.

Introduction

HYPOTHETICAL 6.1

You are an estate attorney. You handle wills, trusts, and end-of-life matters for clients. Years ago, you prepared a joint will and trust for a couple. They came into your office together, and the three of you prepared a single will and trust for them, indicating that they plan to leave their joint assets equally to their two biological children. It was an easy preparation of the documents. You kept one copy, and you handed them a copy to keep. You told them that should they need to change the document, to feel free to come back to you at any time. It has now been ten years, and the wife suddenly appears in your office on a Wednesday afternoon. She has been having an affair with her old college sweetheart, and she is pregnant. Both are still married to their respective spouses, and her husband does not know about the affair or the pregnancy. She wants you to change the will and trust to divide all the assets one-third between her three children.

> Please refer to the interactive ebook in Cognella Active Learning for interactive/media content.

Many times, legal matters which on their surface seem simple can turn out to be complex because of the parties involved, or the subject matter. This is especially true when multiple parties are involved. Having the foresight to identify these complexities is important.

This chapter focuses on the fiduciary duty of loyalty also known as conflict of interest. Recognizing and resolving conflict of interest situations is critical to good lawyering and building relationships with clients.

An important tool for lawyers to routinely check or "screen" for conflicts of interest is a conflict check. Conflict checks are usually facilitated internally by law firms through conflict-checking software and in bigger/national firms through a conflicts department.

Why Check for Conflicts?

Lawyers owe loyalty. If their loyalty is to someone other than their client, they cannot zealously represent such client. Loyalty forms the bedrock of the attorney-client relationship. Lawyers should be wary of anything that threatens to impair this loyalty. As noted in an important California case, "[a] client who learns that his or her lawyer is also representing another party in litigation, or other transactional adversaries, even with respect to a matter wholly unrelated to the one for which counsel was retained, cannot long be expected to sustain the level of confidence and trust in counsel that is one of the foundations of the professional relationships."[1] Clients will not feel comfortable opening up to a lawyer unless they know their lawyers are absolutely committed to advancing their best interests. Even if the rest of the world is against them, they know that their lawyer will remain in their corner.[2]

To facilitate a conflict check, the lawyer should obtain only information sufficient to determine whether a conflict of interest exists. This includes the potential client's identity, potential adverse parties, and any other parties involved in the engagement. Suppose a conflict is highly likely, as in an area of law in a small community or a practice area with a few major clients. In that case, a lawyer may decide not to handle a matter that could create conflicts with other clients (who have more significant matters).

The check for loyalty applies at all stages of representation—before, during, and even after representation. Lawyers continue to owe loyalty to former clients, especially if that loyalty could jeopardize a current case. If a representation initially appears appropriate, but an actual conflict arises during the course of representing the client, the attorney must inform the parties in writing about the conflict and its foreseeable consequences.

Two or More Parties

Be wary of representing two or more parties at once, as they usually present conflicts of interest. Examples of this dynamic can include:

- A divorcing couple
- A husband and wife who want a will or estate plan
- Multiple plaintiffs stemming from a personal injury matter
- Multiple partners forming a new business
- A buyer and seller in a single real estate transaction

Let's look at the example of a divorcing couple. They may seek to split amicably, but that may not always hold during their negotiations. There are also many unknowns to a divorce that can lead to conflicts—who gets the kids? What if one spouse makes more money than the other? What if things change in the future? How do you maintain confidentiality? If one spouse shares a secret with you, do you have to tell the other? The answers to all these questions present challenging issues for a lawyer who chooses to represent both spouses in a divorce. Loyalty cannot be maintained, and only in rare situations should a lawyer agree to represent both sides.

One cannot discuss the duty of loyalty without considering how other duties—like the duty of

---

1. *Flatt v. Superior Court* (1994), 9 Cal.4th 247, at p. 285
2. *State Compensation Ins. Fund v. Drobot*, 192 F. Supp. 3d 1080

competence, the duty of confidentiality, and the duty of communication—influence loyalty. Thus, lawyers will analyze these duties together. Additionally, ABA Model Rule 2.1 requires a lawyer to "exercise independent professional judgment and render candid advice." A part of the duty of loyalty requires lawyers to consider whether they can render candid advice while representing multiple parties in a legal matter.

- **Why competence?** When a conflict clouds an attorney's decision-making, it could impact the attorney's ability to provide legal advice competently.
- **Why confidentiality?** You do not want a situation where the lawyer relies on a client's confidential information in a way that injures the client.
- **Why independent judgment?** You do not want the conflict to cloud the lawyer's judgment and interfere with their ability to render candid advice.

In short, a conflict of interest affects the *quality* of representation.

Please remember! Conflict of interest can sometimes feel overly complicated. It is very "rule-driven." Do not overthink it! Conflict of interest is making sure a lawyer is always loyal to their client and the legal matter. Can the lawyer be devoted to their client and the legal dispute? If they cannot, there is a conflict of interest.

Lawyers must avoid conflicts that do or may affect the quality of representation for their clients. Sometimes, those conflict situations simply "do not feel right" or "do not pass the smell test."

HYPOTHETICAL 6.2

You have a long-time client, Margot, who owns several dry-cleaning businesses in the area. Over the years, you have handled everything for Margot, from a minor slip-and-fall in front of one of her stores to all the contractual work to expand her business. She has been a client for over 20 years and, while you are not social with her, you consider her a loyal client and now a friend. You know she will always come to you for all her legal needs and confidences, and you both have fostered a trusted relationship.

Recently, Syd, who owns a stationery store in town, comes to you and says, "I have an opportunity to expand my business, and I am looking into buying a vacant building." They want you to review the purchase agreement. This would be your first time dealing with this client. However, you remembered years ago, Margot mentioned that Syd was trying to acquire a property by a bid process from the city where Margot expanded her respective businesses. You were not involved in the bid process. The bid process was fairly quick, and as Margot had explained to you after, it had come down to between her and Syd. She felt strongly that Syd was bidding not because he could afford the bid prices but rather to spite Margot and up the bid price.

You are not sure why Margot believed this, but she seemed angry and adamant about her accusation against Syd. You quickly forgot the story at the time, as Margot had won the bid and eventually expanded her dry-cleaning business at the location. It had been there for over ten years now.

You had forgotten about this story until Syd came into your office. Is this an actual conflict? Is there a breach of loyalty? That is something you would have to decide. How would Margot feel if she knew you were representing Syd? Is it something you want to talk to her about? Would it affect your relationship?

> Please refer to the interactive ebook in Cognella Active Learning for interactive/media content.

ABA Model Rule 1.7: Conflicts of Interest

Unless an exception applies, a lawyer shall not represent a client if the representation involves a concurrent conflict of interest. ABA Model Rule 1.7 is important, as evidenced by the 35 comments that accompany it.

A concurrent conflict of interest exists if:

- The representation of one client will be **directly adverse** to another client.
- There is a significant risk that the representation of one or more clients will be **materially limited** by the lawyer's responsibilities to another client, a former client, a third person, or the lawyer's personal interest.

Thus, ABA Model Rule 1.7(a) divides concurrent conflicts into (1) direct adversity conflicts and (2) material limitation conflicts. This rule covers actual conflicts and potential conflicts. In weighing potential conflicts, consider: (i) the likelihood of the conflict; and (ii) the severity of the conflict.

Table 6.1. ABA Model Rule 1.7

Directly Adverse (ABA Model Rule 1.7(a)(1))

Current or existing clients; litigation: A lawyer cannot represent two sides on opposing sides of litigation. For example, if a chef sues their employer—a restaurant—for unpaid wages, a lawyer cannot represent the chef and the restaurant in the lawsuit.

Transactional matters: Direct adversity conflicts can also arise in transactional matters. For example, a lawyer cannot represent the seller of a business in negotiations with a buyer represented by the same lawyer, not in the same transaction, but another, unrelated matter [Comment 7].

Related matters: Simultaneous representation of clients involved in different lawsuits can give rise to a conflict if the suit involves related matters. For example: representing a client who is enforcing a patent infringement case while also representing the potential patent infringer on other matters.

Unrelated matters: Even though the risk of split loyalties is lower in unrelated matters, ABA Model Rule 1.7(a) does not make a distinction. <u>Absent consent</u>, a lawyer may not act as an advocate in one matter against a person the lawyer represents in some other matter even when the matters are wholly unrelated. For example, a lawyer cannot represent an insurance company and pursue a lawsuit against a party who is the insured of the insurance company.

Cross-examining existing clients: A conflict may arise when a lawyer is required to cross-examine a client who appears as a witness in a lawsuit involving another client, and the testimony will be damaging to the client who is represented in the lawsuit [Comment 6]. For example, a law firm represents a client accused of fraud against a university. ©hat same law firm represents the university in other matters. Since the law firm will have to cross-examine university representatives in the fraud case, there will be a conflict. A lawyer may be inclined to choose a soft or deferential cross-examination which will compromise the representation. [Practically speaking, in situations like the university fraud example, law firms might choose to appoint conflicts counsel for the sole purpose of cross-examining their current client.]

Pre-trial litigation: ©he issues presented herein could also apply to taking discovery, whether testimony or documentary, on behalf of one client against another. For example, when a lawyer deposes a non-party witness, who is the lawyer's client in another matter, especially if the deposition is likely to harm or embarrass the witness.

Material Limitation (ABA Model Rule 1.7(a)(2))

Material limitation is broader than direct adversity since it covers conflicts with other clients, third persons, former clients, and personal interests.

1. Impair = weaken
2. Material limitation = any factor that would impair loyalty to a client or interfere with a lawyer exercising independent judgment on behalf of the client. It must be more than just the possibility of a material limitation. Rather, there must be a significant risk that the representation will be materially limited.
3. Ask: Do you have confidential information about a client that could be used against them? Would the quality of your representation be compromised in any way such that you cannot provide diligent and competent representation? Is there a significant risk that you cannot consider, recommend, or carry out an appropriate course of action for the client?

Situations that are commonly analyzed under ABA Model Rule 1.7(a)(2) include:

1. A lawyer asked to represent several individuals seeking to form a joint venture is likely to be materially limited in their ability to recommend or advocate all possible positions that each might take because of the lawyer's duty of loyalty to others [Comment 8].
2. A lawyer asked to represent a new client against a former client [Comment 9].
3. A lawyer for a corporation who sits on its board of directors [Comment 35].
4. Lawyers who are having employment or merger discussions with their current adversaries/law firms [Comment 10].
5. Lawyers related to one another by blood or marriage [Comment 11].

Note: *The comments mentioned in the table are comments to ABA Model Rule 1.7. For each of the examples presented below, remember that a lawyer can still represent the client with consent, among other things. We will discuss the exception to the rule later in this chapter (see ABA Model Rule 1.7(b)).*

Criminal Cases

Lawyers can jointly represent multiple defendants in a criminal case. However, a lawyer's duty of loyalty can be severely limited in these situations and some states even prohibit this. For example, assume a lawyer represents a father and son in a criminal case, where both are charged for arson and conspiracy. After consulting with his clients, getting informed consent, and assessing whether it's reasonable to continue representation, the lawyer decides to represent both the father and son. As the case develops, it becomes apparent that the father and son have different degrees of culpability. The prosecution offers the son a plea deal in exchange for testifying against the father. At this stage, a conflict of interest has materialized. It would be difficult for the attorney to advise both the son and father, especially since the son has a plea deal that directly points fingers at the father. In advising the son to take the plea deal, the lawyer compromises his duty of loyalty to the father.

CASE ALERT: KLEMM V. SUPERIOR COURT

In *Klemm v. Superior Court*,[3] the court grappled with the issue of whether an attorney may represent both husband and wife in a non-contested divorce (marital dissolution). The wife filed a petition for dissolution after six years of marriage. They did not have any community property or substantial personal property. They both waived their right to spousal support. At the dissolution hearing, attorney Catherine Bailey represented the wife. Separately, and due to the close relationship between Bailey and the former couple, she acted without compensation. Throughout the dissolution, Bailey had consulted with both husband and wife and worked out an oral agreement regarding custody. Eventually, the attorney agreed to represent the husband in the hearing for child support, which the wife did not object to. The wife was still a party to the hearing. Even though the attorney had client consent, the court concluded:

> As a matter of law, a purported consent to dual representation of litigants with adverse interests at a contested hearing would be neither intelligent nor informed. Such representation would be per se inconsistent with the adversary position of an attorney in litigation, and common-sense dictates that it would be unthinkable to permit an attorney to assume a position at a trial or hearing where he could not advocate the interests of one client without adversely injuring those of the other.[4]

---

3. *Klemm v. Superior Court*, 75 Cal.App.3d 893
4. Id. at 898–899

After reading the case, ask yourself: why did the attorney choose to represent both parties, knowing that their circumstances could change at any point during the dissolution proceedings? Would you take on the representation of both husband and wife in a non-contested divorce?

Opinion
Brown(G. A.), P. J.

The ultimate issue herein is to what extent one attorney may represent both husband and wife in a noncontested **[75 Cal. App. 3d 896]** dissolution proceeding where the written consent of each to such representation has been filed with the court.

Dale Klemm (hereinafter husband) and Gail Klemm (hereinafter wife) were married and are the parents of two minor children. They separated after six years of marriage, and the wife filed a petition for dissolution of the marriage in propria persona. There was no community property, and neither party owned any substantial personal property. Both parties waived spousal support. The husband was a carpenter with part-time employment.

At the dissolution hearing Attorney Catherine Bailey appeared for the wife. It developed that Bailey is a friend of the husband and wife and because they could not afford an attorney she was acting without compensation. The attorney had consulted with both the husband and wife and had worked out an oral agreement whereby the custody of the minor children would be joint, that is, each would have the children for a period of two weeks out of each month, and the wife waived child support.

The trial judge granted an interlocutory decree and awarded joint custody in accord with the agreement. However, because the wife was receiving aid for dependent children payments from the county, he referred the matter of child support to the Family Support Division of the Fresno County District Attorney's office for investigation and report.

The subsequent report from the family support division recommended that the husband be ordered to pay $25 per month per child (total $50) child support and that this amount be paid to the county as reimbursement for past and present A.F.D.C. payments made and being made to the wife. Bailey, on behalf of the wife, filed a written objection to the recommendation that the husband be required to pay child support.

At the hearing on the report and issue of child support on April 25, 1977, Bailey announced she was appearing on behalf of the husband. She said the parties were "in agreement on this matter, so there is in reality no conflict between them." No written consents to joint representation were filed. On questioning by the court the wife evinced uncertainty as to her position in the litigation. The wife said, "She [Bailey] asked me to come here just as a witness, so I don't feel like I'm taking any action against Dale." The judge pointed out that she (the wife) was still a party. When first asked if she wanted Bailey to continue **[75 Cal. App. 3d 897]** as her attorney she answered "No." Later she said she would consent to Bailey's being relieved as her counsel. She then said she

---

Superior Court of Fresno County, "Klemm v. Superior Court," 75 Cal.App.3d 893, 1977.

didn't believe she could act as her own attorney but that she consented to Bailey's representing the husband. After this confusing and conflicting testimony and a request for permission to talk to Bailey about it, the judge ordered, over Bailey's objection, that he would not permit Bailey to appear for either the husband or the wife because of a present conflict of interest and ordered the matter continued for one week.

At the continued hearing on May 2, 1977, Bailey appeared by counsel, who filed written consents to joint representation signed by the husband and wife and requested that Bailey be allowed to appear for the husband and wife (who were present in court). The consents, which were identical in form, stated: "I have been advised by my attorney that a potential conflict of interest exists by reason of her advising and representing my ex-spouse as well as myself. I feel this conflict is purely technical and I request Catherine Bailey to represent me." The court denied the motion, and the husband and wife have petitioned this court for a writ of mandate to direct the trial court to permit such representation.

Rule 5-102 of the State Bar Rules of Professional Conduct states:

"(A) A member of the State Bar shall not accept professional employment without first disclosing his relation, if any, with the adverse party, and his interest, if any, in the subject matter of the employment. A member of the State Bar who accepts employment under this rule shall first obtain the client's written consent to such employment.

"(B) A member of the State Bar shall not represent conflicting interests, except with the written consent of all parties concerned." (3B **[75 Cal. App. 3d 898]** West's Ann. Bus. & Prof. Code (1974 ed., 1977 cum.supp.) foll. § 6076 at p. 65 [Deering's Cal. Codes Ann. Rules (1976 ed.) at p. 614].)

The California cases are generally consistent with rule 5-102 permitting dual representation where there is a full disclosure and informed consent by all the parties, at least insofar as a representation pertains to agreements and negotiations prior to a trial or hearing. (*Gregory v. Gregory* (1949) 92 Cal. App. 2d 343, 349 [206 P.2d 1122] [marital settlement agreements]; *Davidson v. Davidson* (1949) 90 Cal. App. 2d 809, 819 [204 P.2d 71]; *Lessing v. Gibbons* (1935) 6 Cal. App. 2d 598, 605-606 [45 P.2d 258] [court approved attorney acting for both studio and actress in concluding negotiations and drawing agreements. The court refers to the common practice of attorneys acting for both parties in drawing and dissolving partnership agreements, for grantors and grantees, sellers and buyers, lessors and lessees, and lenders and borrowers].) Where, however, a fully informed consent is not obtained, the duty of loyalty to different clients renders it impossible for an attorney, consistent with ethics and the fidelity owed to clients, to advise one client as to a disputed claim against the other. (*Dettamanti v. Lompoc Union School Dist.* (1956) 143 Cal. App. 2d 715, 723 [300 P.2d 78].)

Though an informed consent be obtained, no case we have been able to find sanctions dual representation of conflicting interests if that representation is in conjunction with a trial or hearing where there is an actual, present, existing conflict and the discharge of duty to one client conflicts with the duty to another. (*See Anderson v. Eaton* (1930) 211 Cal. 113 [293 P.

788]; *Hammett v. McIntyre* (1952) 114 Cal. App. 2d 148, 153-154 [249 P.2d 885]; *McClure v. Donovan* (1947) 82 Cal. App. 2d 664, 666 [186 P.2d 718].) [1] As a matter of law a purported consent to dual representation of litigants with adverse interests at a contested hearing would be neither intelligent nor informed. Such representation would be per se inconsistent with the adversary position of an attorney in litigation, and common sense dictates that it would be unthinkable to permit an attorney to assume a position at a trial or hearing where he could not advocate the interests of one client without adversely injuring those of the other. **[75 Cal. App. 3d 899]**

[2] However, if the conflict is merely potential, there being no existing dispute or contest between the parties represented as to any point in litigation, then with full disclosure to and informed consent of both clients there may be dual representation at a hearing or trial. (*Burum v. State Compensation Ins. Fund* (1947) 30 Cal. 2d 575 [184 P.2d 505]; *Lysick v. Walcom* (1968) 258 Cal. App. 2d 136, 146-147 [65 Cal. Rptr. 406, 28 A.L.R.3d 368]; see *Arden v. State Bar* (1959) 52 Cal. 2d 310 [341 P.2d 6].)

[3] In our view the case at bench clearly falls within the latter category. The conflict of interest was strictly potential and not present. The parties had settled their differences by agreement. There was no point of difference to be litigated. The position of each inter se was totally consistent throughout the proceedings. The wife did not want child support from the husband, and the husband did not want to pay support for the children. The actual conflict that existed on the issue of support was between the county on the one hand, which argued that support should be ordered, and the husband and wife on the other who consistently maintained the husband should not be ordered to pay support.

While on the face of the matter it may appear foolhardy for the wife to waive child support,[3] other values could very well have been more important to her than such support — such as maintaining a good relationship between the husband and the children and between the husband and herself despite the marital problems — thus avoiding the backbiting, acrimony and ill will which the Family Relations Act of 1970 was, insofar as possible, designed to eliminate. It could well have been if the wife was forced to choose between A.F.D.C. payments to be reimbursed to the county by the husband and no A.F.D.C. payments she would have made the latter choice.

Of course, if the wife at some future date should change her mind and seek child support and if the husband should desire to avoid the payment of such support, Bailey would be disqualified from representing either in a contested hearing on the issue. (Rules of Prof. Conduct, rule 4-101; *Goldstein v. Lees* (1975) 46 Cal. App. 3d 614 [120 Cal. Rptr. 253].) There would then exist an actual conflict between them, and an attorney's duty **[75 Cal. App. 3d 900]** to maintain the confidence of each would preclude such representation. (*Industrial Indem. Co. v. Great American Ins. Co.* (1977) 73 Cal. App. 3d 529 [140 Cal. Rptr. 806].)

The conclusion we arrive at is particularly congruent with dissolution proceedings under the

Family Law Act of 1970, the purpose of which was to discard the concept of fault in dissolution of marriage actions (Civ. Code, §§ 4506, 4509), to minimize the adversary nature of such proceedings and to eliminate conflicts created only to secure a divorce. (*In re Marriage of Cary* (1973) 34 Cal. App. 3d 345 [109 Cal. Rptr. 862] (disapproved on other grounds in *Marvin v. Marvin* (1976) 18 Cal. 3d 660, 665 [134 Cal. Rptr. 815, 557 P.2d 106]); *The End of Innocence: Elimination of Fault in California Divorce Law* (1970) 17 UCLA L.Rev. 1306) It is contrary to the philosophy of that act to create controversy between the parties where none exists in reality.

We hold on the facts of this case, wherein the conflict was only potential, that if the written consents were knowing and informed and given after full disclosure by the attorney, the attorney can appear for both of the parties on issues concerning which they fully agree.

It follows that if we were reviewing the order of the trial court after the first hearing held on April 25, 1977, the petition for mandate would have to be denied on the ground that no written consents to joint representation had been procured at that time. Moreover, as a result of the judge's questioning of the wife, he could have reasonably concluded that the wife's consent was not given after a full disclosure and was neither intelligent nor informed.

The order before us, however, is the order entered after the second hearing held on May 2, 1977, at which time the written consents of both the husband and wife, dated that date, were received by the judge without further inquiry of the clients or of the attorney. It could well have been that between April 25 and May 2 and before signing the written consents the parties became apprised of sufficient information to make the written consents intelligent and informed. The situation on May 2 was not necessarily the same as it was on April 25. The record of the May 2 hearing reflects no inquiry whatsoever as to whether the written consents were knowing, informed and given after full disclosure. Thus it appears the trial judge failed to exercise his discretion in accordance with proper legal principles. Accordingly, the cause must be **[75 Cal. App. 3d 901]** returned to the trial court to make the determination of whether the consents were knowing, informed and given after a full disclosure.

[4] A word as to procedure. Initially, the trial court is entitled to accept properly executed written consents to joint representation at their face value. The judge is entitled to presume the attorney is familiar with the law and code of professional ethics and has complied with the proper standards. However, if the judge has any question regarding whether the proper standards have been observed, it is his duty to either require counsel to inquire further or inquire himself regarding the circumstances of the execution of the written consents and the state of mind of the clients for the purpose of making the necessary factual determination in this regard.4

[5] Finally, as a caveat, we hasten to sound a note of warning. Attorneys who undertake to represent parties with divergent interests owe the highest duty to each to make a full disclosure of all facts and circumstances which are necessary to enable the parties to make a fully informed decision regarding the subject matter of the litigation, including the areas of potential conflict and the possibility and desirability of seeking independent legal advice.

(*Ishmael v. Millington* (1966) 241 Cal. App. 2d 520 [50 Cal. Rptr. 592].) [6] Failing such disclosure, the attorney is civilly liable to the client who suffers loss caused by lack of disclosure. (*Lysick v. Walcom, supra,* 258 Cal. App. 2d 136.) In addition, the lawyer lays himself open to charges, whether well founded or not, of unethical and unprofessional conduct. (*Arden v. State Bar, supra,* 52 Cal. 2d 310.) Moreover, the validity of any agreement negotiated without independent representation of each of the parties is vulnerable to easy attack as having been procured by misrepresentation, fraud and overreaching. (*Gregory v. Gregory* (1949) 92 Cal. App. 2d 343 [206 P.2d 1122].) It thus behooves counsel to cogitate carefully and proceed cautiously before placing himself/herself in such a position.

As was said in *Anderson v. Eaton, supra,* 211 Cal. 113, 116: "It is also an attorney's duty to protect his client in every possible way, and it is a **[75 Cal. App. 3d 902]** violation of that duty for him to assume a position adverse or antagonistic to his client without the latter's free and intelligent consent given after full knowledge of all the facts and circumstances. [Citation.] By virtue of this rule an attorney is precluded from assuming any relation which would prevent him from devoting his entire energies to his client's interests. Nor does it matter that the intention and motives of the attorney are honest. The rule is designed not alone to prevent the dishonest practitioner from fraudulent conduct, but as well to preclude the honest practitioner from putting himself in a position where he may be required to choose between conflicting duties, or be led to an attempt to reconcile conflicting interests, rather than to enforce to their full extent the rights of the interest which he should alone represent. [Citation.]"

We have considered respondent's other contentions and find them to be without merit.

It is ordered that a peremptory writ of mandate issue directing the trial court to reconsider Bailey's motion to be allowed to represent both husband and wife, that the court determine if the consent given by each was knowing and informed after a full disclosure by the attorney, and to decide the motion in accordance with the principles set forth in this opinion.

Petitioners shall recover costs.

Gargano, J., and Hopper, J., concurred.

CASE ALERT: IBM V. LEVIN: ANTITRUST

This case involved a motion to disqualify counsel for the respondent from further participation in a private antitrust suit because counsel had represented both respondent and petitioner while the matter was still pending before the district court. The district court disqualified counsel from further representation of the respondent but permitted counsel to submit its past work product to the respondent's substituted counsel. IBM petitioned the court to block the transfer of past work products. Further, IBM contended that counsel should have first obtained consent before representation. The court agreed. Counsel should have disclosed to IBM the facts of its representation and obtain consent.

After reading the case, answer the following question: what was the concurrent conflict of interest?

Opinion
Maris, Circuit Judge

This petition for a writ of mandamus and these appeals and cross-appeals seek our review of an interlocutory order of the United States District Court for the District of New Jersey entered in this private anti-trust suit directing Carpenter, Bennett Morrissey (herein "CBM"), counsel for the plaintiffs, Howard S. Levin (herein "Levin") and Levin Computer Corporation (herein "LCC"), to withdraw from the case and allowing CBM to turn over its past work on the case to substitute counsel for the plaintiffs with consultation with such counsel to effect the turnover permitted for a period of sixty days.

The plaintiffs' lawsuit against the International Business Machines Corporation (herein "IBM"), alleging violations of sections 1 and 2 of the Sherman Act, 15 U.S.C.A. §§ 1 and 2, and of the laws of the State of New Jersey, was filed about ten months after Levin caused LCC to be incorporated under the laws of New Jersey for the purpose, stated in the complaint, of engaging in the business of purchasing for lease certain data processing equipment manufactured by IBM, known as the 370 series or IBM fourth generation computer equipment. When IBM refused to extend installment credit to Levin and LCC on other than terms which the latter considered to be unfair and unreasonable, this action was filed, on June 23, 1972, in the Superior Court of New Jersey, Chancery Division, Essex County. The suit was subsequently removed to the district court.

The amended complaint filed in the district court asserts that IBM illegally perpetuates a monopoly position in the manufacture, distribution and ownership of computers and in particular of fourth generation or 370 series computers in New Jersey and throughout the United States by maintaining policies and practices which discourage sales of that equipment and force users to lease it directly from IBM at arbitrarily high rentals. The relief sought is an injunction against IBM's further use of alleged anticompetitive and discriminatory practices with respect to the distribution of its fourth generation computers as well as damages, an order directing IBM to grant the plaintiffs installment credit on reasonable terms which would permit their purchase of the computers, related items and services and an order directing IBM to sell its fourth generation computers to LCC by installment sale.

Shortly after the filing of the amended complaint, the plaintiffs applied to the district court for a preliminary injunction directing IBM to extend installment credit to LCC for the purchase of IBM computer equipment. The motion was denied. An appeal was taken to this court at our No. 72-1843 and on June 4, 1973, we entered an order affirming the district court's decision.

In December 1973 the plaintiffs moved in the district court for partial summary judgment or in the alternative for a preliminary injunction ordering IBM to rent certain components of IBM

United States Court of Appeals, Third Circuit, "IBM v. Levin," 579 F.2d 271, 1978.

computer equipment to LCC for integration into computers not owned by IBM. This motion also was denied by the district court. On appeal to this court at our No. 74-1304, we affirmed by an order entered October 31, 1974. Thereafter, both parties undertook extensive discovery in the district court and trial before the court was set for September 1977.

In June 1977 IBM moved for an order disqualifying CBM from further participation in the case on the ground that the law firm had represented both the plaintiffs and IBM during the pendency of the action in the district court in violation of the disciplinary rules of the Code of Professional Responsibility of the American Bar Association which had been adopted by the district court as the standards of ethical conduct which practitioners before the court are required to observe.

The district court, on the basis of depositions, affidavits and briefs filed with it and after hearing arguments of counsel for IBM and CBM and new counsel for the plaintiffs, disqualified CBM from further representation of the plaintiffs in the case but permitted CBM to turn over its past work product on the case to the plaintiffs' new counsel and allowed consultation between CBM and the plaintiffs' substitute counsel with respect thereto for a period of sixty days. The order of disqualification was entered in the district court by Judge Meanor December 28, 1977. An amended order which clarified CBM's right to appeal from the order of disqualification was entered January 9, 1978. Since the latter contains all the significant provisions of the original order, we confine our discussion to it.

IBM petitioned this court for a writ of mandamus directing Judge Meanor to prohibit the turnover of CBM's past work product and consultation between CBM and the plaintiffs' substitute counsel for a period of sixty days following disqualification. IBM, in addition, appealed from the portions of the district court's order which permit such turnover of work product and consultation. IBM also moved to stay the portions of the order concerning which it seeks review, to consolidate its appeals and petition for mandamus for review purposes and to expedite briefing.

CBM and the plaintiffs cross-appealed from the district court's order disqualifying CBM. Their appeals raise questions concerning the applicability to CBM of the ban of the American Bar Association's Code against a lawyer's dual representation of adversaries and the appropriateness of the sanctions of disqualification and total withdrawal after sixty days in the circumstances of this case. CBM and the plaintiffs moved this court to dismiss IBM's appeals and petition for mandamus for lack of jurisdiction and for IBM's failure to demonstrate any prejudice or injury to its rights by reason of the portions of the order sought by it to be reviewed.

We granted the stay pending review requested by IBM, deferred IBM's petition for mandamus and CBM's motion to dismiss IBM's appeals and petition for consideration with the merits of the appeals and cross-appeals, ordered consolidation of the related cases and directed an expedited schedule of briefing. The case has now been argued and is before us for decision.

We turn then to outline the facts out of which this controversy arose. It appears that CBM had represented both Levin and the corporation with which he was then associated, Levin Townsend Computer Corporation (herein "LTC"), a computer leasing corporation, from 1965 to 1969. From

1966 to 1969 CBM performed considerable work for LTC including representing the corporation in several disputes with IBM in connection with IBM's installment sale to LTC of IBM computer equipment. In January 1970 when Levin terminated his association with LTC, CBM withdrew as attorneys for LTC but continued to represent Levin sporadically in matters unrelated to LTC. In the latter part of 1971 CBM resumed an active attorney-client relationship with Levin. At that time CBM arranged for the incorporation of LCC on behalf of Levin. One of the firm's partners, Stanley Weiss, became a director of LCC and another, David M. McCann, assumed the office of secretary of the corporation.

LCC's effort in late 1971 and 1972 to secure installment credit on terms acceptable to it for the purchase of IBM equipment was handled by McCann dealing with Joseph W. S. Davis, Jr., counsel for IBM's Data Processing Division located in White Plains, New York. As LCC's prospects for a satisfactory credit arrangement with IBM diminished with IBM's successive rejections of LCC's applications for installment credit, Levin's determination to take legal action against IBM grew. In February 1972 McCann advised Davis of the plaintiffs' intention to file suit to enjoin IBM from imposing more stringent credit requirements on LCC than were applied to prospective lessees of the equipment LCC desired to purchase.

Davis reported this information to Nicholas Katzenbach, IBM vice-president and general counsel, and Chester B. McLaughlin, assistant general counsel, both working out of the general counsel's office located at IBM's corporate headquarters in Armonk, New York.

In March 1972 a meeting, attended by McCann and Weiss of CBM, Davis and R. G. O'Neill of IBM, and Levin and the treasurer of LCC, was held at LCC's New York City office in an unsuccessful attempt to resolve the dispute. IBM, thereafter, engaged the law firm of Riker, Danzig, Scherer Debevoise to represent it in any ensuing suit. On June 23, 1972, CBM filed the present suit on behalf of the plaintiffs and has prosecuted it until the present time.

In April 1970 a member of IBM's legal staff in the general counsel's office at Armonk, Robert Troup, contacted Edward F. Ryan, a CBM partner and one of five members of the firm specializing in labor matters, for the purpose of retaining CBM's services in the preparation of an opinion letter for IBM regarding a jurisdictional dispute with an electrical workers' union. The CBM partners considered and rejected the possibility that acceptance of the IBM assignment in the labor matter might create a conflict of interest in the light of CBM's former representation of LTC. Ryan prepared an opinion on the jurisdictional dispute question and accepted a second assignment from Troup in July 1970 dealing with a union's right to picket IBM in the event IBM cancelled a subcontracting arrangement and a third assignment in May 1971 relating to the availability of injunctive relief against certain union picketing.

In April 1972 Ryan accepted Troup's telephoned request for another opinion letter in a labor matter concerning the right of temporary employees to form a separate bargaining unit. At this point Ryan's account of the facts diverges from that of Troup. Ryan's sworn statement is that his acceptance of IBM's fourth assignment caused him some concern since he was aware of CBM's current representation of LCC and LCC's difficulty in procuring credit from IBM. Consequently, a few days after Troup's call, Ryan consulted with McCann and Weiss about a possible conflict of interest in CBM's representation of both IBM and LCC simultaneously. Weiss informed Ryan of the contemplated antitrust suit against IBM and advised him to obtain IBM's consent to the firm's representation of both IBM and the plaintiffs. Ryan stated that shortly thereafter he called Troup at his Armonk office and in a conversation lasting about three minutes brought to Troup's attention the contemplated antitrust suit against IBM by CBM's client, Levin. Troup's response, according to Ryan's testimony, was that the matter was not significant from IBM's point of view and he directed Ryan to proceed with the assignment given him. Various members of the CBM firm testified to their understanding at the time that Ryan had obtained IBM's consent to the dual representation. Troup, however, by affidavit and deposition, denied ever having been informed by Ryan of the proposed Levin lawsuit or that CBM might represent another client in a suit against IBM. CBM obtained Levin's consent to CBM's representation of IBM in labor matters and the antitrust suit was filed by Weiss acting for the firm June 23, 1972, one week after the completion of CBM's fourth opinion letter for IBM.

Weiss testified, also, in connection with IBM's knowledge of CBM's possible conflict of interest involving IBM, that in July 1973 while he and Charles Danzig, a partner of Riker, Danzig, Scherer Debevoise, IBM's counsel in the antitrust suit, rode together in a train from Philadelphia to Newark, Weiss mentioned that CBM performed occasional work for IBM in labor matters. Danzig denied that such a statement was made to him by Weiss.

It is undisputed that during CBM's prosecution of the antitrust suit, Ryan accepted four additional labor relations assignments from Troup without further discussing with Troup CBM's concurrent representation of Levin and LCC. On February 2, 1974, Ryan was asked to represent IBM in effecting the recovery of IBM equipment from a warehouse in Edison, New Jersey operated by an employer who was experiencing labor problems with the Teamsters Union. Ryan's work in this matter included the preparation of a complaint in replevin against the warehouse operator which was never filed and an application for a writ of possession which was granted by the Superior Court of New Jersey, Law Division, Middlesex, but was not executed since the union and employer arranged for union members to deliver the equipment to IBM. Preparation of the application for a writ required CBM's receipt from IBM of a schedule identifying the various pieces of equipment and IBM customers involved.

In June 1974 Ryan was requested by Troup to represent IBM in a matter involving a claim of the Division of Weights and Measures of the State of New Jersey of jurisdiction over certain IBM equipment necessitating its approval of the sale and use of the equipment in New Jersey and the possible licensing of IBM maintenance engineers. Ryan referred the assignment to a CBM partner, Jerome J. Graham, Jr., who accepted it after being assured that CBM's representation of LCC in the pending antitrust suit had been previously cleared with IBM. Graham's participation in the matter, according to his affidavit, ended in August 1976.

In June and July 1976 Ryan was contacted by IBM attorneys requesting two opinion letters, one dealing with an employer's obligation in regard to supervisory employee's performance of certain work during a work stoppage and the second having to do with restrictions under New Jersey law on registered nurses' performance of certain medical examination procedures. The opinion letters were completed by CBM in July 1976.

Subsequently, at a law school alumni luncheon in New York City on January 28, 1977, John Lynch, a partner of CBM, met Richard McDonough, then a member of IBM's legal staff, and Lynch mentioned to McDonough his role in prosecuting the plaintiffs' antitrust suit against IBM. McDonough indicated surprise in that CBM was, to his knowledge, representing IBM in labor matters. In April 1977, at a dinner attended by McDonough and counsel for IBM in the antitrust suit, McDonough expressed to the latter an interest in knowing how CBM's conflict of interest had been reconciled to permit CBM's representation of Levin and LCC in the suit against IBM. McDonough's remarks caused IBM to investigate the matter further and led to the filing in June 1977 of the motion to disqualify CBM.

These being the facts we turn to the consideration of the questions raised by the parties. We first consider the questions of jurisdiction which have been raised. It is clear that we have jurisdiction under 28 U.S.C. § 1291 to hear the appeals of the cross-appellants from the district court's order disqualifying CBM. *Akerly v. Red Barn System, Inc.*, 551 F.2d 539, 542-543 (3d Cir. 1977); *Kramer v. Scientific Control Corp.*, 534 F.2d 1085, 1088 (3d Cir. 1976); *Kroungold v. Triester*, 521 F.2d 763, 765 (3d Cir. 1975); *American Roller Co. v. Budinger*, 513 F.2d 982, 983 (3d Cir. 1975); *Greene v. Singer Co.*, 509 F.2d 750 (3d Cir. 1971), cert. denied, 409 U.S. 848, 93 S.Ct. 54, 34 L.Ed.2d 89 (1972). The disqualification order is a "collateral order" which, although it does not terminate the claims in litigation, does finally dispose of an issue entirely separable from and independent of those claims which involves the risk of irreparable injury and the loss of an important right if immediate review is denied. *See Cohen v. Beneficial Industrial Loan Corp.*, 337 U.S. 541, 546-547, 69 S.Ct. 1221, 93 L.Ed. 1528 (1949).

Our jurisdiction over the order of disqualification being clear, we think it extends, notwithstanding the restrictive nature of the collateral order doctrine, to those portions of the district court's order which spell out the nature and extent of the disqualification ordered. Our holding in *Akerly v. Red Barn System, Inc.*, 551 F.2d 539 (3d Cir. 1977), is distinguishable. In *Akerly* we concluded that our jurisdiction over an appeal from an order denying a motion to disqualify opposing counsel did not empower us to consider the district court's denial of a related motion to dismiss the complaint and the denial of dismissal did not become an appealable collateral order by reason of its basis in alleged attorney misconduct. Here, our jurisdiction is invoked only with respect to the grant of disqualification since the other portions of the district court's order which are sought to be reviewed are, in fact, integral parts of the disqualification proper.

The way is thus open to us to consider the contention raised by the cross-appellants that the district court abused its discretion in requiring CBM's total withdrawal from the case after sixty days. Since this issue is properly before us on the cross-appeals, we may entertain IBM's opposing contention, either on its separate appeals or as appellee on the cross-appeals, that the district court abused its discretion in granting the sixty-day consultation period. *Compare Consolo v. Federal Maritime Commission*, 383 U.S. 607, 615, 86 S.Ct. 1018, 16 L.Ed.2d 131 (1966). Moreover, even if the turnover issue had not been raised in the appeals or cross-appeals, our power of review over the disqualification order, once established as it is here, encompasses what is plainly an aspect of the reviewable order. *See Rhoads v. Ford Motor Co.*, 514 F.2d 931, 934 (3d Cir. 1975); *McCreary Tire Rubber Co. v. CEAT S.p.A.*, 501 F.2d 1032, 1038 (3d Cir. 1974); 9 Moore's Federal Practice ¶ 110.25[1] at 273 (2d ed. 1973).

Since we conclude that we have authority to review all aspects of the district court's order raised in the appeals and cross-appeals, we need not consider further CBM's contention that that part of the district court's order which deals with the turnover of CBM's past work is not independently appealable under the *Cohen* collateral order doctrine nor its argument that IBM, not having been prejudiced by the turnover decision, lacks standing as an aggrieved party to take an appeal from it. Accordingly, CBM's motion to dismiss IBM's appeals will be denied. CBM's motion to dismiss IBM's petition for a writ of mandamus will be granted, however. Since IBM is entitled to raise on the appeals and cross-appeals the issues which it has sought to raise by mandamus, the remedy of that extraordinary writ is foreclosed to it. *See Kerr v. United States District Court*, 426 U.S. 394, 403, 96 S.Ct. 2119, 48 L.Ed.2d 725 (1976); *Ex parte Fahey*, 332 U.S. 258, 67 S.Ct. 1558, 91 L.Ed. 2041 (1947); *Roche v. Evaporated Milk Association*, 319 U.S. 21, 27-28, 63 S.Ct. 938, 87 L.Ed. 1185 (1943).

We turn then to consider the order under review. If the facts found by the district court establish that practitioners before it have acted in a way which disqualifies them under its rules and established standards of professional conduct, it would ordinarily be error for the court to fail to declare the disqualification. But in its order of disqualification the court has a wide discretion in framing its sanctions so as to be just and fair to all parties involved. Except where purely legal issues are involved, the district court's action in these matters may be reversed only for a clear abuse of this discretion. *Kramer v. Scientific Control Corp.*, 534 F.2d 1085, 1088 (3d Cir. 1976); *Kroungold v. Triester*, 521 F.2d 763, 765 (3d Cir. 1975).

CBM's principal contention does raise a legal question, however. It is that under a proper interpretation of the disciplinary rules of the American Bar Association's Code of Professional Responsibility which are in force in the district court an attorney who has asserted a claim against a client pursuant to his representation of a second client may continue to represent the first client with respect to matters unrelated to the lawsuit without disclosing fully the facts of the dual representation to the client being sued and without obtaining his consent.

The pertinent rule of the Code of Professional Responsibility, which Code the district court adopted in 1970 under its Local Rule 6 as the controlling standard of conduct for the members of the bar practicing before it, provides as follows:

"DR 5-105 Refusing to Accept or Continue Employment if the Interests of Another Client May Impair the Independent Professional Judgment of the Lawyer.

"(A) A lawyer shall decline proffered employment if the exercise of his independent professional judgment in behalf of a client will be or is likely to be adversely affected by the acceptance of the proffered employment, except to the extent permitted under DR 5-105(C).

"(B) A lawyer shall not continue multiple employment if the exercise of his independent professional judgment in behalf of a client will be or is likely to be adversely affected by his representation of another client, except to the extent permitted under DR 5-105(C).

"(C) In the situations covered by DR 5-105(A) and (B), a lawyer may represent multiple clients if it is obvious that he can adequately represent the interest of each and if each consents to the representation after full disclosure of the possible effect of such representation on the exercise of his independent professional judgment on behalf of each.

"(D) If a lawyer is required to decline employment or to withdraw from employment under DR 5-105, no partner or associate of his or his firm may accept or continue such employment."

CBM argues that clauses (A) and (B) of DR 5-105 are not applicable since no effect adverse to IBM resulted from CBM's concurrent representation of both IBM and the plaintiffs and no adverse effect on CBM's exercise of its independent professional judgment on behalf of IBM was likely to result from CBM's representation of these clients in two entirely unrelated areas. Since clauses (A) and (B) do not apply, CBM argues, the consent requirement of clause (C) of DR 5-105 also is not applicable.

We think that CBM takes too narrow a view of the meaning of the phrase "adversely affected" in clauses (A) and (B), and that a somewhat more generous interpretation is called for. The rule does not define the nature or extent of the adverse effect contemplated on the attorney's exercise of independent judgment. However, DR 5-105(C) makes clear that situations entailing the likelihood of an adverse effect include circumstances in which such an effect may be minor permitting the performance of adequate services in spite of it. In those cases the multiple representation may take place if the attorney believes in good faith that he can adequately represent both clients and if the consent of the clients is obtained.

We think, however, that it is likely that some "adverse effect" on an attorney's exercise of his independent judgment on behalf of a client may result from the attorney's adversary posture toward that client in another legal matter. *See Cinema 5, Ltd. v. Cinerama, Inc.*, 528 F.2d 1384, 1386-1387 (2d Cir. 1976); *Grievance Committee of the Bar of Hartford County v. Rottner*, 152 Conn. 59, 65, 203 A.2d 82, 84 (1964); Advisory Committee on Professional Ethics of the Supreme Court of New Jersey, *Opinion No. 282*, 97 N.J.L.J. 362 (1974), and *Opinion No. 301*, 98 N.J.L.J. 209 (1975). For example, a possible effect on the quality of the attorney's services on behalf of the client being sued may be a diminution in the vigor of his representation of the client in the other matter. *See Cinema 5, Ltd. v. Cinerama, Inc., supra* at 1387. A serious effect on the attorney-client relationship may follow if the client discovers from a source other than the attorney that he is being sued in a different matter by the attorney. The fact that a deleterious result cannot be identified subsequently as having actually occurred does not refute the existence of a likelihood of its occurrence, depending upon the facts and circumstances, at the time the decision was made to represent the client without having obtained his consent.

The cases relied upon by CBM do not support its argument that the Code rule can never be violated by concurrent representation of several clients absent a showing of a relationship in the subject matter of the multiple representation. Most of the cases cited by CBM concern instances where ethical improprieties were found and are, therefore, not authority here. In *Moritz v. Medical Protective Co.*, 428 F. Supp. 865 (W.D.Wis. 1977), the challenge to multiple representation came from a former and not a current client. But as the Court of Appeals for the Second Circuit stated in *Cinema 5, Ltd. v. Cinerama, Inc.*, 528 F.2d 1384 (2d Cir. 1976), in connection with the prosecution of a lawsuit by an attorney or his partner against an actively represented client as opposed to a former one, "The propriety of this conduct must be measured not so much against the similarities in litigation as against the duty of undivided loyalty which an attorney owes to each of his clients." 528 F.2d at 1386. The case of *City of Cleveland v. Cleveland Electric Illuminating Co.*, 440 F. Supp. 193 (N.D.Ohio 1977), aff'd 573 F.2d 1310 (6th Cir. 1977), *cert. denied*, ___ U.S. ___, 98 S.Ct. 1648, 56 L.Ed.2d 85 (1978), also cited by CBM, involves a waiver of objections to an attorney's continuing representation of another client and is, therefore, also not apposite.

An attorney must be cautious in this area and, if he is to adhere to the high standards of professional responsibility, he must resolve all doubts in favor of full disclosure to a client of the facts of the attorney's concurrent representation of another client in a lawsuit against him. As the Second Circuit Court of Appeals has stated, "Putting it as mildly as we can, we think it would be questionable conduct for an attorney to participate in any lawsuit against his own client without the knowledge and consent of all concerned." *Cinema 5, Ltd. v. Cinerama, Inc.*, 528 F.2d 1384, 1386 (1976). Indeed, in the present case the record indicates that the members of CBM themselves apparently took the same view of the applicability of the disciplinary rules to their situation both during the course of the dual representation and, it appears, in their arguments and admissions in the district court.

During the course of CBM's representation of the plaintiffs and IBM, the firm twice considered the possibility of the existence of a conflict of interest which might require some responsive action by CBM, once in 1970 and again in 1972. It is significant that in the second instance, the one pertinent here, which occurred when IBM requested CBM to represent it in a labor matter shortly before the filing of the antitrust suit, Weiss, CBM's partner in charge of the prosecution of the antitrust suit against IBM, advised Ryan, the partner involved in the representation of IBM, to obtain IBM's consent to the dual representation. Ryan testified that he then made the disputed telephone call to Troup. Other CBM partners, Lynch and Graham, who became involved in the situation, Lynch in assisting Weiss and Graham in taking an assignment for IBM from Ryan, testified to their perception of the dual representation as one requiring full disclosure to IBM and its consent. Thus, at the time they were faced with the question of the propriety of their continuing representation of a client about to be sued or being sued by them, the involved members of the firm apparently considered that the better course was to obtain consent. Moreover, at the hearing on IBM's motion to disqualify CBM, held August 31, 1977, CBM's counsel twice indicated to the court his understanding that a law firm could not, with impunity, sue a client with whom it had a currently ongoing relationship.

Having, in spite of CBM's concession in the district court, nonetheless considered the legal point it raises here and having decided that the continued representation of a client being sued in an unrelated matter without the client's consent may be violative of the Code, in particular DR 5-105, we turn to the question of whether the district court erred in disqualifying CBM and, if not, whether the court abused its discretion in permitting CBM to turn over its work product to plaintiffs' new counsel during a period of sixty days.

The district court concluded that its rule applying the Code required that CBM obtain IBM's consent to the firm's representation of it after full disclosure of the facts of CBM's representation of the plaintiffs. In support of this conclusion the court made several findings. The court found as a fact that at all relevant times CBM had an on-going attorney-client relationship with both IBM and the plaintiffs. This assessment of the relationship seems entirely reasonable to us. Although CBM had no specific assignment from IBM on hand on the day the antitrust complaint was filed and even though CBM performed services for IBM on a fee for service basis rather than pursuant to a retainer arrangement, the pattern of repeated retainers, both before and after the filing of the complaint, supports the finding of a continuous relationship.

The court also found that although the services required of CBM by IBM dealt consistently exclusively with labor matters, this was not the result of any special arrangement between them and that at any time IBM, unaware of CBM's participation in the plaintiffs' action, might have sought CBM's assistance in legal matters more closely related to the lawsuit. Thus, it was perhaps fortuitous that CBM, as the court found, never acquired any confidential information from IBM useful in the prosecution of the antitrust suit.

These findings, with which we agree, support the district court's conclusion, which seems to us reasonable and just, that CBM was obligated in these circumstances at the very least to disclose fully to IBM the facts of its representation of the plaintiffs and obtain its consent.

The district court determined that CBM did not meet its burden of proving that such a full disclosure was made and that consent by IBM to CBM's dual representation was obtained thereafter. CBM asserts that disclosure and consent were not necessary in that IBM had constructive knowledge of the pertinent facts since its labor lawyers knew of CBM's representation of IBM in that area and its lawyers handling the defense of IBM in the antitrust action knew of CBM's participation in that matter. This assertion is without merit. Clause (C) of

DR 5-105 specifically imposes upon an attorney the burden of affirmatively providing disclosure and obtaining consent. Clearly, full and effective disclosure of all the relevant facts must be made and brought home to the prospective client. The facts required to be disclosed are peculiarly within the knowledge of the attorney bearing the burden of making the disclosure. To accept CBM's position would be to engraft an unwarranted exception on the requirement of DR 5-105 that disclosure must be sufficient to enable the prospective client himself to make an informed decision as to whether in the circumstances counsel will be retained. *See E.F. Hutton Co. v. Brown*, 305 F. Supp. 371, 398 (S.D.Tex. 1969); *In re Kushinsky*, 53 N.J. 1, 4, 247 A.2d 665 (1968).

CBM alternatively argues that IBM's consent was in fact obtained. As we have stated earlier, Ryan testified that he called Troup at the IBM Armonk headquarters in April or May 1972 for the express purpose of informing Troup of the facts of CBM's representation of the plaintiffs and that Troup, after hearing the disclosure, directed Ryan to proceed with the preparation of the requested opinion in the labor matter. It appears that a telephone call lasting no more than three minutes was placed from Ryan's Newark office on May 3, 1972, to Troup's office in Armonk. Troup denied that he ever received the information which Ryan alleged had been conveyed and denied having given the consent Ryan alleged he sought to elicit or having had the authority to do so. Weiss testified that in July 1973 he had in a casual conversation with Danzig, IBM's counsel in the antitrust suit, mentioned that IBM employed CBM to perform occasional legal services in labor matters. Danzig denied that the statement was made to him by Weiss.

The district court did not deem it necessary to resolve these issues of credibility between Ryan and Troup and between Weiss and Danzig since it determined that even accepting CBM's version of this disputed testimony a full and adequate disclosure as required by DR 5-105 had not been made to IBM and that the IBM antitrust attorneys did not in fact know during the relevant period that CBM was representing IBM in labor matters. We conclude that the district court did not err in so determining and in concluding that since IBM's informed consent to the concurrent representation by CBM of it and the plaintiffs had not been obtained, CBM had violated DR 5-105. While we accept the district court's finding that the antitrust lawyers in IBM's legal department did not know that its labor lawyer in the same department was repeatedly retaining the services of CBM in labor matters, we cannot refrain from expressing our belief that such a situation could not have existed for over five years if the activities of the IBM legal department had been properly coordinated and controlled. Apparently in IBM's case the practice was to "let not thy left hand know what thy right hand doeth", a Biblical injunction directed to almsgiving which is hardly applicable to the internal operation of a corporate legal department.

CBM and the plaintiffs urge that even if CBM is held to have violated DR 5-105, the district court's disqualification of CBM from the case is too harsh a sanction and penalizes the plaintiffs unnecessarily in view of the termination of CBM's relationship with IBM and the district court's finding that, in the course of its representation of IBM, CBM did not obtain any information which would aid it in the prosecution of the antitrust suit against IBM.

In considering this contention, we bear in mind the proposition that the plaintiffs do not have an absolute right to retain particular counsel. *Kramer v. Scientific Control Corp.*, 534 F.2d 1085, 1093 (3d Cir. 1976). The plaintiffs' interest in retaining counsel of its choice and the lack of prejudice to IBM resulting from CBM's violation of professional ethics are not the only factors to be considered in this disqualification proceeding. An attorney who fails to observe his obligation of undivided loyalty to his client injures his profession and demeans it in the eyes of the public. The maintenance of the integrity of the legal profession and its high standing in the community are important additional factors to be considered in determining the appropriate sanction for a Code violation. *See Hull v. Celanese Corp.*, 513 F.2d 568, 572 (2d Cir. 1975). The maintenance of public confidence in the propriety of the conduct of those associated with the administration of justice is so important a consideration that we have held that a court may disqualify an attorney for failing to avoid even the appearance of impropriety. *Kramer v. Scientific Control Corp.*, 534 F.2d 1085, 1088-1089 (3d Cir. 1976); *Richardson v. Hamilton International Corp.*, 469 F.2d 1382, 1385-1386 n. 12 (3d Cir. 1972), *cert. denied*, 411 U.S. 986, 93 S.Ct. 2271, 36 L.Ed.2d 964 (1973). *See also Cinema 5, Ltd. v. Cinerama, Inc.*, 528 F.2d 1384, 1387 (2d Cir. 1976). Indeed, the courts have gone so far as to suggest that doubts as to the existence of an asserted conflict of interest should be resolved in favor of disqualification. *Hull v. Celanese Corp.*, 513 F.2d 568, 571 (2d Cir. 1975); *Chugach Elec. Ass'n v. United States D.C. for Dist. of Alaska*, 370 F.2d 441, 444 (9th Cir.), *cert. denied*, 389 U.S. 820, 88 S.Ct. 40, 19 L.Ed.2d 71 (1967). Mindful of these considerations, we cannot say that the district court erred in ordering the disqualification of CBM.

It is true that the plaintiffs will be injured by the disqualification of CBM, their counsel for a number of years. Here the district court ameliorated the harsh effect upon the plaintiffs of its sanction against CBM by permitting the turnover to substitute counsel for the plaintiffs within sixty days of the past work product of CBM on the case. IBM contends that the allowance of a turnover of work product with consultation, particularly work product prepared after the filing of IBM's motion, was an abuse of discretion.

In support of its contention IBM cites *First Wisconsin Mortgage Trust v. First Wisconsin Corp.*, 571 F.2d 390 (7th Cir. 1978), and *Fund of Funds, Ltd. v. Arthur Andersen Co.*, 567 F.2d 225 (2d Cir. 1977). To the extent that the Seventh Circuit Court of Appeals lays down a legal tenet in *First Wisconsin Mortgage Trust* against permitting the turnover of a disqualified attorney's work product, we disagree, but we note that the court in that case expressly limited its holding to the facts of the case. 571 F.2d 390, 399. *Fund of Funds, Ltd. v. Arthur Andersen Co.*, 567 F.2d 225 (2d Cir. 1977), also cited by IBM, involves a complex situation not comparable to the facts present here. It deals with the question of the disqualification of counsel because of his relationship with disqualified co-counsel and in it the court does not address the question of the turnover of a disqualified attorney's work product.

As we have already indicated, disqualification in circumstances such as these where specific injury to the moving party has not been shown is primarily justified as a vindication of the integrity of the bar. We think the turnover provisions of the district court's order of disqualification are sufficient for that purpose and a proper exercise of the court's discretion.

We have considered the other contentions of the parties but find them so lacking in merit as to require no discussion here.

The petition for a writ of mandamus will be dismissed and the order of the district court as amended will be affirmed.

Can a Lawyer Still Represent Each Client Despite a Conflict?

The short answer is yes. However, before a lawyer can proceed, they must complete four steps. If any one of these steps cannot be completed, the lawyer may not proceed with the representation. This is known as an **impermissible conflict**.

1. Determine if they can provide competent and diligent representation (that is, the lawyer reasonably believes they can competently and diligently represent the client despite the conflict).
2. Confirm that the representation is not prohibited by law. Some matters are outright prohibited. For example, a former prosecutor cannot consult with the defense if they were previously involved as the prosecutor.
3. Confirm that the representation does not involve the assertion of a claim by one client against another in the same litigation or proceeding. For instance, a lawyer would not be able to represent an employer and an employee in the same lawsuit.
4. Get the client's informed consent confirmed in writing.

Get the client's informed consent confirmed in writing.[5]

Recap: What Practical Steps Should a Lawyer Follow in Assessing Conflicts?

1. Clearly identify the client or clients.
2. Determine whether a conflict of interest exists.
3. Decide whether representation may be undertaken despite the conflict.
    - If yes, consult with the affected clients and obtain informed consent. Typically, lawyers describe conflicts, consequences, or material risks resulting from conflicts and describe any actual and

---

5. Informed consent is defined in ABA Model Rule 1.0(e). It requires the lawyer to explain the material risks and foreseeable adverse consequences presented by the conflict.

reasonably available alternatives in the engagement letter or a separate conflicts letter.[6] They must provide sufficient information to enable the client to give informed consent.
- If no, STOP! If a conflict exists and representation cannot continue, depending on where the attorney-relationship is, an attorney should either decline to take the case, advise multiple clients to get separate counsel, or withdraw.

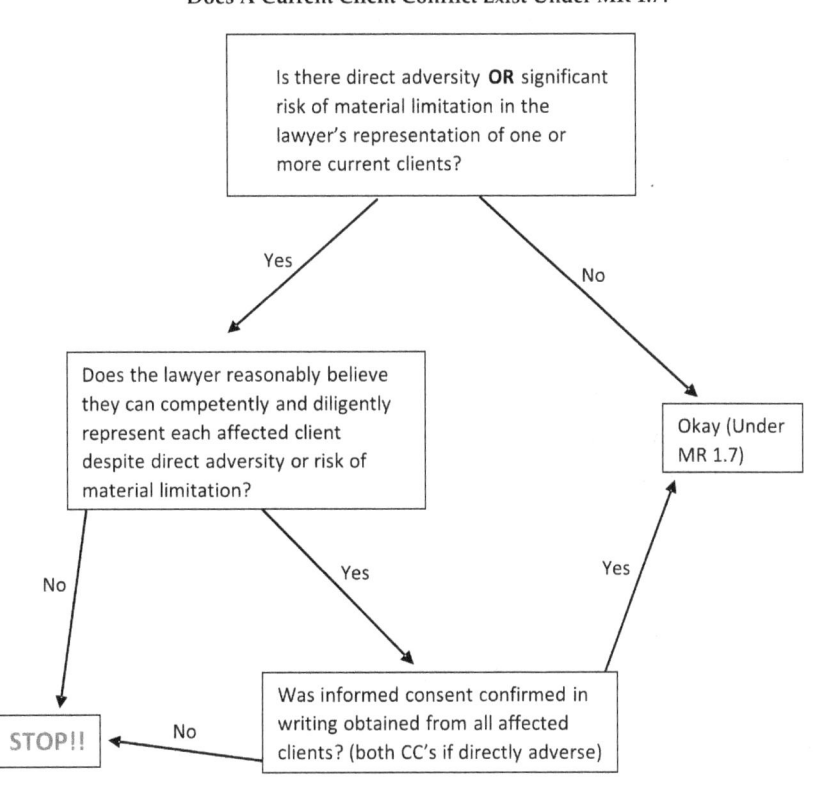

Does A Current Client Conflict Exist Under MR 1.7?

FIGURE 6.1   Does A Current Client Conflict Exist Under MR 1.7? (Note: "CC" stands for Current Client; "MR" stands for Model Rule.)

WOULD YOU REPRESENT THESE CLIENTS?
Scenario #1: Maya and Diego are thinking about starting a new fitness company. As former

---

6. ABA Model Rule 1.0(e).

athletes, they have tremendous expertise in everything from running, biking, and swimming. Their business will sell clothing and gear that supports triathletes. Maya will invest $500,000 into the business, while Diego will provide marketing and social media expertise. They ask a fellow triathlete, Alisha, who happens to be a lawyer, to help them with all the relevant paperwork and legal documentation needed to start and run the company. Should Alisha represent them both? Are there any actual and potential conflicts?

Scenario #2: Maya and Diego were involved in a four-car collision off Interstate 5. Maya has minor injuries, while Diego has more long-term injuries. They both ask Alisha, a personal injury lawyer, to represent them in a lawsuit against one of the other drivers involved in the collision. Should Alisha represent them both? Are there any actual and potential conflicts?

Waivers

A waiver is informed client consent reflected in a written agreement. As discussed above, for consent to be effective, it must contain a detailed explanation of the various issues causing a conflict and explain any potential adverse consequences that might arise if the client waives the conflict. A link to a sample conflict waiver letter can be found at the end of the chapter.

In practice, you will find that waiver letters are extremely detail oriented and specific to the matter and parties. The following guidelines are helpful:

- Write in clear, simple English.
- Identify the current/actual conflict.
- Identify potential future conflicts.
- Outline risks of joint representation like sharing of confidential information and the need to withdraw.
- Emphasize confidentiality.

HYPOTHETICAL 6.3
When things get complicated: Toxic torts

Sludge Corp. and Slime LLC were recently brought into a multiparty complex toxic tort litigation. A group of homeowners in Belclaire Shores is suing both corporations and approximately 50 other chemical manufacturers for alleged dumping of toxic chemicals in their nearby lake, causing wildlife to become sick, and in some cases, die.

Your firm, ABC Law Firm, is a well-known toxic tort defense firm. You have represented both Sludge Corp. and Slime LLC in individual matters before. They are both being sued in this case, and both have come to you to represent and defend them.

You bring in the CEO of each company to discuss the conflict and to see if the three of you can agree to a waiver.1

1 ABA Model Rule 1.7 (a) defines that a concurrent conflict of interest exists if: (1) the representation of one client will be directly adverse to another client; or (2) there is a significant risk that the representation of one or more clients will be materially limited by the lawyer's responsibilities to another client.

> Please refer to the interactive ebook in Cognella Active Learning for interactive/media content.

SAMPLE WAIVER

Sludge Corp. and Slime LLC have asked ABC Law Firm to represent each of them in a complex toxic tort litigation brought by homeowners from Belclaire Shores. Both understand that this law firm has represented the other in prior toxic tort-related matters. Both being jointly sued as defendants, we have discussed that some defenses in this litigation may be similar and also adverse to each defendant. Because there may be defenses for each defendant that may be adverse to the other, there may be a conflict in ABC Law Firm representing each defendant. This includes the possibility that each defendant may need to argue that the other party is wholly and solely liable. Sludge Corp. and Slime LLC, both having been involved in the litigation process before and having been defendants in toxic tort matters before, understand the potential conflicts discussed.

Both have agreed to waive the conflict and agree to this firm representing both defendants jointly. Both defendants further understand that it is possible that circumstances could arise where the continued representation of one, or both parties, may not be possible by ABC Law Firm, and ABC Law Firm may be required to withdraw from representation.

Both Sludge Corp. and Slime LLC understand that confidentiality cannot be maintained in this joint representation, and both agree to waive attorney-client confidentiality and privilege.

Signatures

Sludge Corp.   Slime LLC

Advance Waivers (ABA Model Rule 1.7)

An advance waiver is where a client consents to future/potential conflicts. These conflicts have not yet occurred but could in the future. Whether an advance waiver is effective depends in large part on the degree of specificity.

Generally, advance waivers are scrutinized closely. Comment 22 to ABA Model Rule 1.7 states that the general test of enforceability of forward-looking waivers will be "the extent to which the client reasonably understands the material risks that the waiver entails." Some states like California and New York allow advance waivers provided the client is "sophisticated," like in the case of a Fortune 500 company with in-house counsel and familiarity with legal matters. If the client has consulted independently with a lawyer before signing the waiver, that's a plus. Careful drafting is a must.

Read the following article about a case involving the law firm of Sheppard, Mullin, Richter, & Hampton to learn more about the requisite disclosures for enforceable advance conflict waivers: https://www.americanbar.org/groups/business_law/publications/blt/2019/06/req-disclosures/.

> **SAMPLE LANGUAGE REFLECTING ADVANCE WAIVER BETWEEN A CLIENT (WHO IS A CORPORATION AND IDENTIFIED AS COMPANY BELOW) AND THEIR OUTSIDE COUNSEL.**
>
> *The Company agrees that, notwithstanding our representation of the Company in general corporate matters we may, now or in the future, without seeking or obtaining your further consent, represent other persons, whether or not they are now clients of our law firm, in other matters, including litigation, where those other persons are adverse to the Company. The Company also agrees not to seek disqualification of our law firm. The Company also agrees not to seek disqualification of our law firm should the firm sue the Company in the future.*

Imputation and Screening

A conflict to one is a conflict to all! Lawyers associated with law firms are frequently confronted with imputed conflicts of interest (also known as the rule of imputed disqualification). An imputation is when a conflict with one lawyer disqualifies all lawyers at the law firm. In other words, the duty of loyalty applies with equal force to all lawyers at the law firm. The rationale supporting this rule is that lawyers at the same firm have direct access to the client's confidential information, and therefore have a duty to protect it. This rule applies to all lawyers—private or public (such as a district attorney or public defender's office).

As noted in ABA Model Rule 1.10, *while lawyers are associated in a firm, none of them shall knowingly represent a client when any one of them practicing alone would be prohibited from doing so by Rules 1.7(concurrent conflicts)or 1.9(successive conflicts).*For example, a lawyer represents a client in a property dispute. The client loses and decides to appeal but chooses another firm for the appeal. Neither the lawyer nor anyone at the lawyer's law firm could represent the party defending the appeal (against the former client) as they would be conflicted.

Note that ABA Model Rule 1.10 does not extend imputation to lawyers where a conflict arises due to a personal interest of the disqualified lawyer and does not represent a significant risk of *material limiting* the representation.

Imputation is a significant problem in large law firms. When running a conflict check, the system will reveal a potential conflict of interest because of a representation by another lawyer in an unrelated matter. That client might even be in a different city or state. In such matters, the lawyer may have to decline representation due to the conflict.

Imputation issues also arise in the following matters:

- A former judge now practices law and represents a client who once appeared in their court (ABA Model Rule 1.12).
- A lawyer who served as an arbitrator, mediator, or other third-party neutral now represents one of the parties involved in a former arbitration, mediation, or other dispute resolution process (ABA Model Rule 1.12).
- A former government employee now in private practice (ABA Model Rule 1.11).
- A prospective client situation where the lawyer cannot represent a current client who has interests materially adverse to the prospective client because the lawyer received confidential information from the prospective client that could be significantly harmful (ABA Model Rule 1.18). No lawyer at the law firm can undertake the representation.
- Where the lawyer represented a former client while the lawyer worked at another firm.

Can a Lawyer Overcome Imputation?

Generally, yes.

First, **identify the conflict**. Lawyers and law firms must screen for potential or actual conflicts before taking on a client or legal matter. This process is called a "conflict check." Screening for conflicts is the process of checking for potential or actual conflicts. The process can vary from law firm to law firm, but it must be done. This is true whether the lawyer is a public or government lawyer or one in private practice.

Such conflict checks can be done by inputting basic information about the parties and legal matters into various screening software available on the market. The information would include the names of the parties, names of any businesses, addresses, or other identifying matters. The software would compare the information to that in the law firm's database to see if there are cases with similar identifying information. It would then be up to the lawyer to review the information in depth to confirm whether a potential or actual conflict exists. In larger, multinational law firms, the conflict checks are usually conducted through a dedicated conflicts department. However, the lawyer still has the final duty to confirm that no actual or potential conflicts exist.

Second, get **client informed consent** from all affected parties.

Next, **create a screen**. Here, the conflicted lawyer is isolated from the other lawyers at the firm to "protect information that the isolated lawyer is obligated to protect."[7] For a screen to be effective, remember the following:

- No one at the firm should communicate with the isolated lawyer about the matter.

---

7. See ABA Model Rule 1.0(k).

- Remind everyone at the firm about the conflict frequently.
- Cut off access to anything related to the issue, including electronic files.

Consequences for Representing a Client When There Is an Impermissible Conflict of Interest

1. **Discipline:** Lawyers can be disciplined for violating conflict rules.
2. **Disqualification:** Parties can file motions to disqualify counsel where conflicts persist. California has even recognized motions by non-parties to disqualify counsel. The non-party is a party of interest in the lawsuit and has shared confidential information with the attorney whose disqualification is sought.

Key Takeaways

- A conflict of interest is typically impairments of a lawyer's duty of loyalty.
- It is possible to represent multiple clients in the same matter with constraints.
- Informed consent is key.
- Effective conflict waivers need to explain the conflicts, risks, and consequences.
- Advance waivers can be effective sometimes.
- At times, a waiver just is not enough.
- Consider the relationship between confidentiality, privilege, and conflicts of interest.
- The following YouTube video is an excellent primer on concurrent conflicts of interest:

> Please refer to the interactive ebook in Cognella Active Learning for interactive/media content.

Ethics in Action

Read the following disciplinary action(s) in which the state bar used the rules discussed in this chapter to bring disciplinary charges against an attorney.

1. Failure to provide written disclosures about conflicts [pending]: *In the Matter of Foster*
   https://www.statebarcourt.ca.gov/Portals/2/documents/opinions/Foster-Richard-James-17-O-00414-Opinion-filed%203-16-20.pdf
2. Conflict with Former Client [90-day suspension]: *In re Larry Elliot Klayman*

https://www.cadc.uscourts.gov/internet/opinions.nsf/0/
8B3A1624667231A3852586A400509860/$file/20-7110-1891862.pdf

End-of-Chapter Discussion Questions

1. Should lawyers be required to purchase screening software to check for conflicts of interest? If so, what are the parameters? Do they need to update it monthly or yearly? What if it is too expensive to purchase or maintain?
2. Are the current conflicts of interest rules too burdensome?
3. Other than the ones discussed already, can you think of scenarios where lawyers should not attempt to get conflict waivers?
4. Although allowed, do you think you could fully and accurately represent two clients who have waived a known conflict? Discuss.

Additional Resource

A sample conflict waiver letter can be found on the Nevada State Bar website. https://www.nvbar.org/wp-content/uploads/sample-conflict-waiver-joint-representation-nv.pdf

CHAPTER 6

Conflict of Interest [Part 2]

> Visit your interactive ebook to download the Chapter 6b Outline.

Learning Objectives

- Identify situations that create personal conflicts of interest.
- Apply conflict of interest rules involving former clients.
- Apply conflict of interest rules involving prospective clients.
- Understand how fees can create an inherent conflict of interest.

Key Terms

- **Personal conflict:** A conflict that arises due to the lawyer's own interests.
- **Former client:** A client who used to be represented by a lawyer.
- **Prospective client:** A person who consults a lawyer to retain the lawyer or secure legal service or advice from the lawyer, also commonly referred to as a potential client.
- **Withdraw:** Terminating the representation due to a conflict or potential of an ethical violation.

Introduction

Lawyers owe loyalty to clients. If their loyalty is to someone else, they cannot zealously represent a client. Chapter 6, Part 1 discussed how a conflict of interest might arise when two or more clients oppose one another. What happens when it's the lawyer's own personal situation that creates a conflict of interest? How do we identify those personal situations, and when do they become potential or actual conflicts? Lawyers can easily insert their own personal emotions or biases into a case or representation. Personal emotions or biases can affect a case.

Therefore, a lawyer needs to know when to identify personal conflicts and step away. We will explore those personal conflicts in this chapter.

We will also explore conflicts relating to former clients—a client who used to be represented by a lawyer but is no longer being represented. Remember, even though a lawyer may not currently represent a client, the fiduciary duties to that client continues. What if you have a new client coming into your office and that new client presents a conflict of interest with a former client? How can you overcome such a conflict, and what happens if you cannot?

We also explore conflicts with prospective clients in this chapter. Prospective or potential clients generally consult lawyers to retain the lawyer or secure legal service or advice from the lawyer. Even if a prospective client does not ultimately retain the lawyer's services, certain fiduciary duties are owed to them, including maintaining the confidentiality and avoiding conflict of interest.

When you think of conflicts of interest, a conversation about legal fees must be a part of the discussion. Legal fees create an inherent conflict of interest for lawyers. Consider this: what is a lawyer's product? It is not like we are baking a loaf of bread or manufacturing a TV. No, our "product" is our legal expertise. It's our minds. Exchanging our legal thinking for money, or what we think our legal expertise is worth, can be emotional and can create conflicts. Every lawyer thinks they are worth $10,000 an hour or more! Asking for money in exchange for our legal services and maybe getting some pushback will create a conflict. We need to recognize and discuss the conflict that money can create.

Personal Conflicts and Other Sticky Situations

Loyalty is compromised when the lawyer cannot exercise independent professional judgment due to a personal interest. Some examples of personal interest conflicts include the following:

- A lawyer married to opposing counsel in a current case.
- A lawyer has stock/equity in the company they are defending or opposing.
- A lawyer does not believe in his or her client's case.

These examples present issues that create a personal conflict of interest. In these situations, the lawyer's own interest in defending themselves might interfere with representing the client. We discuss personal conflicts separately to highlight ABA Model Rule 1.7(a)(2). Personal conflicts can create a significant risk that a lawyer's representation may not serve the client's best interests.

Besides ABA Model Rule 1.7(a)(2), some situations are treated separately in ABA Model Rule 1.8, as they involve conflicts between a client's interest and a lawyer's interest. These are situations where a lawyer may be tempted to put their personal interests before the client. Unless otherwise noted, the prohibitions and requirements apply equally to other lawyers in the lawyer's firm. Table 6.2 outlines specific examples/scenarios/cases where personal conflicts arise.

Table 6.2 ABA Rule 1.8

Situation	Rule and Supporting Information	Examples/Scenarios/Cases
Soliciting Gifts from Clients [ABA Model Rule 1.8(c)]	A lawyer may not seek a substantial gift from the client. This includes preparing legal instruments (like a will) transferring property to the lawyer or the lawyer's spouse, child, grandchild, parent, or grandparent. It also includes anyone with whom the lawyer or the client maintains a "close, familial relationship." This rule would not prevent the lawyer's own family from preparing legal instruments that leave property to the lawyer or his family! A lawyer may not ask a client to appoint the lawyer the executor to the client's estate. Similarly, a lawyer may not ask the client to name them in their will as a recipient of the property. The rule is supported by the fact that lawyers often hold positions of power and influence over their clients and might persuade them to give them anything.	**Example #1** A client may not gift a car to his or her lawyer under this rule. A car would be considered a substantial gift. They may, however, gift an inexpensive bottle of wine as a thank you. **Example #2** A lawyer prepares a will for a client who is 85 years old. The client has the requisite capacity to execute the will. The lawyer cannot ask the client to add a provision that will leave the client's house to the lawyer. This would be considered unethical under ABA Model Rule 1.8(c).
Literary and Media Rights [ABA Model Rule 1.8(d)]	A lawyer cannot acquire literary or media rights in the client's "case" before the conclusion of the representation. This rule bars both parties from entering and negotiating an agreement. We have this rule because a lawyer might be tempted to try the case consciously or unconsciously in a manner that could be opposed to the client's interests. In other words, the lawyer: 1. May want to do things to create publicity. 2. May not want to raise certain defenses like insanity, questioning the validity of the agreement between lawyer and client. Both scenarios create a personal conflict of interest.	A lawyer represents Kim Kardashian in a high-profile product liability case involving one of Kim's companies. If the lawyer agrees to write a book about Kim's case while it is still pending before a court, the lawyer will violate ABA Model Rule 1.8(d).

(Cont'd)

Table 6.2 ABA Rule 1.8 (Cont'd)

Situation	Rule and Supporting Information	Examples/Scenarios/Cases
Financial Assistance [ABA Model Rule 1.8(e)]	A lawyer may not generally provide financial assistance in a pending or forthcoming litigation matter. There is no restriction on providing financial assistance in a non-litigation matter (however, it is still subject to ABA Model Rule 1.8(a)). This rule is supported by the general notion that lawyers should not encourage litigation. Clients should not be choosing lawyers because the lawyer will support the lawsuit financially. Rather, they should pick a lawyer based on things like competence and diligence. Exceptions: A lawyer may advance court costs and expenses of litigation for an indigent client or where the client will repay the lawyer later, as in contingency cases, where repayment can be contingent on the successful conclusion of the matter. Notes: Advancing living and medical expenses for an indigent client is also acceptable under the rule since they are considered non-litigation expenses. Expenses of litigation include anything that supports collecting evidence like the medical examination of the client, paying an investigator to collect information on a potential witness, interviewing expert witnesses, etc. Non-litigation expenses include things like living expenses, such as paying rent or groceries.	A lawyer agrees to pay for court costs and expert fees in a matter that is billed by the hour. This would violate the rule on financial assistance.
Compensation from a Third Party for Representation [ABA Model Rule 1.8(f)]	Generally, lawyers should not accept third parties' fees, as it is likely to interfere with the attorney-client relationship. When someone else pays the lawyer's fees, it could interfere with that lawyer's independent judgment and confidentiality obligations as they feel obligated to keep the "financier" of their services reasonably informed and happy. However, the client and the financier may not always have the same interests, and by no means should the lawyer feel compelled under the financier's direction. However, there are situations where a third party needs to pay another's fees. In those cases, lawyers can accept compensation from someone other than the client, provided that: 1. The client gives informed consent. 2. The lawyer must maintain confidentiality and not disclose information to that third party. 3. The lawyer conducts the representation such that there is no interference with the lawyer's independent professional judgment.	**Example #1** A parent paying for their child's defense in a criminal shoplifting case is allowed, provided the steps outlined in ABA Model Rule 1.8(f) are followed. **Example #2** A father can pay for his daughter's divorce attorney, provided the steps outlined in ABA Model Rule 1.8(f) are followed. **Example #3** A business partner paying for their partner's lawsuit is allowed, provided the steps outlined in ABA Model Rule 1.8(f) are followed.

Situation	Rule and Supporting Information	Examples/Scenarios/Cases
Aggregate Settlements [ABA Model Rule 1.8(g)]	A lawyer who represents two or more clients shall not participate in making an aggregate settlement of the claims of or against the clients in a civil matter, or in a criminal case, an aggregated agreement as to guilty: 1. Unless each client gives informed consent; and 2. The lawyer's disclosure shall include the existence and nature of all the claims or pleas involved and the participation of each person in the settlement.	In a multiparty personal injury matter where the lawyer represents more than one plaintiff, the lawyer shall not agree to any settlements adverse to other clients.
Acquisition of Proprietary Interest in the Cause of Action of the Subject Matter of Litigation [ABA Model Rule 1.8(i)]	A lawyer may not acquire a proprietary interest in a client's cause of action or litigation because lawyers should not invest in their own client's cases. By giving a lawyer an interest in the case (e.g., an agreement whereby the client agrees to give the lawyer 10 percent of the share of the proceeds in the litigation matter in exchange for $10,000), they might be tempted to act in a way that protects their financial interest rather than the client. Exception 1: A lawyer can acquire a lien authorized by law to secure the lawyer's fee or expenses. States recognize two types of liens: a statutory charging lien and a retaining lien. 1. A charging lien gives the lawyer a claim to be paid for the lawyer's services out of the recovery in the matter. 2. A retaining lien gives the lawyer the right to retain client materials (like documents, case files, etc.) until the lawyer is paid. Exception 2: A lawyer can enter into a contract with a client for a reasonable contingency fee in a civil case. A contingency fee presents a situation where the lawyer can still get a percentage of the recovery.	**Example #1** A lawyer is asked to represent a client in litigation involving a wrestling ring. The client agrees to give the lawyer an ownership interest in the wrestling ring as payment. This is prohibited, as the client is giving a part of the subject matter of the litigation. **Example #2** A lawyer representing a client in a dispute involving the ownership of a patent cannot buy an interest in the client's patent (e.g., enter into a contract for 5 percent of any royalty payments), since the patent is the subject matter of the litigation.

(Cont'd)

Table 6.2 ABA Rule 1.8 (Cont'd)

Situation	Rule and Supporting Information	Examples/Scenarios/Cases
Sexual Relationships [ABA Model Rule 1.8(j)]	A lawyer shall not have sexual relations with a client unless the relationship predates the formation of the client-lawyer relationship or involves a former client. This is a strict prohibition, as evidenced by the use of the word shall. Why? These rules exist for the same reasons they do in other professions, like doctor-patient, teacher-student, or coach-athlete. 1. First, there is always a possibility that a client's involvement with a lawyer is due to the lawyer's influence on the client. Given that clients usually engage with lawyers at their most difficult times, they are emotional and vulnerable. Thus, there is potential for a lawyer's abuse of power over the client. Lawyers are often in a superior position and can easily persuade a client to enter a relationship. 2. Second, such a relationship creates a conflict of interest. The lawyer may not be able to exercise independent professional judgment because the personal relationship might get in the way. 3. Lastly, it could jeopardize candid communication. Due to the personal relationship, the client may not want to open up to the lawyer fully. This interferes with the need for information to represent the client properly. Imputation: This is the only rule where imputation does not apply. It will not apply to the other lawyers in the firm.	*You can take your lover as your client, but you cannot take your client as your lover!* **Case Alert** In *In re Disciplinary Proceedings Against Atta*, an attorney represented a client in a divorce proceeding. Soon after, they began having a sexual relationship. Between April 2012 and February 2013, the attorney and client had numerous telephone calls, a majority of them being lengthy and after midnight. In one telephone conversation, the attorney told his client that he had strong feelings for her and that he would marry her one day. By the end of May 2013, the lawyer's relationship with his client had deteriorated, and their sexual relationship had ended. Subsequently, the client accused the attorney of intentionally delaying the filing of divorce documents after she terminated the relationship. The Supreme Court of Wisconsin found that by representing the client while engaging in a relationship with her, the attorney had violated Wisconsin's rules on sexual relationships. This rule also applies when the client is an organization. It prevents inside or outside counsel from having a sexual relationship with those responsible for supervising, directing, or regularly consulting with that lawyer concerning the organization's legal matters.

Situation	Rule and Supporting Information	Examples/Scenarios/Cases
Positional Conflicts [ABA Model Rule 1.7, Comment 8]	A positional conflict is where a lawyer may score a victory for one client that would establish a precedent that harms another client. Suppose there is a substantial risk that the firm's representation of the one client will create a legal precedent that is *likely to undercut the firm's other clients' legal position materially*. In that case, the lawyer should refuse the first representation, or withdraw, *unless* they can get informed consent from both clients after informing them of the consequences.	**Example #1** Let's say an attorney is representing a client in a case that challenges the constitutionality of a statute. They could not represent a client in another case that asks the court to uphold the constitutionality of the statute. Victory, in either case, would create a legal precedent that will likely undercut the client's legal position. **Example #2** The firm bids on and wins a commercial property at an auction on behalf of a client to the detriment of another client. **Example #3** A law firm represents an oil company but then takes on a pro bono case for an environmental company that seeks to file a lawsuit that makes an argument for a stronger interpretation of current regulations, which will add further obligations on oil companies. If the law firm were successful in the pro bono matter, it would establish a precedent that hurts the oil company client, despite the oil company client not being involved in the suit or in any way litigating the regulations.

Table 6.2 ABA Rule 1.8 (Cont'd)

Situation	Rule and Supporting Information	Examples/Scenarios/Cases
Advocate Witness Rule [ABA Model Rule 3.7]	This rule prohibits a lawyer from acting as an advocate at trial where the lawyer is likely to be called as a witness, unless: 1. The testimony relates to an uncontested issue; 2. The testimony relates to the nature and value of legal services rendered in the case; or 3. Disqualification of the lawyer would cause substantial hardship on the client. The lawyer may continue to advocate where another lawyer in the lawyer's firm may be called a witness.	**Example #1** A lawyer represents a client in the drafting and negotiating of a contract. A few years later, there is a dispute, and the lawyer is a possible witness as to what occurred in the negotiation. **Example #2** A lawyer is testifying about the specific date of hiring by the law firm of a legal expert in a case where an expert's files are being introduced into evidence at trial. **Example #3** A lawyer testifies that legal bills provided in a case are accurate regarding the dates of services provided, individuals who worked on a matter, and amount of legal fees. **Example #4** A lawyer provides testimony relating to legal work done by the law firm and a particular lawyer, that there is an upcoming trial date, and disqualification of a lawyer now would be severely prejudicial to a client due to the amount of work that would need to be duplicated by another lawyer so close to trial.

Attorneys and Fees: Inherent Conflict of Interest

Attorneys should be paid for their services. However, when it comes to fees, any combination of fees for services can create an inherent conflict of interest. The court in the California case of *Maxwell v. Superior Court*,[1] best stated that almost any fee arrangement between attorney and client may rise to a conflict.

Attorneys must get paid. This is a service-based industry, and their service is their legal expertise and work. Setting a fee for such legal effort can be difficult sometimes. What if you and your client do not agree on the fees set? What if you are overcharging or even undercharging for your legal work according to the industry standards? Fees are amorphous and can be personal. They can be based on the number of years you have been in practice, your reputation and expertise in a field, or because you are part of a particular law firm with a certain fee structure. However, it can be difficult to place a dollar value on any of these parameters, as variables can exist throughout.

The ABA has allowed for flexibility between lawyers and clients in setting fees. They even allow for some creativity by allowing lawyers and clients to choose which of the most common fee arrangements

---

1. (1982) 30 C3d 606

would best suit the relationship and the type of work the lawyer will be undertaking—for example, fixed, contingency, or an hourly fee arrangement. Some lawyers and clients may even choose a hybrid of these options.

No matter what fee set-up model is decided upon, a recognition must exist that any model of a fee set-up between a lawyer and a client may lead to conflict. The court in *Maxwell* cited these three most common types of fee arrangements used and the potential conflicts:

- In a case where the lawyer was working for a flat fee, the court noted that a lawyer might "dispose of the case as quickly as possible, to the client's disadvantage."
- In a contingency case, both the lawyer and the client may have a potential conflict. As the court opined, "The contingent fee contract so common in civil litigation creates a 'conflict' when either the attorney or the client needs a quick settlement while the other's interest would be better served by pressing on in the hope of a greater recovery."
- While in an hourly fee arrangement, the court thought an attorney "would have a 'conflicting interest' to drag the case on beyond the point of maximum benefit to the client."

These are valid concerns that clients likely all have as they write out checks for legal fees. At the beginning of the attorney-client relationship, a candid discussion about the scope of work, expectations, and fees between the attorney and client is absolutely necessary to alleviate some of the conflicts of interest inherent in fees.

HYPOTHETICAL 6.4
Investing in your client's business

In 2004, BE FIT, a company started in Los Angeles, California, created a chain of gyms that promoted a "unique fitness experience". Customers could individually workout or take classes at the gym while also focusing on their post workout recovery. They had a section of the gym dedicated to recovery—massage rooms, foam rolling stations, essential oils, and saunas. BE FIT hired lawyer Jessica to help them with their business. In addition to handling the business's initial incorporation, she was responsible for drafting contracts with suppliers, employment policies, liability waivers, and other important legal documents. Over the years, she continued to be BE FIT's lawyer. During this relationship, BE FIT has tried to convince Jessica to invest in their business. Eventually, as a customer of BE FIT herself, and a huge believer in their concept, she decides to invest in the client's business. She will own 12% of the company in exchange for $500,000.

Please refer to the interactive ebook in Cognella Active Learning for interactive/media content.

Successive or Former Client

As we have seen in Chapter 6, Part 1, lawyers owe a duty of loyalty to former clients. ABA Model Rule 1.9 addresses when a lawyer may not represent a current client adverse to a former client in a subsequent representation.

Who Is a Former Client?

The first step in assessing whether a former client conflict exists is ensuring the client knows that they are a former client. In other words, the client needs to know that their relationship has ended. Most cases come to a natural close when the matter resolves because they either won at trial or received a settlement. However, this may not always be clear, if, say, the client loses and is thinking about appealing. Similarly, in a transactional matter, the representation might end when the lawyer communicates to the client about the matter ending (by sending a final bill or email to close the matter) or when the list of services indicated in the *scope of representation* clause has been satisfied.

Thus, as an initial matter, ensure the client knows that they are a *former* client. The rules follow a subjective test in that they rely on what the client believes. Consider whether significant time passed from when services were last offered. Make sure a final bill was sent. If there is any chance of ambiguity, make it clear! Send a letter saying the representation has ended and ensure the client receives it and understands it.

What Is the Rule on Former Client Conflicts? ABA Model Rule 1.9

According to ABA Model Rule 1.9, a lawyer may not represent a client in the following scenario:

- The interests of the client are materially adverse to the interests of a former client.

- The representation is in the "same or substantially related matter"[2] as the former client's representation.

- The former client does not give informed consent, confirmed in writing.

Note: Playbook information is information about client "tells" and "attitudes." Playbook information about a client does not create a conflict of interest. It could be something as simple as information indicating that a client is aggressive during negotiations or more detailed, such as information that a client usually settles employment issues or that a client is conservative and will do anything to settle a case over going to trial.

---

2. Comment 3 to ABA Model Rule 1.9: "Matters are 'same or substantially related' for purposes of this rule if they involve the same transaction or legal dispute or if there is a substantial risk that confidential information as would normally have been obtained in the prior representation would *materially advance* the client's position in the subsequent matter."

Former Client

A v. B (Lawyer represents B).

Representation ends.

A appeals.

The lawyer cannot now represent A against B without B's informed consent.

Substantially Similar Matter: Illustration

Laura previously represented Cindy in a matter involving Cindy's business. As a result, she learned about Cindy's financial situation. A few years later, Doug (Cindy's husband) asks Laura to represent him in his divorce against Cindy. ABA Model Rule 1.9 would prevent Laura from representing Doug without Cindy's consent. The primary reason for this is the confidential information Laura has about Cindy's financial situation. Laura could use this information to advance Doug's position against Cindy (the former client). Additionally, Laura would need Doug's permission, as Doug is a current client, and Laura's previous representation of (and loyalty to) Cindy could impair her ability to represent Doug (see ABA Model Rule 1.7(a)(2).

Does a Former Client Conflict Exist Under MR 1.9(a) & 1.7?

```
          Is the matter the same or
          substantially related to work
          done for the former client?
         /                          \
       Yes                           No
        |                             |
        v                             v
   Are the interests               Okay under MR 1.9(a)*
   materially adverse? ---No--->
        |
       Yes
        |
        v
   Informed consent            *Note that if there is significant risk of
   confirmed in writing from    material limitation in representation
   former client is required*   of CC, then you must have reasonable
                                belief + consent from CC required by
                                MR 1.7
```

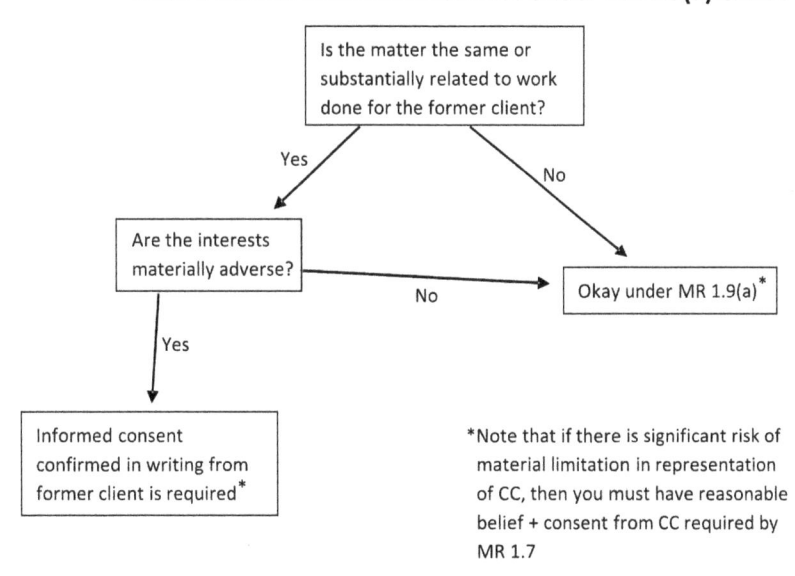

FIGURE 6.2   Does a Former Client Conflict Exist Under ABA Model Rules 1.9(a) and 1.7?

If significant time has passed between Laura's representation of Cindy and the impending divorce, any confidential information that Laura might have about Cindy would be obsolete, as the financial information has likely changed.

HYPOTHETICAL 6.5
When you disagree with your client

Larry, an attorney, is a member of Freedom For All (Freedom), a nonprofit organization that seeks to help LGBTQ+ individuals defend themselves in lawsuits involving their liberty interests under the Constitution. Larry does not represent Freedom as an attorney. Recently, Freedom helped to get a statute enacted that requires all employers to hire at least 10 percent of their workforce from the LGBTQ+ community.

ABC Corporation (ABC) is a corporation that wants to challenge the statute. Rashida, president of ABC, asked Larry to represent ABC and Larry agreed. Larry does not personally agree with ABC's objective but moves forward with the representation nonetheless by filing a complaint challenging the statute. Larry personally thinks the statute is good law and secretly hopes that ABC loses the lawsuit.

Please refer to the interactive ebook in Cognella Active Learning for interactive/media content.

Prospective Clients

- ABA Model Rule 1.18 (a): Someone who consults with a lawyer about the possibility of forming a client-lawyer relationship with respect to the matter.

The rule recognizes a conflict only when there is a possibility that the prospective client gave the lawyer information that could be significantly harmful to a prospective client.

A lawyer cannot represent another client without consent if

- the matter is the "same or substantially related matter" as the prospective client consultation,
- the client's interests are "materially adverse" to the interests of the prospective client, or
- the prospective client gave the lawyer information that could be "significantly harmful" to the prospective client.

Generally, when lawyers meet with prospective clients, they ask clients not to reveal facts or confidences about the case until conflicts have cleared. Lawyers might also obtain advance consent that any information disclosed in the consultation cannot be the basis for future disqualification.

In Chapter 2, you read *Flatt v. Superior Court* (1994).[3] In this case, a prospective client (Daniel) met with an attorney (Flatt) about an issue involving his former lawyer (Hinkle). Hinkle happened to be an existing client of Flatt's law firm, albeit in an unrelated matter. Did Flatt have to inform Hinkle about the meeting with Daniel? What about Daniel?

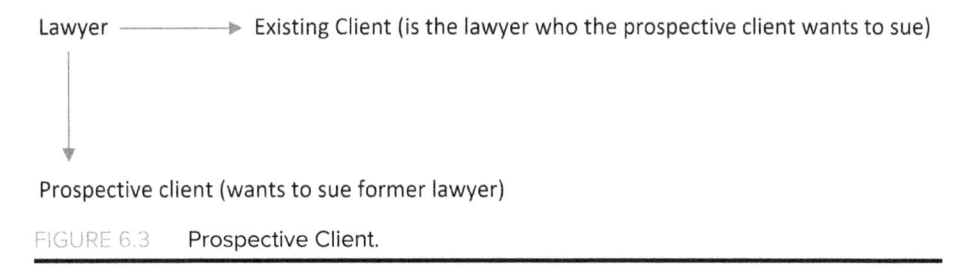

Lawyer ⟶ Existing Client (is the lawyer who the prospective client wants to sue)

↓

Prospective client (wants to sue former lawyer)

FIGURE 6.3   Prospective Client.

In a narrow opinion, the California court held that the consulted lawyer had to maintain the prospective client's confidentiality but did not have to tell the prospective client about any pending statute of limitations because of his duty to the existing client. Further, the court held that the lawyer has an unwaivable duty of loyalty not to represent the prospective client in light of an irremediable conflict with the existing client and should act promptly to terminate the relationship after learning about the client. As noted in the opinion, "One's loss ought not to be another's gain," and any advice given to Daniel would have been contrary to Hinkle's interests and the firm's duty to provide undivided loyalty to him.

3. 9 Cal.4th 275

Does a Prospective Client Conflict Exist Under MR 1.18 & 1.7?

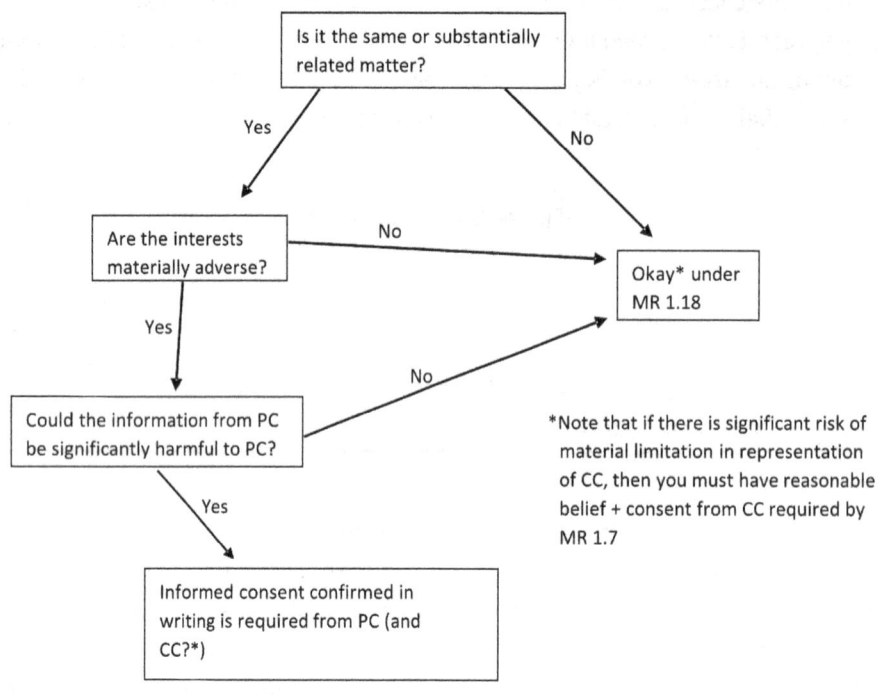

FIGURE 6.4   Does a Prospective Client Conflict Exist Under ABA Model Rules 1.18 and 1.7?

Moving to Another Law Firm: Lateral Transfers

In the legal profession, it is common for lawyers to make lateral moves to other firms. These are often called lateral moves or lateral hires. One lawyer or even an entire department moves from one law firm to another law firm. The conflict of interest rules still apply in these situations, and both the lawyer or lawyers that have made a move and the law firm taking on the new laterals must ensure there are no conflicts of interest with any new clients that come on board with the new lawyers or with existing clients.

Lateral lawyers may take clients that may now be adverse to clients at the new firm. Even if the lawyers do not take any clients, the new firm they are joining may have established clients that the lawyer may have once been adverse to, which would now present a conflict of interest with the lateral hires. What can the lawyer, and the law firm, do to address such conflicts? Remember that conflicts can be imputed to the entire firm.

Below is a comprehensive framework that addresses the questions one must ask in assessing whether a lateral lawyer and their new law firm are disqualified from representing a client adverse to a former client (when the lateral lawyer leaves, the clients at the old firm become former clients).

FRAMEWORK TO ANALYZE CONFLICT IMPUTATION: THE LATERAL MOVE
ABA Model Rule 1.10

Linda Lawyer is making a move from MNO Law Offices to RST Law Offices. This is the lateral move she has been working on for years, and she is excited to join the employment department of RST. She will be taking three associates with her and a good number of clients. She has been doing employment law at MNO for 10 years and both MNO and RST have well-known and established defense-based employment law departments.

As Linda and her associates join the new firm, here are three questions to ask to figure out if there are any conflicts of interest associated with Linda and the new associates joining RST Law Offices:

Three questions to ask:

1. While working at the former law firm, did the lawyers *represent* any clients whose interests are adverse to their new law firm's client?
2. Are the two matters in question the *same or substantially related*?
3. Is the lateral moving lawyer's conflict *imputed* to all lawyers in the new firm, such that the entire firm would be disqualified if the lateral lawyer is personally disqualified?

The answers to questions 1 and 2 tell you whether only the lateral moving lawyer or lawyers would be disqualified or screened; the answer to question 3 tells you whether the entire new firm would be disqualified.

Notes:

- There is a *rebuttable* presumption that the lateral lawyer learned confidential information about the old client while at the old law firm. However, if the lawyer did not perform any work for the old client, he or she did not represent the client.
- There is a *rebuttable* presumption that the lateral lawyer *will* share confidential client information regarding the old client with the new law firm. This presumption can be rebutted with an effective screen.
- While an effective screen will protect against attorney discipline, it may not protect against malpractice liability and disqualification claims.

What about Linda's old firm? Can they continue to represent a person with interests' material adverse to those of a client represented by the formerly associated lawyer and not currently represented by the firm? The short answer is yes, provided the matters are not the same or substantially related. No lawyer remaining in the firm has information from the prior representation protected by ABA Rules 1.6 and 1.9 that is material to the matter.

HYPOTHETICAL 6.6
An insurance company on both sides

In 2020, Lawyer L moved from Firm ABC to Firm XYZ. At Firm ABC, Lawyer L represented several insurance companies. After moving to Firm XYZ, it turns out that XYZ has clients who want to sue several of the insurance companies that Lawyer L previously represented.

> Please refer to the interactive ebook in Cognella Active Learning for interactive/media content.

What about Relationships That Simply Do Not Feel Right?

What do you do in a situation when taking on the legal relationship simply does not feel right? Many clients or cases come across a lawyer's desk where there may be some hesitancy in taking on the case. But when considering why there is hesitation, one cannot really put their finger on the reason. The representation simply does not feel right. There can be many examples of this:

- Maybe you feel the client was not completely forthright?
- Maybe you felt that you and the client would have conflicts down the road on how the case should be progressed?
- Maybe you knew your significant other would be disappointed that you took on this client or case?
- You do not like a potential client.
- You do not like the subject matter of the case.

These are not necessarily examples of concrete conflicts. But would they—and could they—hinder a lawyer's ability to be absolutely loyal to their client? Yes. What did we say from the very beginning of this book? Lawyers are simply human, and as humans, we are imperfect and emotional beings. You cannot take emotions out of the law!

The lawyer needs to recognize these personal biases early to prevent conflicts. It is okay to walk away from a representation or a case because of personal biases.

Key Takeaways

- Lawyers owe a duty of loyalty to their clients. Loyalty is compromised when the lawyer cannot exercise independent professional judgment due to a personal interest.
- When it comes to fees, any fees or combination thereof creates an inherent conflict of interest.

- Lawyers cannot represent new clients against former clients when there is a risk that confidential information will be used against the former client.
- Lawyers must be mindful of conflicts with prospective clients.
- Lawyers and law firms need to screen for potential conflicts when lawyers make lateral moves to a new firm.
- A lawyer's personal biases can create conflicts of interest.

Ethics in Action

Read the following disciplinary action(s) in which the state bar used the rules discussed in this chapter to bring disciplinary charges against an attorney.

- Improper transfer of property [one-year suspension]: *In re Lee C. Grevemberg*
  https://www.lasc.org/opinions/2003/02b2721.pc.pdf

End-of-Chapter Discussion Questions

1. A lawyer's personal relationships (by blood or marriage) with opposing counsel may create a conflict. This definition does not include nontraditional settings, like live-in partners, roommates, and close friendships. Should the rules include nontraditional relationships?
2. Some lawyers argue that strict conflict of interest rules interfere with a lawyer's ability to enter contracts and earn a livelihood freely. Do you agree? Why or why not?
3. Clients are our bread and butter, and we cannot make money without them. What situation can you think of where you would transfer jobs and leave your clients behind due to a conflict? What about a situation where your current law firm was dissolving and you had to find a new law firm for yourself, but this new law firm created too many conflicts for you to bring over one, some, or even many of your clients? What would you do?
4. What if a client started creating a conflict for you by engaging in a personal relationship with you during the legal relationship? What if you were interested, but it was against your law firm's policies to engage in relationships with clients? What if you were completely uninterested and the client continued to pursue you, making the legal relationship difficult and uncomfortable?
5. Consider a situation where you solely did work for a particular client for years. From time to time, you would bring in your law partner to help with very big matters, but most of the time you, and your law firm understood the client to be yours. The next time the client needed legal work, they called your law partner instead and asked if they could handle the matter and not you. Is there a conflict? Why or why not?

CHAPTER 7

The Lawyer as Advocate

> Visit your interactive ebook to download the Chapter 7 Outline.

Learning Objectives

- Evaluating how to avoid frivolous litigation.
- Balancing the duty of advocacy with the duty to the legal system.
- Evaluating how to maintain fairness to your adversary.
- Identifying a lawyer's duties to non-clients.

Key Terms

- **Perjury:** Willfully or intentionally lying after taking an oath or affirmation to tell the truth.
- **Frivolous:** Not being of serious value.
- **Candor:** Being honest.
- **Officer of the court:** A responsibility to promote honesty, justice, and the integrity of the legal system.
- **Integrity:** The quality of being honest and upholding ethics and morals.
- **Agent:** Someone who has authority (called a principal) to act on behalf of another due to their fiduciary relationship.

Introduction

HYPOTHETICAL 7.1
This is it!

You are in the middle of the biggest trial of your career. The courtroom is packed with interested parties, curious spectators, and those just enthralled with the legal escapades that have transpired back and forth between you and opposing counsel up to this point. The case has been complicated, difficult, but both sides have done a fair, hard, and smart workup of the case and the legal precedent. You know you have a sizable adversary on the other side, and the respect is mutual. It is high stakes, the pressure is on, and the press is on the edge of their seats, and You. Are. In. Your. Element.

Your client is on the stand, and you are beautifully questioning her as you did the last few times during trial practice. She is genuine, likable, and she has everyone's attention, including the jury's. You quickly glance over at them, noticing that they are hanging on her every word. They are convinced of her story, of her version of the facts. You are starting even to ease a little bit, as you know she is winning over the jury. And then, just like that, all of a sudden, you go ice cold. As you start to process the weight of what just happened, you realize the deception you feel!

Your client just blatantly lied on the stand.

You look over at her, and she knows she lied, and you know she lied, and she knows you know she lied! You look at her to explain why she would lie when everything is going so well, but she just stares at you for the next question. You quickly look over at opposing counsel, who you can tell is not sure if a lie was just told, but the wheels are certainly starting to turn.

You quickly try to rehabilitate your client by making your next question so that she can correct herself and say she made a mistake and recant the lie, but she does not. She wants to stay the course. She is lying to try to make her case stronger, but she just committed perjury on the stand.

She just jeopardized everything … or did she?

Please refer to the interactive ebook in Cognella Active Learning for interactive/media content.

We have spent a lot of time in this book so far talking about a lawyer's duties to their clients and how to zealously advocate on their behalf. But what about other duties as lawyers? Being a lawyer is not just about advocating for your client. Rather, it's working to help your client within the complex net of the justice system. It's solving problems while working within the confines of the ethical rules provided by our legal structure and protocols. We do not have rules like "Do not commit perjury" for no reason. Such rules make sure that we are all operating on an equal level when resolving legal disputes. Such rules make sure we are vested in looking at the applicable facts and the law at the center of the dispute rather than spending time, money, and resources on ill-suited or deceitful tactics that would take away from what is really important when trying to come to some kind of resolution for the parties. All lawyers are advocates within the legal system, and we cannot be operating on a different set of ethical rules.

While we absolutely must zealously represent our clients, we have a duty also to maintain the integrity of the legal system. If lawyers, for example, allow clients to commit perjury on the stand, how are they maintaining the integrity of our legal system? How can anyone have faith in a system lawyers will not fight to uphold? We are advocates, but we are also officers of the court.

> **OFFICER OF THE COURT**
> n. any person who has an <u>obligation to promote justice and effective operation of the judicial system</u>, including judges, the attorneys who appear in court, bailiffs, clerks and other personnel. As officers of the court lawyers have an <u>absolute ethical duty to tell judges the truth, including avoiding dishonesty or evasion</u> about reasons the attorney or his/her client is not appearing, the location of documents and other matters related to conduct of the courts.[1]

As we will explain in this chapter, it is our duty to not bring lawsuits or defend lawsuits unless there is a valid basis in the law and in fact to do so. It not only makes a mockery of our legal system, but it takes up precious resources from our courts, administrators, juries, and other lawyers to entertain such frivolous matters.

We will also explain what to do if you have a client who commits perjury on the stand. Lawyers have a duty to try to rectify the perjury, and we will explain what the options are if you cannot rectify the issue.

We will also explain the duty of candor to the tribunal. Lawyers shall not knowingly make a false statement of fact or law to a tribunal or fail to correct a false statement or fact or law to a tribunal. Lawyers must also disclose adverse legal authority, even if the other side fails to disclose it, and they absolutely cannot offer evidence that they know to be false.

You get the picture here. It takes truthful, honest lawyers who work within the ethical rules to make our legal system work its best for those who need it. And for this reason, the ABA Model Rules specifically prescribe duties that lawyers owe to the public and other lawyers.

As Simon H. Rifkind so perfectly stated in *The Lawyer's Role and Responsibility in Modern Society*[2], "The object of a trial is not the ascertainment of truth but the resolution of a controversy by the principled application of the rules of the game. In a civilized society these rules should be designed to favor the just

---

1. Officer of the Court legal definition (thefreedictionary.com).
2. 30 The Record of The Assoc. of the Bar of the City of New York, 1975.

resolution of controversy; and in a progressive society they should change as the perception of justice evolves in response to greater ethical sophistication."

Meritorious Claims and Contentions

ABA Model Rule 3.1 uses the words *meritorious claims and contentions* in its title to remind lawyers that they must only bring legal claims after fully researching and understanding a case.

This duty is closely tied to ABA Model Rules 1.1 and 1.3 on competence and diligence.

ABA Model Rule 3.1 uses the word *shall* to emphasize an affirmative duty. Simply put, a lawyer shall not bring or defend a claim unless there is a basis to do so in law and fact.

The policy supporting this rule is that frivolous lawsuits trigger waste. It requires wasteful expenditure for other parties in litigation while also wasting the court's time and resources. Our legal system already endures unreasonable delays, backlogs, and jammed courts, thus making this rule even more important.

The rule does not, however, require lawyers to act as judges in their client's case. In other words, a lawyer can take a position to further a client's goal even if the lawyer believes the client will ultimately lose or has a weak case. What is important is that the lawyer communicates his or her position to the client, the strength and weaknesses of a case, and proceeds accordingly.

The standard for showing that a claim is "frivolous" is high. Filing a case that proves to be meritless is okay. The rule includes a "good faith" exception, where lawyers can argue for an extension, modification, or reversal of existing law. Lawyers should not fear discipline for making aggressive and creative arguments for expanding or limiting the application of the law. We have seen time and time again examples of lawyers advocating for legal change, which has significantly impacted the country—as in the cases of *Brown v. Board of Education*[3] and *Loving v. Virginia*,[4] among others.

In sum, it's okay for lawyers to file a claim, even if the claim is weak. That said, they cannot take a position that has no basis in law or facts.

- **No basis in facts.** This requirement goes back to the lawyer's duty of competence and diligence, where lawyers must investigate the facts of a case. For example, in a medical malpractice case, the very minimum required of a lawyer is to ask for and examine the patient's medical records before determining relevant facts of the case. Similarly, if a client has a landlord-tenant dispute regarding a lease provision, the lawyer needs to determine what the lease says before rendering advice. In both of these examples, if the facts do not support a claim, the lawyer would be violating ABA Model Rule 3.1.
- **No basis in law.** A lawyer should not take a position that has no law to back it up. That does not mean a lawyer cannot argue that a law should be changed or interpreted in a way that includes the client's situation. Rather, in advocating for change, the lawyer must argue in good faith. Here, too, the lawyer's duty of competence and diligence applies. The lawyer must research the current status

---

3. 347 U.S. 483 (1954)
4. 388 U.S. 1 (1967)

of the law, to whom it applies, whether an argument for change is supported by legal precedent, and so on.

Thus, filing an action or taking a defense for a client is not frivolous merely because the facts have not first been fully substantiated or because the lawyer expects to develop vital evidence only by discovery.

CASE ALERT
Friedgood v. Axelrod

In *Friedgood v. Axelrod*,[5] the court determined whether defendants in a civil rights case are entitled to attorney fees under Section 1988 upon a showing that the complaint is frivolous without regard to the state of mind of either plaintiff or counsel. In this case, the case was deemed frivolous and in bad faith as the plaintiff had fabricated his story, claiming that he was asked to remove asbestos without any protective clothing. The court concluded that no such thing happened because the plaintiff's times and alleged circumstances were incorrect. The court did not find that the attorney engaged in any misconduct and professionally conducted himself. He responsibly conducted discovery and thoroughly investigated the case.

Please refer to the interactive ebook in Cognella Active Learning for interactive/media content.

Real-Life Example
Review the disciplinary action against a pro se litigant (a former judge) who sued his dry cleaners for $67 million in damages for losing a pair of pants (linked below). Do you agree with the disciplinary panel that a 90-day suspension was appropriate for violations of ABA Model Rules 3.1 and 8.4?

Pants Judge Suspended:

https://lawprofessors.typepad.com/legal_profession/2020/06/a-seemingly-endless-saga-involving-the-pants-judge-has-ended-in-a-discipline-decision-by-the-district-of-columbia-court-of-ap.html

---

5. 593 F. Supp. 395 (S.D.N.Y. 1989)

> **Ripped from the Headlines**
>
> Review the article linked below from the *Washington Post* about whether Trump's lawyers could get in trouble for frivolous lawsuits. Do you agree with the author's conclusion?
>
> **Can Trump's Lawyers Get in Trouble for Frivolous Lawsuits?**
>
> https://www.washingtonpost.com/politics/2020/12/11/can-trumps-lawyers-get-trouble-frivolous-lawsuits/

Criminal Law Exception

ABA Model Rule 3.1 provides that a lawyer representing a defendant in a criminal proceeding or in any other proceeding that could result in incarceration of the client may defend the proceeding as to require every element of the case be established. This rule implies that the prosecution will always have the burden of proof to establish that every element of the case be met and insisting that the prosecution meet this burden does not violate the rule. For example, if a criminal defense lawyer rejects a plea deal and maintains the position that the client is not guilty (even if the client confesses to the lawyer about his guilt), the lawyer would not be violating ABA Model Rule 3.1.

ABA Model Rule 3.4: Extends to Discovery Requests

ABA Model Rule 3.4(d) prohibits lawyers from making frivolous discovery requests. The requirements regarding a basis of law and fact and good faith exceptions apply here. For example, suppose a lawyer knows that a certain request is protected by a nondisclosure agreement or is a trade secret. In that case, they should not request that information unless they are making a good-faith argument that the existing law is incorrect or inapplicable to their client.

Consequences

Violating the rule on frivolous litigation can lead to disciplinary action. It can also result in court-imposed sanctions or a tort action for abuse of process and/or malicious prosecution.

Honesty and Candor

Our legal system relies on a system of honor and candor. This includes honesty to the court and our judicial officers. We trust our courts to hand down decisions that vary from small fines or warnings to rulings that are monumental to our society and our way of life. In doing that our courts depend on—and more importantly, trust—the information lawyers present to them. It is this information, whether it is in the form of witness testimony, written briefs, applicable case law, or other facts or evidence, that our courts dissect and study to make decisions. It must be candid, correct, and current.

ABA Model Rule 3.3 governs candor and honesty to our courts. The standard for ABA Model Rule 3.3 is *knowledge*: "A lawyer shall not knowingly misrepresent a fact or law to a court." This information has to be in the lawyer's control. But we all know of instances of clients and witnesses who will do things without the lawyer's knowledge. Clients have been known to all of a sudden lie on the stand to better their cases, or simply because they are nervous, forgetful, etc. They have been known to not share the full truth of facts with their lawyers because of embarrassment, or they do not think it is material, or they forgot. Lawyers cannot control what they do not know, and the ABA does not expect them to do so. When it comes to the facts, lawyers are at the mercy of their clients, witnesses, and other evidence to educate them and help them piece together what happened as best they can. That is the simple truth!

At the same time, lawyers do not always make the best researchers of case law. They may not find all the cases relevant to their case—both good or bad cases for their case. Or they do find bad cases and they take the chance and do not disclose the bad case to the court. They may ask a client or witness to lie to the court. A lawyer may withhold material evidence! Whatever the reason may be, all of these examples above translate into one thing: falseness to our courts and a breakdown of out courts' ability to make true decisions.

- **False statement of fact or law:** Lawyers are prohibited from making a false statement of law or facts to a tribunal. The evidence a lawyer presents to a court must be accurate to the best of the lawyer's knowledge.
- **Duty to correct false statements:** ABA Model Rule 3.3 further requires that a lawyer correct material laws or facts previously made to a tribunal by a lawyer.
    - Lawyers must not make false statements to the court. The *material* element applies only to correcting previous false material facts, and not the statements to the court.

This rule defines perjury, i.e., lying to the court. Perjury presents two duties for a lawyer, depending on whether the lying has or has not yet occurred:

1. **Prospective duty:** Lawyers have a duty to prevent the perjury. Lawyers cannot make a false statement of facts or law.

For example: Lawyers cannot offer made-up facts.

2. **Retrospective duty:** Lawyers have a duty to remediate or correct the perjury, but only if the perjury is *material*.

For example: Witness testified that she saw the defendant who is accused of robbing the local bank drive away in a red car. In prior deposition testimony, the same witness testified that she witnessed someone drive away in a green car just around the time of the bank robbery. The lawyer knows the witness is lying on the stand now because her client, the defendant, has a green car. Also, just before trial, the defendant told his lawyer that he and the witness have formed a recent romantic relationship.

The lawyer cannot let the testimony of the red car stand, as the color is material in this situation, even though it would likely be detrimental to her client.

The material element comes into play only when there is a retrospective duty. Something is deemed material if there is a substantial chance that it could impact the outcome.

> The duty of candor to the tribunal *trumps* the duty of confidentiality (ABA Model Rule 1.6) in regard to perjury. False statements to the court, especially material ones, cannot stand.

- **Disclosure of legal authority:** Lawyers must offer all relevant legal evidence that is controlling in their jurisdiction. This includes legal authority in the jurisdiction that is directly adverse to a lawyer's position. A lawyer must disclose adverse legal authority, even if opposing counsel failed to disclose it.

> **PRACTICE NOTE**
> When submitting a motion to the court, your hearing can often be a month or more after your original motion has been submitted. If during that time adverse authority has come down against your motion, but before your hearing date, be transparent about it. You have a few options here:
>
> - File a supplemental brief outlining the adverse authority for the court's consideration.
> - Withdraw your motion.
> - Depending on the nature of the hearing, and your hearing date, and the context of the adverse authority, bring it up at the hearing.
>
> Bottom line: You need to bring it up!

- **Offering false evidence:** If the lawyer knows that an opposing lawyer, a client, or witness called by the lawyer has given material evidence that is false, the lawyer must take reasonable remediable measures.

> Let's call this what this is: You know you or your client or a witness has committed perjury!

What now? You have a duty to remediate the perjury, even if this involves disclosing to the court in breach of confidentiality (ABA Model Rule 1.6). The duty to remediate only triggers when the lawyer knows of the perjury. A lawyer's reasonable belief will not prevent the evidence from being considered by the jury.

But before you disclose the perjury to the court, there are steps that can be taken to remediate:

1. Recess—If in a formal hearing such as a deposition, hearing, or a trial, ask for a brief recess to speak to your client privately.
2. Remonstrate—Persuade the client or witness to correct the perjury. There may be a good chance that the perjury is not necessarily due to lying, but rather a nervous, forgetful, or tired witness. Testifying can be a stressful event, especially if it is regarding a traumatic event or if the testimony goes many hours or days. It can be exhausting. Think about the person testifying and the factors that may have led to the perjury unrelated to lying. Could they be tired? Are they on a medication that makes them forgetful, tired, confused, dizzy, or even thirsty or hungry? Did something happen on the way in to the testimony? Did they have a stressful morning or going through something stressful in their lives? These could all have an impact on the testimony.
3. Resign—If a client or witness does not correct a material fact, then a lawyer may resign or withdraw from the case if there is no other option to remedy the perjury. Withdrawing can be difficult and may require both the client's and the court's consent.
4. Reveal—If there is no other option, a lawyer may reveal the perjury to the court only if it is appropriate.

Fairness to Your Adversary

In an adversarial system like ours, fairness is an essential ingredient to maintaining integrity and decorum. Fairness attempts to create a system of rules for attorneys to follow, thus promoting fairness in competition. Ultimately, the court benefits from parties treating each other fairly, as it helps in presenting the truth—that is, a true version of the events that took place. Below is a list of fairness concerns that every lawyer should be aware of.

- **Unlawful obstruction [ABA Model Rule 3.4(a)]:** This rule prohibits a lawyer from unlawfully altering, destroying, or concealing anything with potential evidentiary value. Destroying evidence is a crime in most jurisdictions. Additionally, a lawyer should not counsel or assist anyone else in taking this action. For example, if a client appears at your office with the gun he used to commit a crime, the rules require that you not "hide" or "get rid of" the gun for your client. Such an action would amount to a violation of ABA Model Rule 3.4(a), among other violations. In fact, the rules go as far as requiring you to inspect the gun and hand it over to appropriate authorities (law enforcement or other prosecuting authority). Similarly, the lawyer could not advise the client on "how to get rid of the gun" for the same reasons.

In the case of *In re Ryder*,[6] a lawyer was disciplined because he put a weapon used in a robbery and money from the robbery in a safe deposit box. Initially, the money and weapon were in the client's safe deposit box. The lawyer moved it to his own safe deposit box and thus obstructed the authority's ability to access it.

The example above is quite extreme. What about subtle destruction of evidence due to negligence? For example, where a lawyer inadvertently destroys an important document as part of the firm's annual shredding policy. In these cases, courts have imposed discovery sanctions against lawyers or have granted an adverse evidentiary presumption.

Similarly, what if a lawyer advises a client to take down a controversial social media/Facebook post? The New York Bar concluded that an attorney could advise clients to keep their social media privacy settings turned on so long as the "evidence" is generally preserved in cyberspace or on the user's computer.[7]

- **Improperly influencing witnesses [ABA Model Rule 3.4(b)]:** Preparing witnesses for trial is a common procedure in any litigation. The lawyer may not falsify evidence or counsel or assist a witness to testify falsely. For this reason, lawyers are careful about telling witnesses the importance of speaking the truth. Following this rule becomes problematic when lawyers coach witnesses to say things to obtain a favorable result.

OKAY WITNESS PREPARATION VS. NOT-OKAY WITNESS PREPARATION

Example #1

Okay: Telling a witness that they can testify as to what they remember.

Not Okay: Telling a witness that if they forget facts, they can make them up.

Example #2

Okay: Coaching a witness on the stand who may be nervous to remember facts they previously testified to during a deposition:

Attorney: Do you remember the color of the car that you saw on the day of September 16th that was involved in the drive-by shooting?

Witness: I do not.

---

6. 263 F.Supp 370 (E.D. VA) aff'd, 381 F.2d 713 (4th Cir. 1967)
7. See NYCLA Ethics Op. No. 745 (Jul. 2, 2013); see also Op. No. 14-1, Professional Ethics of the Florida Bar (Jun. 25, 2015, approved Oct. 16, 2015); N.C. Formal Ethics Opinion 5 (July 25, 2014).

(Witness previously testified under oath during a deposition that the car was red.)

Attorney: Do you recall that you previously testified during your deposition that it was red? (Submits deposition testimony into evidence to corroborate testimony.)

Witness: Yes, I now remember.

Not Okay: Same facts as above, but there is no prior deposition testimony.

Attorney: Do you remember the color of the car that you saw on the day of September 16th that was involved in the drive-by shooting?

Witness: I do not.

(Attorney to witness during a break, "Say the car was red, it will help our case.")

After break, witness is back on the stand:

Attorney: Do you now remember the color of the car?

Witness: Yes, I now remember it was red.

Example #3

Okay: Telling a witness to explain what they did after a question that calls for a simple yes or no answer.

Attorney: Did you call the police after your car accident?

Witness: No, because the other party was calling the police to come to the scene.

Not Okay: Telling a witness to lie!

Additionally, it goes without saying that lawyers cannot pay witnesses for favorable testimony. They can reimburse witnesses for expenses relating to serving as a witness, and an expert witness can be paid for time spent preparing for testifying and time spent testifying. This is usually an expense that clients are aware of.

- **Knowingly disobeying the rules of the tribunal [ABA Model Rule 3.4(c)]:** If lawyers disobey the rules of a tribunal, they will be sanctioned. An example would be failing to respond to a court order to produce documents. If the lawyer plans to challenge the order or document, they should do so immediately, like in the case of a court order requiring documents subject to attorney-client privilege. The lawyer can seek a protective order for the documents. However, the lawyer should simply not ignore the court's order.
- **Referring to irrelevant or inadmissible facts [ABA Model Rule 3.4(e)]:** Lawyers must not refer to facts that are not supported by admissible evidence. Recall the last time you watched a legal show when a lawyer vigorously objects because the opposing counsel attempts to state something that was clearly ruled as inadmissible. The judge then proceeds to ask the lawyers to approach the judge away from the jury. The judge admonishes the lawyer who made a scene in court and then

asks the jury to disregard the statement just made. This is a classic example of a lawyer attempting to refer to irrelevant or inadmissible facts.

- **Stating personal knowledge of factual maters or expressing an opinion about culpability, credibility, guilt, or justness [ABA Model Rule 3.4(e)]:** This rule goes to the very nature of the courtroom experience. When a lawyer speaks, the jurors and judges listen. For this reason, a lawyer should not express his personal opinion about a case or express personal knowledge on factual matters at trial. The following statements would violate ABA Model Rule 3.4(e).
    - "There is no way my client did this. I know him personally."
    - "This witness is telling the truth. I have never seen him lie before."
    - "The only just thing to do in this case is to acquit this defendant because he did not commit this crime."
    - "The defendant did not run a red light. I saw him driving."
- **Cooperating with other parties [ABA Model Rule 3.4(f)]:** A lawyer usually cautions their client against providing information to opposing counsel/the other side without first consulting them. Lawyers do not want clients voluntarily furnishing information about a case when they do not have to do so legally. However, what about witnesses and other parties associated with a case who are not parties and are not represented by counsel? Can a lawyer prevent them from cooperating with opposing counsel? The short answer is no, unless the person is a relative or an employee or **agent** of a client or the lawyer reasonably believes that the person's interests will not be adversely affected by not talking with the opposing counsel/other side.

MARK AND SOO
ABA Model Rule 3.4(f)

Mark and Soo were involved in a car accident on a neighborhood street. The street was filled with single-family houses. Mark was driving on the street for the first time, looking for his friend Carl's home. He was going to Carl's house for the first time for dinner. Soo lives on the street and lives two houses down from Carl and is his neighbor and friend. He is driving behind Mark. As Soo gets closer to Mark's car, Soo notices that Mark is driving relatively slowly down the street but does not think much of it. Mark is wondering why the guy behind him is driving so close to him and speeds up a little bit. In his desire to avoid Soo, Mark all of a sudden notices Carl's address pop up on the house next to him and he quickly brakes. Soo is unable to avoid him and rear-ends Mark's car. Carl, waiting for Mark, sees the entire accident out of his window and rushes out of the house, making sure his friends are okay.

A few months later, both Mark and Soo are unable to agree on who was at fault for the accident, and their insurance companies will not pay for any claims for damages to the cars or injuries they both received because they cannot agree on what happened. Mark claims that Soo hit his car, but Soo claims that Mark stopped so suddenly that he could not avoid him.

> Both men hire lawyers and sue one another. Now the question really will be, what will Carl say in all this? Both Mark and Soo will want Carl to be "on their side" of the lawsuit. But under ABA Model Rule 3.4(f), neither lawyer can prevent Carl from talking to the other side and explaining what he saw happen. No one party has control over Carl as a witness.

A Lawyer's Duties to Non-Clients

The general rule is that while lawyers owe duties to their clients, they do not owe any duties to people and entities that they do not represent. However, there are some cases where lawyers can be held liable to a non-client for the lawyer's malpractice or breach of fiduciary duty.

In some jurisdictions, an attorney may be liable where the third party was an intended beneficiary of the attorney's services or where it is foreseeable that negligent services or advice could cause harm to others.

In a 2004 case, *Vega v. Jones Day*,[8] the court concluded that a non-party could claim fraud against transactional counsel for actively concealing facts material to the transaction. Similarly, a recent Bloomberg Law News report identified fraud, conversion, conspiracy, aiding and abetting, and professional negligence as common examples of popular third-party claims against lawyers.[9]

Most jurisdictions require privity to determine how far and to whom the lawyer's duties of loyalty and care to the client extend. California is one jurisdiction where the courts have created a third-party beneficiary test via case law. In *Lucas v. Hamm*,[10] the court considered several factors in favor of holding a lawyer responsible to the beneficiaries of a will for faulty drafting of the will. These factors include:

- The extent to which the transaction was intended to affect the plaintiff
- The foreseeability of harm.
- The degree of certainty that plaintiff suffered injury.
- The closeness of the connection between the defendant's conduct and the injury.
- Whether imposing liability on an attorney would impose an undue burden on the profession.[11]

In sum, lawyers have to also think about how their actions affect other interested parties.

Key Takeaways

- Our justice system relies on honesty and candor to courts, lawyers, and one another to work

---

8. 121 Cal.App. 4th
9. Helen Gunnarsson, Conference Report: Suits against Lawyers Aren't Just for Clients Anymore, available at bloomberglaw.com (March 11, 2021).
10. 56 Cal.2d 583
11. Id. at 587

effectively.
- Lawyers have a duty to only bring and defend lawsuits that have a value basis in law and in fact.
- Lawyers have a duty to rectify known perjury of a witness.
- Lawyers have a duty of candor to the tribunal.
- ABA Model Rule 3.4(a) prohibits a lawyer from altering, destroying, or concealing anything with potential evidentiary value in a legal proceeding.
- ABA Model Rule 3.4(b) prohibits lawyers from improperly influencing a witness.
- Lawyers are expected to cooperate with one another within the ethical rules and obey the rules of the tribunal.

Ethics in Action

Read the following disciplinary action(s) in which the state bar used the rules discussed in this chapter to bring disciplinary charges against an attorney.

- Honesty and Fairness [Disbarred]: *In the Matter of Millard Farmer*, https://www.gasupreme.us/wp-content/uploads/2019/11/s19y1156.pdf

End-of-Chapter Discussion Questions

1. To what extent do you think the adversarial nature of our legal system discourages honesty and fairness?
2. If a client wants their lawyer to hide something from the other side, what should a lawyer do? Is withdrawing simply passing the buck on to someone else?
3. If your client says something during a deposition that you are hearing about for the first time, were you a bad lawyer? In other words, why did you not know about these facts before? Does it reflect purely on the trust that the client places in you?
4. In most cases, frivolous lawsuits occur because a party wants to harass the other side. Being sued is incredibly frustrating, time consuming, and costly. Is our litigious system to blame? Could one solution be to increase the monetary limits on cases that go to small claims courts? Should alternate dispute resolution methods be more widely available?

CHAPTER 8

Decision-Making in a Lawyer-Client Relationship

> Visit your interactive ebook to download the Chapter 8 Outline.

Learning Objectives

- Recognize the challenges in representing someone who is impaired.
- Assess and identify the role lawyers play when they represent clients.
- Assess and identify the role clients play.
- Know when not to represent a client.

Key Terms

- **Settlement:** An agreement between two parties intended to resolve a legal dispute between them.
- **Plea:** An agreement between the prosecution and the defendant where the defendant pleads guilty to criminal charges in exchange for a reduced sentence or dropped charges.
- **Bench trial:** A trial before a judge
- **Diminished capacity:** When an individual may not have the mental capacity to make a decision (due to age, mental impairment, or for some other reason).
- **Guardian ad litem:** When a person involved in a suit cannot adequately represent their own interests, the court may appoint a guardian ad litem to protect the person's interests.
- **Conservator:** A situation where a court appoints a responsible person (called the "conservator") to care for another adult (called the "conservatee") who cannot care for themselves or their finances.

Introduction

The ABA Rules say little about the day-to-day responsibilities of a lawyer. There are many such responsibilities, including communicating with the client about the relationship, the terms of the agreements, how decisions will be made, understanding the client's goals and objectives for representation, etc. Furthermore, the rules clarify that an attorney is the client's advocate, a fiduciary meant to promote the client's best interests. So, what happens when the lawyer and client disagree? Is the lawyer simply a hired gun, or should the lawyer play a more active role when clients decide to take drastic decisions that the lawyer disagrees with?

HYPOTHETICAL 8.1
When a startup has trouble starting!

You have been representing a client and her blood-testing startup from its inception. She claims that is it is now valued at $9 billion. You have been assisting with legal issues, including patent applications, raising money from investors, and hiring employees. You take her word on the valuation, as you are the lawyer and not the "finance guy." What do you know about money? You know documents and applications.

It turns out the entire premise of the startup is a hoax. You suspected this a while ago when you were filling out a patent application, and one of the researchers shared with you that "the thing doesn't work. We keep testing it, but we keep getting unusable results." You take the issue back to your client, who simply shrugs it off as "don't worry, it's just in the initial phases. It works. We are just working out the kinks." You continue to draft investor documents for your client that include future revenue projections based on valuation documents that she gave you, but you suspect they are wrong. You are just trying to be a "team player." During an investor meeting, your client exclaims, "Oh, I know someone at the FDA. We will get approval." You know that this is an outright lie because the FDA rejected your application. You have had enough. You quit the next day.

Please refer to the interactive ebook in Cognella Active Learning for interactive/media content.

Pause for Reflection

In terms of Comment [9] to Paragraph (d), lawyers can give their honest opinion about the actual consequences that appear likely to result from a client's conduct. Even if the client continues to use the lawyer's advice, the lawyer will not necessarily be deemed complicit in the criminal or fraudulent conduct of the client. There is a fine distinction between presenting an analysis of all legal aspects of questionable conduct and furthering the commissioning of a crime or fraudulent conduct.

Although a somewhat extreme scenario (and partially inspired by the company Theranos), it helps us understand the role lawyers play in advising clients. When a client uses the lawyer's services to commit fraud, the lawyer must not further assist in the commission of fraud.

Decision-Making Authority

There is a high likelihood that lawyers and clients will disagree on issues concerning decision-making. Thankfully, the rules help outline some areas that are exclusively within the domain of clients. An overarching principle is that clients decide the goals (the ends) of the representation, while lawyers decide the means to achieving those goals. For example, the client's goal might be to draft a will that leaves property to both his children. The lawyer will assist in this goal by preparing a document that reflects these objectives, keeping in mind certain provisions in the will that are important to ensure the will is legally valid. Decisions on how to draft and execute the will fall within the lawyer's territory—as lawyers decide the means to achieving the client's objectives. Thus, clients make decisions on the objectives of their representations, while lawyers are responsible for tactical and strategic decisions. As aptly stated in *Blanton v. Womancare, Inc.*,[1]

> In the course of a trial, there be but one captain per ship. Any attorney must be able to make such tactical decisions as whether to call a particular witness, and the court and opposing counsel must be able to rely upon the decisions he makes, even when the client voices opposition in open court. (Blanton, 38 Cal. 3d at 404)

Ultimate Authority

Clients have ultimate authority on certain types of decisions. ABA Model Rule 1.2(a) expressly outlines decisions clients are entitled to make. Table 8.1 below provides a breakdown of these areas reserved for the client and the reasons supporting them.

Table 8.1. ABA Model Rule 1.2(a) Scope of Representation

Whether to appeal	Clients have the final say because of the emotional toll and cost of a continuing lawsuit.
Whether to settle	Clients bring lawsuits to vindicate their rights. When they settle a case and forgo trial, they have to feel comfortable with the final outcome.
Whether to accept a plea deal	A plea deal could put a client in jail. They should have the final say on the terms of those deals.

Cont'd

---

1. (1985) 38 Cal.3d 396

Whether to testify	The Fifth Amendment of the US Constitution protects the client's right against self-incrimination. For these reasons, the client can decide whether it is in their best interests to testify.
Whether to waive jury trial	The Sixth and Seventh Amendments of the US Constitution recognize the right to a jury in civil and criminal trials, respectively. This is a fundamental right that only the client can choose to forgo.

In each of these decisions, a lawyer is still a counselor. They can advise clients on the benefits and consequences involved in any of the decision areas listed above.

What Happens When a Lawyer and Client Disagree?

On occasion, there can be situations where the lawyer and client disagree on the means to establish the client's objectives. In these situations, clients normally defer to the lawyer's expertise. Similarly, lawyers will defer to clients on issues related to expenses and concerns for third parties. But what happens if their disagreement is serious enough to lead to a complete breakdown of the relationship? In such cases, the lawyer should consider withdrawing, as neither the lawyer nor the client benefits.

CASE ALERT
The case of *McCoy v. Louisiana*[2] is a good example of this type of disagreement.

Here, the defendant and his lawyer disagreed on whether to take a plea deal. The defendant did not want to concede guilt by taking the plea deal. In contrast, the lawyer wanted to concede guilt, as he felt he could get a lighter sentence through accountability and arguing for diminished capacity. Over the objection of the client, the lawyer conceded to the client's guilt. The lawyer argued for a verdict of second-degree murder on a theory of diminished capacity. The jury returned a verdict of first-degree murder and recommended the death penalty.

McCoy appealed his verdict. The Louisiana Supreme Court denied the appeal and affirmed the conviction, reasoning that defense counsel's admission of guilt was simply a strategic choice by counsel. The Supreme Court of the United States disagreed. In a 6–3 opinion, the court concluded that McCoy's right to assistance of counsel was violated when defense counsel conceded guilt over the client's objection. The court distinguished decisions made by counsel and those reserved to the client. Counsel is responsible for all decisions relating to "trial management," such as calling on a witness or raising objections. On the other hand, the client has the exclusive right to decide whether to plead guilty, waive the right to a jury trial, testify on one's own behalf, and forgo an appeal. Whether to assert innocence as a defense is also within those decisions reserved to the client.

2. 138 S.Ct. 1500 (2018)

> Please refer to the interactive ebook in Cognella Active Learning for interactive/media content.

Criminal, Fraudulent, and Prohibited Transactions

ABA Model Rule 1.2(d) prohibits a lawyer from counseling or assisting clients in conduct that they know is criminal or fraudulent. In short, do not teach a client "how to get away with murder" or "how to hide the money" they just stole. Public interest and integrity require lawyers to be good representatives of the legal system and uphold the law.

Let's say a potential client tells you that he is an agent for an anonymous government official from a "high-risk" jurisdiction who wants to buy an expensive property in the United States that would be owned through a corporation. The potential client is vague about the source of the funds. Can you represent them? A competent attorney will want to know if the source of the client's funds is legitimate, since a lawyer cannot help a client launder illegal money.[3]

That said, if the lawyer simply discusses the consequences of a course of conduct, they would not be violating ABA Model Rule 1.2(d). There is an important distinction between presenting an analysis of legal aspects of questionable conduct and recommending how a crime or fraud might be committed. Thus, in the previous example, if instead of forming a corporation to help buy the property, the lawyer simply discusses a legal path to buying a property and an illegal path to buying the property and specifically discourages the illegal path, the lawyer will be acting within the confines of ABA Model Rule 1.2(d).

Similarly, lawyers may counsel or assist a client in making a good faith effort to determine the law's validity, scope, meaning, or application. Using the same example, if it is unclear whether the law allows certain types of funds to be used in the purchase of the property, the lawyer can make a good faith effort to determine if the client's proposed conduct falls within the scope of the law.

Real-Life Application

ABA Model Rule 1.2(d) is best understood with the issue surrounding marijuana. Marijuana is legal in many states but still illegal under federal law. Thus, in the states where it is legal, can lawyers advise clients despite their conduct being illegal under federal law? California State Bar Formal Opinion 2020-22 is a helpful resource to understand what a lawyer can and cannot do under these circumstances.

---

3. This example was based on a CBS investigation for *60 Minutes* called Anonymous, Inc. You can find the original episode here: https://www.cbsnews.com/news/anonymous-inc-60-minutes-steve-kroft-investigation/.

> Read the following California State Bar Formal Opinion 2020-202:
>
> http://www.calbar.ca.gov/Portals/0/documents/ethics/Opinions/Formal-Opinion-2020-202-17-0001.pdf
>
> - Pay attention to the definitions assigned to the words *counsel* and *assist*.
> - Ask yourself:
>   - What can a lawyer do for a cannabis business?
>   - What can a lawyer not do for a cannabis business?

Diminished Capacity

Everybody deserves and needs access to legal representation, legal help, and justice, even those who may not be able to articulate the help they need. These individuals may actually need help from the law even more, and lawyers must find a way to assist them as they would any other client. Working with individuals with diminished mental or physical capacity may present unique challenges. Our duty as lawyers to them requires that we maintain a normal attorney-client relationship as reasonably as possible. The empathetic beings in us also recognize that these individuals may need something more. They may need more than the legal assistance we would provide to other clients who do not have the same needs. If a person who needs legal help cannot make decisions on their own or does not understand what is happening around them, what can we as lawyers do to help them?

Who are individuals with diminished capacity? These are persons who are unable to understand the legal issues they may be involved in or make a decision in connection with those legal matters due to things such as age (being a child), mental or physical impairment (an adult who possesses the mental age of a four-year-old, an adult who has suffered a brain injury resulting in diminished ability to speak or communicate as before, a person in a coma), or some other reason. These are simple examples and not a complete list.

ABA Model Rule 1.14 guides lawyers who have clients with diminished capacity.

ABA Model Rule 1.14: Client with Diminished Capacity

1. When a client's capacity to make decisions in connection with a legal representation is diminished, the lawyer shall, as far as reasonably possible, maintain a normal attorney-client relationship with the client.
    - **Side note:** Clients with diminished capacity are owed all the fiduciary duties as other clients would have from their lawyer. A lawyer must maintain competence, candid communication, confidentiality, and be aware of conflict of interest with clients with diminished capacity.
    - **Practical steps in representing someone with diminished capacity:**
        - When you represent a client with diminished capacity, explain to them that your

goal is to keep them safe and healthy. Build rapport with them just like you would with any other clients.
   - Explain the court process and what they should expect.
   - Ask often, and in a manner they understand, if they have questions.
2. When a lawyer reasonably believes that the client has diminished capacity and is at risk of substantial physical, financial, or other harm unless action is taken, the lawyer may take reasonable action to protect the client's interest. This includes consulting with individuals or entities that have the ability to take action to protect the client. The lawyer may also, in appropriate cases, have a guardian ad litem, guardian, or conservator appointed.
   - **Side note:** Lawyers may not always understand the nature, medical reasoning, or even severity of a client's diminished capacity. Get help if you do not! You have a duty to maintain the fiduciary duties to the client, but you need to help your client. As explained further below, it may be okay to breach the fiduciary duties if reasonably necessary to best assist your client.
3. Information relating to the representation of a client with diminished capacity is protected by ABA Model Rule 1.6 (Confidentiality); however, if a lawyer needs to take protective actions as referenced in (b) above, the lawyer is impliedly authorized under ABA Model Rule 1.6(a) to reveal information about the client, but only to the extent necessary to protect the client's interests.

Comment 6 of ABA Model Rule 1.14 directs lawyers to balance certain factors when working on determining the extent of a client's diminished capacity.

Factors to balance:

- client's ability to articulate reasoning leading to a decision
- variability of state of mind throughout the relationship and ability to appreciate the consequences of a decision
- the substantive fairness of a decision
- the consistency of a decision with the known long-term commitments and values of the client

Practically speaking, as a lawyer, you may not be able to fully assess these factors on your own. We are lawyers and not medical professionals, and it is important to remember that. If you cannot determine, or if you have any doubts about your ability to determine a client's state of mind, or if they will really understand the long-term consequences of a legal decision, then seek the appropriate guidance for your client.

Diminished Capacity and Confidentiality

Lawyers can breach confidentiality to the *extent necessary* to help clients with diminished capacity.
Some examples include the following:

- Suppose you need to explain to a medical professional a certain portion of the legal representation and explain why you believe your client did not understand it. In that case, the medical

professional can best help your client.
- Telling the court that you believe it would be best to have a guardian ad litem appointed for your client because your client is a child and did not understand certain aspects of the legal consequences of the decisions that needed to be made in a lawsuit. A guardian would be better able to make those decisions on his or her behalf.

Again, only provide the confidential information necessary to effectuate representation for a client with diminished capacity. One of the most common scenarios where confidentiality may need to be breached is when obtaining a guardian ad litem or conservator for a client with diminished capacity. Both of these individuals are just that: guardians for the client.

A guardian ad litem is there to act on and serve in the best interests of the client. They can often make the decisions for the client when the client themselves would not be able to. The guardian ad litem is generally a title maintained during the course of a legal representation, but it can extend after such representation is over if necessary. A common example would be where a child is injured, and a lawsuit is filed on behalf of the child. Often a parent will be the guardian ad litem for the child and will help make decisions on behalf of the child or client's best interests. But it may not always be the parent. If the parents and the child were involved in a single-car accident, for example, and the parents are unable to serve as guardians because of their own injuries, then it may be another family member, medical professional, or someone else that the court may appoint. When appointing a guardian, the question should always be, who will look out for the best interests of the client?

A conservator is also someone who would serve to act in the best interest of the client, but the conservator generally is in place long after the legal matter is over. A conservator may be appointed long term to manage the financial affairs or even the daily life of a client due to physical and/or mental incapacities. A regular check-in with the court, such as every month to every year, with the conservator would also be implemented to make sure the relationship is still in the client's best interests.

Once that guardian is appointed, the lawyer will have to share and discuss aspects of the case with the conservator or guardian ad litem, almost as if that person were the client. Careful here—we say *almost*! Lawyers need to provide adequate and enough information to the guardian so that they can serve in the best interests of the client, but only to the extent necessary to do so. If certain aspects of the attorney-client confidence are not needed to be revealed to this individual, then do not reveal them. For example, an attorney represents families with children who have developmental disabilities. In looking out for the children's best interests, parents are often appointed as conservators when the disabled child turns 18. In these cases, you want to ask whether the parents are the best people to be conservators.

HYPOTHETICAL 8.2
How would you help your client?

Think about the following scenarios. These are all examples of clients with diminished capacity. As their lawyer, how would you make sure you maintain a normal attorney-client relationship while still considering their diminished capacities?

- A client who is in a coma and the family and hospital are in dispute over whether to take the patient off of life support.
- A client who was injured on a construction job site when a steel beam fell on his head causing massive brain injuries. He has episodes of violent outbursts since the accident, forgetfulness, and physical pain. He is in a wheelchair full time because of difficulties with walking.
- A client who has an opioid, drug, or alcohol addiction.
- A client who is elderly; during your representation, you see signs of forgetfulness, such as your name, their name, and what year it is.
- A client who has been diagnosed with multiple personalities.

Please refer to the interactive ebook in Cognella Active Learning for interactive/media content.

Cultural Competence

Lawyers and clients need to have a trust-based relationship to effectively make decisions together. But how do you establish such a relationship if both of you are from different cultural backgrounds? If you both speak different languages? If the way that each of you shows respect, understanding, and empathy is different due to unique cultural upbringings? How can you even communicate, let alone form a relationship where a client will let you make critical decisions that may affect their personal outcome?

Lawyers have a fundamental duty to become culturally competent to the extent necessary to establish a trust-based relationship with a client. The ABA Standards for the Provision of Civil Legal Aid provides:

> Cultural competence involves more than having the capacity to communicate in the language of the persons from each community and involves more than an absence of bias or discrimination. It means having the capacity to interact effectively and to understand how the cultural mores and circumstances of persons from diverse communities affect their interaction with the provider and its practitioners and govern their reaction to their legal problems and to the process for resolving them.[4]

It can be a normal reaction when someone does something differently from you that they are the ones who are odd! But maybe it's you? Or maybe it is no one, and we need to recognize we all live in a uniquely diverse, but small, world. Be careful not to impose what you do or what you think is common or normal on everyone. You will be doing a great disservice to your clients if you do. Small things, such as a gesture or

---

4. Standard 2.4 on Cultural Competence (americanbar.org)

even family dynamics, can be interpreted differently, depending on the cultural values of one's clients. It is important for lawyers to understand these cultural values of a client. They may be highly impactful to a client when making a decision. Not taking time to understand the culture can and will lead to miscommunication between the client and lawyer.

Examples of cultural differences:

1. In some cultures, it is highly important to take the advice of parents, elders, or even a community (religious affiliations) before making big decisions. A lawyer may interpret this as overreaching or even undue influence over a client. But understanding the underlying culture of the client helps a lawyer recognize the decision-making process of the client.
2. Not all cultures recognize shaking of hands as a greeting. Some even consider it rude to extend one's hand for a handshake.
3. Some cultures call for business or legal decisions to be made not in a conference room, but rather over a meal. Enjoying a meal together while discussing a legal impact of a case helps to take down the serious tone of the discussion and can allow for a trust-based relationship to be formed.

These are merely a few examples of cultural differences. There are hundreds, maybe even thousands, that can be discussed. These cultural differences between us all are also developing and continue to evolve. So, the question remains, how can lawyers bridge the cultural gap?

TIPS ON CONNECTING WITH CLIENTS

- Learn about your client's culture before an initial meeting. Use the internet, talk to colleagues, friends, or even experts on cultural differences. Travel books to the region from where your client may be from can also be helpful.
- If your client speaks a different language, find an interpreter who also speaks their language. Have the interpreter present at meetings, even meals, to help with communication.
- Watch your client. If you are unsure about how certain gestures will be interpreted, watch your client and mimic what they do.
- Ask them. Be open, transparent, and respectful to your client. If you are unsure about how to approach perceived differences, then have a conversation with your client. Explain that you want to understand their culture. What is important to them and their decision-making process? Asking a client and having a conversation with them demonstrates that you want to learn, be respectful, and also be cognizant of what is important to them. This will lead to a more successful trust-based relationship.

Being mindful of cultural differences will allow for better communication, decision-making, and trust between you and your client.

Professional Independence

You are not your client. Maintaining professional independence as a lawyer is crucial to the lawyer-client relationship. Recall ABA Model Rule 1.2 (b): A lawyer's representation of a client, including representation by appointment, does not constitute an endorsement of the client's political, economic, social, or moral views or activities.

Being a lawyer can mean having clients whose views you are opposed to. This does not mean that you cannot effectively represent such clients. Like cultural differences, the key is to learn, understand, and respect such disparities and recognize how they may weigh on your client's decision-making process. ABA Model Rule 2.1 provides guidance to lawyers:

> In representing a client, a lawyer shall exercise independent professional judgment and render candid advice. In rendering advice, a lawyer may refer not only to law but to other considerations such as moral, economic, social and political factors, that may be relevant to the client's situation.

Being a lawyer is not easy. It is an inherently adversarial career choice. You are a lawyer to help resolve, prevent, or mitigate, in one way or another, some type of dispute. On top of that, you now have an added burden of connecting with clients who are different from you. It is a lot, but it is a necessity. Not understanding and respecting what is important to your client can lead to great misunderstandings, miscommunications, and misinterpretations that can have dire consequences for your client. We have seen examples of such mistakes trickling into decisions or communications with opposing parties or even tribunals. You represent your client. You must understand whom you represent. As a client, wouldn't you want the same?

Key Takeaways

- While the lawyer has the legal knowledge, it is the client who usually has the ultimate decision-making authority.
- A lawyer cannot counsel or assist a client in conduct that they know is criminal or fraudulent.
- When representing clients with diminished capacity, a lawyer shall maintain a normal attorney-client relationship with the client as far as reasonably possible.
- Lawyers have a fundamental duty to become culturally competent to the extent necessary to establish a trust-based relationship with a client.
- Maintaining professional independence as a lawyer is crucial to the lawyer-client relationship.

Ethics in Action

Read the following disciplinary action(s) in which the state bar used the rules discussed in this chapter to bring disciplinary charges against an attorney.

- Assisting a client in conduct the lawyer knows is fraudulent [three-year suspension]: *In re Vincent DeMarti Porter*, https://www.iardc.org/HB_RB_Disp_Html.asp?id=13150

End-of-Chapter Discussion Questions

1. Dependency and conservatorship courts usually provide court-appointed lawyers to clients. Why do you think that is the case?
2. Some believe that a lawyer is not a social worker or doctor, and thus they should not be required to make judgment calls on diminished capacity or conservatorships. Clients are sophisticated enough to make informed decisions. For this reason, should lawyers have to consult clients about tactical decisions in a case? Or are strategic and tactical decisions best addressed by the lawyer without client involvement?
3. How would you go about forming a trust relationship with a client of a different background?
4. If you are in-house counsel, how much do you think you need to know about your employer's business? Do you need to know about how they develop the product that is being sold? To what extent? For example, let's say the company manufactures candles. Do you need to know the type of wax, the type of wick, how it is packaged, and how it is marketed? As a lawyer, how intimately involved do you need to be with what the company is doing?

CHAPTER 9

Advertising and Solicitation

Visit your interactive ebook to download the Chapter 9 Outline.

Learning Objectives

- Analyze current rules on advertising and solicitation.
- Identify when ads are misleading.
- Understand how lawyers use technology to advertise and solicit and how that might lead to liability.

Key Terms

- **Communication:** Making it known that you are available for professional employment.
- **Solicitation:** Communication directed to a specific person whom the lawyer knows or reasonably should know needs legal services.
- **Advertising:** Promoting one's services and availability.

Introduction

HYPOTHETICAL 9.1
Thank you for your help!

It's a Friday afternoon, and you are just leaving work after a long, hard week. You get on the freeway which is, of course, right in the middle of rush hour. But you don't care. You are going home! You merge into traffic, and even though it is a combination of bumper-to-bumper traffic and quicker sections where you speed up so the car in the next lane does not merge in front of you, you can feel the tension of the week slowly melting off you. You settled into a lane, turn on the radio a little louder, slouch into your seat a little bit, and start to drift off into thinking about what to have for dinner while enjoying movie night with the family. Then, suddenly, BANG! You have been rear-ended. Hard! So hard that you lose control and go screeching into the car in front of you. The double impact sets off your airbags, breaking your nose. One of the two impacts also bruises your chest and breaks a rib.

Your car is stopped in the middle of the freeway, and you are disoriented. It takes what you think is an hour to come to your senses and realize exactly what happened. By that time, police are on the scene directing traffic, your car is set to be towed, and you are being prepped to be taken via ambulance to the local hospital. You are scared, still confused and in pain. You are looking for a kind face, a familiar face, but everyone is tending to the scene or the injuries of those involved.

Before you are put into an ambulance, a woman you see talking to the police for a while comes over to you. She looks concerned. "Are you all right?" she asks. "I saw the entire accident. It was awful. I'm so sorry this happened to you. I am a lawyer, here is my card. Call me, and I will make this right for you." She hands you her card and waves goodbye as they lift you into an ambulance.

A seemingly nice gesture from a stranger—and a lawyer, no less! Maybe this person will need legal aid in this situation, but was this the right approach for the lawyer to take?

> Please refer to the interactive ebook in Cognella Active Learning for interactive/media content.

You also seem to recall hearing a radio ad for a personal injury attorney with a catchy jingle. You think about calling them instead. You think about how tacky the ad was but consider that lawyers need to advertise their services just like everyone else.

> Please refer to the interactive ebook in Cognella Active Learning for interactive/media content.

"Hurt in An Accident? Free Consultation. No Fees Unless We Win." Anyone who lives in Los Angeles (and likely other cities in the US) has seen dozens of billboards with law firms advertising their services for accidents and personal injury claims. Lawyer advertising is a relatively new concept, with the Supreme Court case *Bates v. State Bar*[1] paving the way. Before *Bates*, the legal profession was deemed an *old boys' club* with several barriers to entry. Most clients came by way of referrals. As a result, there was a gap in the availability of legal services to the general public, which prompted states to consider allowing legal advertising to lawyers. It would help inform underserved and underrepresented communities about the scope of legal representation available to them.

This concern had to be balanced against client sophistication. Regulators considered and distinguished legal advertising from other forms of advertising. Legal advertising poses special risks that are not present in other forms of advertising because the public often lacks sophistication and experience concerning the <u>nature</u> and <u>variety</u> of legal services. Regulators also had to look at whether the legal advertising was presented in a way that could be interpreted as a "guarantee" of a particular successful outcome to a potential client. Advertising one's legal services to the general public is one thing, but to say that if you hire a particular lawyer, you will have a successful outcome is another. Think for a moment of the incredible diversity of the American population. While we have different cultural backgrounds and ethnicities, we also range vastly in age, language, literacy, education, and even our savviness in technology. All of these play a factor in how we interpret advertisement—legal or otherwise.

Furthermore, there were concerns that legal ads might suggest lawyers are profit-hungry instead of showcasing legal skills. They also feared that the costs of advertising would be passed on to the consumer.

On the flipside, these fears had to be balanced against whether restrictions on advertising violated the lawyer's First Amendment free speech rights. When states introduced restrictions on advertising, lawyers challenged them. In many instances, the US Supreme Court struck down certain provisions in these states as violating the First Amendment guarantee of free speech.

Read the following advertisement from the Legal Clinic of Bates & O'Steen. What concerns you about the ad? Is anything potentially misleading?

---

1. 433 US 350 (1977)

> **ADVERTISEMENT**
>
> # DO YOU NEED A LAWYER?
> ### LEGAL SERVICES AT VERY REASONABLE FEES
>
> - Divorce or legal separation--uncontested (both spouses sign papers)
> $175.00 plus $20.00 court filing fee
>
> - Preparation of all court papers and instructions on how to do your own simple uncontested divorce
> $100.00
>
> - Adoption--uncontested severance proceeding
> $225.00 plus approximately $10.00 publication cost
>
> - Bankruptcy--non-business, no contested proceedings
>   Individual
> $250.00 plus $55.00 court filing fee
>
>   Wife and Husband
> $300.00 plus $110.00 court filing fee
>
> - Change of Name
> $95.00 plus $20.00 court filing fee
>
> Information regarding other types of cases furnished on request
>
> **Legal Clinic of Bates & O'Steen**
> 617 North 3rd Street
> Phoenix, Arizona 85004
> Telephone (502) 252-8838

FIGURE 9.1 Legal Clinic of Bates & O'Steen Advertisement.

CASE ALERT

In *Bates v. State Bar*, Bates, a partner in an Arizona law firm, sought to provide legal services to moderate-income people and who did not qualify for public legal aid. A part of their services depended on raising money from charitable patrons. The firm decided to advertise its availability and low fees. At the time, Arizona, where Bates had a law firm, restricted legal advertising. After publishing the ad shown in Figure 9.1 in a local newspaper, the state bar brought disciplinary charges against Bates, which he challenged. He claimed that Arizona's restriction on advertising violates his First Amendment right to free speech. The case went all the way to the US Supreme Court.

Keeping a lawyer's First Amendment rights in mind, the Supreme Court concluded that lawyer advertising is commercial speech entitled to protection under the First Amendment. Any stated prohibition was an antiquated rule of etiquette. By allowing lawyer advertising, legal services would become more accessible to the general public and improve the overall administration of justice. The court concluded that the government still had an interest in protecting false, deceptive, or misleading ads and could impose appropriate restraints.

In looking at Bates's ad, the court held that advertising referring to an office as a "legal clinic" is not misleading if geared toward providing subsidized services. Similarly, advertising "very reasonable fees" for an uncontested divorce is not inherently misleading if the lawyer charges lower fees comparable to those charged by lawyers in the same geographic area.

<u>Bottom Line</u>: Although state regulation of lawyer advertising violates a lawyer's First Amendment rights, the state may include an outright prohibition of false and misleading speech.

Please refer to the interactive ebook in Cognella Active Learning for interactive/media content.

SUMMARY OF ABA MODEL RULES ON ADVERTISING AND SOLICITATION

- **ABA Model Rule 7.1**: No false or misleading communications.
- **ABA Model Rule 7.2**: Lawyers may use any form of media to communicate.
- **ABA Model Rule 7.3**: Prohibits in-person solicitation.
- **ABA Model Rule 7.6**: Prohibits pay to play; that is, accepting legal engagement or appointment by a government entity or judge if the lawyer or law firm made a political contribution to them.

Every state has adopted a rule against false and misleading ads, but their rules vary widely with other aspects of advertising. Many states have also deviated from the ABA's approach. In 2018, the ABA updated its advertising and solicitation rules. In this chapter, we address these changes.

Note: Recall ABA Model Rule 8.4(c). It is misconduct for a lawyer to engage in conduct involving dishonesty, fraud, deceit, or misrepresentation. The advertising rules go hand-in-hand with ABA Rule 8.4(c).

Lawyer Communications: Websites, Blogs, and Legal Ads

ABA Model Rule 7.1 prohibits false or misleading communications about the lawyer or lawyer's services. This includes all forms of communications, including advertising. A communication is false or misleading if it contains a material misrepresentation of fact or law or omits a fact necessary to make something not materially misleading.

> **BELOW, WE HAVE OUTLINED SOME INITIAL QUESTIONS ON COMMUNICATIONS:**
>
> 1. What is communication?
>
> **Answer:** Communication is any means used to make known a lawyer's services (ABA Model Rule 7.1, Comment 1).
>
> 2. Are the following statements "communications?" Why or why not? Assume the lawyer posted each statement on his public Facebook profile.
>
> - Trial is finally over. Celebrating tonight!
> - Got my client's arrest expunged. Who wants to be next?
> - Won a million-dollar verdict today. Tell your friends to check out my website.
>
> **Answer:** Examples 2 and 3 are communications. They address the lawyer's services and availability. They also run afoul of the advertising rules (see below). They imply that future clients will win.
>
> 3. Since communications include all forms of communications, what are some examples of written, recorded, or electronic communication?
>
> - Lawyer business cards
> - Attorney newsletters
> - Radio ads
> - Television ads
> - Live chat on lawyer website
> - Text messages
>
> 4. Can a lawyer/law firm have a website?
>
> **Answer:** Law firm or lawyer websites are a form of communication that falls under ABA Model Rule 7.1. In 2010, the ABA issued Formal Opinion 10-457 on the rules governing lawyer websites. Specifically, they felt that websites were a 24/7 marketing tool that clients rely on for information about legal services. The main issue is that the website might give rise to a prospective client relationship, even without the knowledge or intention of creating one. Prospective clients might visit a website to ask questions, which is why lawyers must carefully manage inquiries invited through the website. ABA Model Rule 7.2(d) requires websites to list the name and contact information of at least one lawyer or law firm responsible for its content. They should contain

disclaimers stating that "legal advice is general and should not be relied on as legal advice." The disclaimer must be understandable and placed properly within the view of a website visitor.

5. What about blogs?

Answer: Like websites, blogs serve as an important marketing tool and are therefore subject to false and misleading restrictions. In *Hunter v. Va. State Bar*, Horace Hunter authored a trademark blog. His blog posts, while containing some political commentary, were commercial speech. Hunter admitted that the reason for starting a blog was partly economically driven. He mostly discussed cases in which he had a positive outcome. His blog did not have a disclaimer. The Virginia Supreme Court held that his blog posts were subject to the state bar's advertising disclaimer requirements. The posts were potentially misleading commercial speech that the Virginia State Bar could regulate.

On the other hand, if a lawyer writes a blog but does not discuss legal topics in a way intended to solicit legal business, it will not be subject to ABA Model Rule 7.1.

ABA MODEL RULE 7.1: TRANSPARENCY IN ADVERTISING

It does not matter what means a lawyer uses to advertise their services to the public. The communications must be truthful. ABA Model Rule 7.1 clarifies what false or misleading communication by the lawyer services would be. Communication will be false or misleading if it contains a material misrepresentation of fact or law or omits information necessary to make a statement (when read in its entirety) not materially misleading.

PRACTICAL GUIDE
Questions for lawyers to ask before putting their communications out to the public. Think about how it would be received.

- Is your communication misleading so that it would cause a reasonable person to believe something for which there is no reasonable factual foundation?
- Does your communication create an unjustified expectation that prior results for one client can be obtained for them?
- Does a truthful communication about achievement on behalf of a client or former client create an unjustified expectation of the same

or similar result for future clients? Additionally, would a truthful communication about fees or any kind of services for clients or former clients cause a reasonable person to believe that they can also expect the same fees or services?

The purpose of advertising is to bring in business. And, yes, let's not beat around the bush here ... there is plenty of puffery in advertising in all industries. While some legal businesses will come in through referrals and the like, almost all lawyers will engage in advertising. This may be television commercials, radio ads, or even billboards, but even biographies on a firm website can be considered a form of advertising. They do talk about the lawyer and the lawyer's services. Some even highlight achievements. But as lawyers, we highly caution you against engaging in any type of misleading or confusing marketing. Be transparent with your marketing and consider the perception any and all of your advertising would bring. There are plenty of ways to let the public know you are a competent, ethical, reputable, and skilled lawyer without having to be deceptive.

The way we communicate is constantly changing. We talk more over social media (whatever that social media is nowadays) or over email more than over the phone. How many of us use a fax machine anymore? We predict the rules of advertisement will continue to develop as ways in which we communicate will change. There will be nuances in this area of the ethical rules, so be on the lookout for changes. Here are some examples of some of those nuances:

- An ABA 2020 Report provided that you could include a "Best Lawyer" award in your advertising if you received such an award that was not based on paying for it and if you include details about the award you won.
- When it comes to law firm names, you can include the name of deceased lawyers on the firm's title, Sidley Austin, for instance. But you cannot include the names of lawyers currently working for the government, including lawyers who have left to take on judicial positions. The law firm must change the name even if that means a change to the firm title.
- Advertisements in any manner can include the client names (with client consent), lawyer's or law firm's areas of expertise, awards recovered for a client (with a disclaimer that results are not to be expected by all clients). But a lawyer cannot advertise themselves to be a specialist in an area of law unless they are certified by an appropriate agency (i.e., a lawyer claiming to be an appellate specialist on their website must be certified by the state bar or another appropriate agency).

Have non-lawyer friends and families look at your advertisements or whatever you are putting out to the public before you put it out there. What is their take on it? What would their "expectation" be from it? We are not saying not to put the best version of yourself out there but to be mindful of what image you are giving off. And always be transparent!

MISLEADING OR OKAY?
Consider these various forms of lawyer advertising.

- Lawyer billboard on the freeway. There is a picture of a single man in a suit with the tagline, "Got into an accident? Call us, we can help," with the phone number listed.
- Lawyer's email always has the following sign-off: I am the best trial lawyer in the state. Do not make the mistake of picking another lawyer when you can choose James K. Pick as your lawyer.
- TV commercial comes on. The accident victim shares his traumatic incident of being struck by a motorcyclist. "My lawyer got me $3.4 million in recovery. She can help you, too." At the bottom of the TV commercial, in small print, is a disclaimer "Results not typical. Individual results may vary, and recovery will depend on the individual facts of your case. We make no guarantees."
- A lawyer (who generally practices in civil court) recently defended and won her first and only criminal defense case for a long-time client. Her website now lists vague details of the criminal trial win and says "Criminal Attorney."

ABA MODEL RULE 7.2: COMMUNICATIONS REGARDING A LAWYER'S SERVICES AND REFERRALS

There is no limitation in the methods which lawyers can use to advertise. They can be creative and can use written, recorded, or electronic means to advertise. We have all seen lawyer advertisements on TV, heard them on radios, seen them while browsing the internet. We have even seen them on bus benches, buses, or billboards. ABA Model Rule 7.2 addresses when a lawyer uses, for example, a past client who discusses their personal experiences with the lawyer. For the person listening to that past client, this constitutes a referral to that lawyer—that can be interpreted as— "Come use the lawyer I used because I got an amazing result."

ABA Model Rule 7.2 is a type of safeguard. It limits giving anything of value to the lawyer in exchange for the recommendation made to, for example, that past client.

ABA Model Rule 7.2 (a)—A lawyer may communicate information regarding the lawyer's services through any media.

ABA Model Rule 7.2 (b)—A lawyer shall not give anything of value to a person who recommended that lawyer's services except that a lawyer may refer clients to another lawyer pursuant to an allowed reciprocal referral agreement provided that (i) the agreement is not exclusive (i.e., they can refer to others); and (ii) the client is informed about the existence and nature of the agreement.

Advertisements will often contain recommendations for a lawyer's services. This is especially the case if you have a past client telling the world about the awesome service and recovery the lawyer got for them. Comment 2 to ABA Model Rule 7.2 tells us that a recommendation is something that endorses or vouches for a lawyer's credentials, abilities, competence, character, or other professional qualities. Directory listings and group advertisements that list lawyers by practice area, without more, do not constitute impermissible "recommendations."

ABA MODEL RULE 7.3: SOLICITATION

Please refer to the interactive ebook in Cognella Active Learning for interactive/media content.

HYPOTHETICAL 9.2
Slipping up—Using agents to solicit

After ten years as a civil litigation associate for a national law firm, you start your own law practice. To attract clients, you ask friends and family to "spread the word that you have started a practice specializing in personal injury law." Your sister works at a hospital emergency room as a nurse. Whenever she interacts with a patient who shares that they were in an accident, she calls you immediately. You show up at the hospital and immediately give your business card to the accident victim. You tell them about your law firm practice and encourage them to get a lawyer.

Please refer to the interactive ebook in Cognella Active Learning for interactive/media content.

Solicitation and ABA Model Rule 7.3 are covered in the video presentation. All lawyers need to know the meaning and limitations of solicitation by lawyers and their agents.

ABA MODEL RULE 7.6: PARTICIPATING IN THE POLITICAL PROCESS

Many of the people at the forefront of our political process in the United States are lawyers. Whether local or national politics, lawyers can be passionate about political participation, especially judicial elections or appointments. Many politicians and most judges and justices in the United States were once lawyers. While the engagement is well placed, there is a fine line between passionate engagement and "pay to play." ABA Model Rule 7.6 prohibits pay to play; that is, accepting legal engagement or appointment by a government entity or judge if the lawyer or law firm made a political contribution to them.

KEY TAKEAWAYS

- Advertisements in any form are generally allowed, provided they are not false or misleading.
- Think about the creation of an attorney-client relationship due to law firm websites and blogs.
- Ensure that any "results" your firm obtains does not give the impression that future cases will obtain similar results.
- Do not solicit, especially when an individual has asked you to leave them alone.
- A lawyer can solicit family, someone they have a close personal or prior professional relationship with.
- Every ad or solicitation should include the words "advertising materials" on them.

ETHICS IN ACTION

Read the following disciplinary action(s) in which the state bar used the rules discussed in this chapter to bring disciplinary charges against an attorney.

- False and deceptive advertising [90-day suspension]: *Grievance Administrator v. Gary Nitzkin*, https://www.adbmich.org/getattachment/3ce3b7b8-83ca-4fb9-8d1b-0fa9ea43771f/3ce3b7b8-83ca-4fb9-8d1b-0fa9ea43771f.aspx

END-OF-CHAPTER DISCUSSION QUESTIONS

1. Do you think lawyer advertising rules are too restrictive? Why or why not? If you do believe it is too restrictive, how would you propose changing it?
2. Should lawyers be able to solicit the general public for legal services? Why or why not?
3. Do the current rules on lawyer advertisement and solicitation restrict access to the general public to legal help?
4. Lawyers can access public arrest records. For this reason, it is not uncommon for a recent arrestee to receive flyers from local defense attorneys regarding their services. Why is this allowed? Should it be banned? Is this a violation of privacy?

Image Credits

Fig. 9.1: U.S. Supreme Court Appendix, "Legal Clinic of Bates & O'Steen advertisement," https://www.floridasupremecourt.org/content/download/328934/file/10-1014_081610_Comments%20(8LawFirms).pdf, State of Florida, 1977.

GLOSSARY

ABA
The American Bar Association is a national organization of lawyers who participate in law reform, law-school accreditation, and continuing legal education for lawyers to help improve the legal system.

Actual conflicts
Conflicts that have materialized.

Advertising
Promoting one's services and availability.

Agent
Someone who has authority (called a principal) to act on behalf of another due to their fiduciary relationship.

Alternative Fee Agreements (AFAs)
An AFA is any fee agreement in which a client pays an attorney something other than a standard hourly rate for the legal work performed. Sometimes, AFAs are rereferred to as "value-based billing." Here, a lawyer is paid for the value delivered rather than the time taken to provide the service.

Attorney-client relationship
Relationship between attorney and client where attorney promises to provide legal services, usually for a fee.

Bench trial
A trial before a judge.

Candid communication
A requirement to reasonably communicate with the client at all times to ensure effective communication.

Candor
Being honest.

Communication (Chapter 5)

The exchange of information by speech, writing, gesture, conduct, or other means.

Communication (Chapter 9)

Making it known that you are available for professional employment.

Competence (Chapter 2)

Legal knowledge, skill, thoroughness, and preparation reasonably necessary for representation.

Competence (Chapter 3)

Having the legal knowledge, skills, and thoroughness to represent a client. In some states, this also includes having the mental, emotional, and physical ability to perform legal services.

Complaint

An expression of dissatisfaction with legal services that is filed with the state bar.

Concurrent conflicts

Conflict between two current clients with adverse/opposing interests.

Confidentiality (Chapter 2)

A duty not to disclose or use information about the client's representation.

Confidentiality (Chapter 5)

Information that cannot be disclosed because of the attorney-client relationship.

Conflict of interest

A duty of loyalty to the client by avoiding other lawyers', clients', or third-party interests.

Conflict waiver

Agreement to proceed in light of a conflict after informed consent is provided.

Consent

(Generally) Agreement, approval, or permission.

Conservator

A situation where a court appoints a responsible person (called the "conservator") to care for another adult (called the "conservatee") who cannot care for themselves or their finances.
EDIT

Contingency fees
A sum of money, usually a previously set percentage, that a lawyer receives for a fee only if the matter is successful.

Diligence
Devoting adequate care and attention to each client's matter.

Diminished capacity
When an individual may not have the mental capacity to make a decision (due to age, mental impairment, or for some other reason).

Disbarment
The revocation of an attorney's right to practice law.

Discipline
A penalty ranging from a permanent loss of a law license to a private warning, imposed for violating the ethical rules.

Ethics
A system of moral tenets or principles; the collective doctrines relating to the ideals of human conduct and character.

Fiduciary duty
Duty owed by attorney to client. Fiduciary means trust. Consequently, an attorney should act in the client's best interests. There are four fiduciary duties. They are confidentiality, candid communication, conflict of interest, competence.

Flat or fixed fees
A fixed amount paid to a lawyer irrespective of the number of hours spent on the case.

Former client
A client who used to be represented by a lawyer.

Frivolous
Not being of serious value.

Guardian ad litem
When a person involved in a suit cannot adequately represent their own interests, the court may appoint a guardian ad litem to protect the person's interests.

Hourly fees
A set hourly rate a lawyer will receive for legal service throughout the legal representation.

Hybrid-hourly contingency
A mixture of the hourly rate and contingency fee models, it involves the attorney being paid a guaranteed hourly fee and then being paid a bonus fee if the client's claim receives strong recovery.

Incompetence
Acting without competence.

Informed consent
The process of getting permission from a client after providing them with information about the conflict and an explanation of risks and alternatives.

Integrity
The quality of being honest and upholding ethics and morals.

Malpractice
A lawsuit filed by a client against an attorney (or any professional for that matter) for damages. Malpractice lawsuits occur due to improper or negligent conduct by an attorney.

Model Rules of Professional Responsibility
A set of ethical guidelines for lawyers, some of which are mandatory while others are not. Each rule has comments that help explain the rule.

Morality
The doctrine of right and wrong in human conduct.

Negligence
When an attorney makes a mistake that causes "damages" to a client, which a reasonable attorney in a similar situation would not have made.

Objection
Opposition, legal reason for disapproval.

Officer of the court
A responsibility to promote honesty, justice, and the integrity of the legal system.

Perjury
Willfully or intentionally lying after taking an oath or affirmation to tell the truth.

Personal conflict
A conflict that arises due to the lawyer's own interests.

Plea
    An agreement between the prosecution and the defendant where the defendant pleads guilty to criminal charges in exchange for a reduced sentence or dropped charges.

Potential conflicts
    Conflicts that could arise in the future but have not yet materialized.

Privilege
    (Generally) A special legal right, exemption, or immunity granted.

Prospective client
    A person who consults a lawyer to retain the lawyer or secure legal service or advice from the lawyer, also commonly referred to as a potential client.

Reasonable or reasonably
    When used in relation to conduct by a lawyer denotes the conduct of a reasonably prudent and competent lawyer (ABA Model Rules, Rule 1.0(a) Terminology, 2020 Edition).

Reasonably should know
    When used in reference to a lawyer, it denotes that a lawyer of reasonable prudence and competence would ascertain the matter in question (ABA Model Rules, Rule 1.0(j) Terminology, 2020 Edition).

Referral fees
    A lawyer who refers a matter to another lawyer for a portion of the total fees paid for the case, usually one-third.

Retainer
    An advance or deposit against future work.

Screening for conflicts
    The process of checking for actual or potential conflicts before taking on a client or legal matter.

Secrets
    Things that are kept from the knowledge of others or shared only with those concerned. Usually, information shared as a course of the professional relationship.

Settlement
    An agreement between two parties intended to resolve a legal dispute between them.

Solicitation
Communication directed to a specific person whom the lawyer knows or reasonably should know needs legal services.

State Bar (or Bar Association)
An organization of members of the legal profession that license and discipline lawyers.

Statutory fees
Fees in some cases may be set by statute or a court may set and approve a fee. Often seen in probate, bankruptcy, or other proceedings.

Successive conflicts
Conflict between a former client and a current client.

Suspend
To temporarily remove an attorney's right to practice law.

Waive
To surrender, abandon, or give up.

Withdraw
Terminating the representation due to a conflict or potential of an ethical violation.